THE PRICK

A Novel

The Prick

A Novel

By

D.C. Wales

www.penmorepress.com

The Prick by D.C. Wales
Copyright © 2017 D C Wales

ISBN-13: 978-1-946409-00-3(Paperback)
ISBN-13: 978-1-946409-01-0 (e-book)

BISAC Subject Headings:

LAW013000 Law/Civil Rights
LAW054000 Law/ Labor and Employment
LAW064000 Law/ Litigation
Editor Susan Wenger
Editor Chris Paige
Art Work by Jessica Richardson
Cover Illustration by Christine Horner

Address all correspondence to:
Penmore Press LLC
920 N Javelina Pl
Tucson AZ 85748

Book One

Chapter 1

Friday, March 29th
The Law Offices of Jason Hunter, Esq.
Ponce de Leon, Atlanta

"Okay, Maggie. Tell me what happened," Jason Hunter said, looking over his cheap IKEA desk at the fleshy and distraught woman. She maintained a low whimper that escalated to full-on heaving sobs at regular intervals.

"Slowly," he instructed. Jason had pen and yellow legal pad at the ready to record any actual words that came out of her mouth. At the top of the pad, he wrote, "ATTORNEY-CLIENT PRIVILEGED."

This was going to get ugly. She had been crying since she arrived. Like, nonstop from the parking lot to the door to the chair. She must be dehydrated, Jason thought. Her hand was wet when he shook it. Most unpleasant. He'd resisted the urge to pull away immediately. Compassion, compassion, compassion, the plaintiff's attorney's credo.

Jason, Maggie Moxley, and her dumb-as-a-mule husband, Pete Moxley, were sitting in Jason's office, a windowless room painted a sickly yellow. The color reminded Jason of a dentist's office for some reason. Didn't understand the association, but they were both unpleasant places to spend any time. The nascent firm bearing Jason Hunter's name only had two rooms, the entryway and this office. He had hung bright pictures at window height in an attempt to avert claustrophobia. It didn't work. There was no circulation and it always felt stuffy. The plan was to upgrade ASAP. Which he might be able to do at some point in the goddamn future if he could convince this wreck of a woman to tell him what the goddamn hell happened.

The details had been opaque when Jason first spoke with Pete on the phone. Something along the lines of, "My wife's boss is a fuckin' deviant pervert and I want to see what we can do." Maggie was a legal secretary for a well-respected, well-known, well-everything international law firm with an office downtown. Jason didn't know the purported harasser personally, but he knew who he was. Robert Spelkin III. Spelkin was a big shot, and his smiling face occasionally appeared next to stories about important cases in the news. Jason told Pete to come into his office, and to bring his allegedly victimized wife.

Maggie Moxley was a forty-two-year-old, white high school graduate. Her outfit consisted of light jeans and an AC/DC T-shirt. The flesh on her arms and neck shook as she blubbered and dabbed her eyes with a balled-up tissue. Not exactly a sex symbol. In person, Pete Moxley turned out to be massive. Just a towering idiot. And a Monster Truck enthusiast. He wore a black T-shirt featuring a large truck gleefully rolling over its lesser auto brethren. Glowering seemed to be his expression of choice, and he had a good glower going in the chair to Maggie's right.

"He told me … that if I didn't touch it, then he was going to fire me," Maggie managed.

"Touch what?"

The Prick

"His fuckin' dick, what the fuck you think?" Pete interjected. "I'm gonna kill the sumbitch."

"All right," Jason said in his best soothing tone. "I know you've heard the story already, Pete, but I need to hear it now. And I need to hear it from her, okay?"

The brim on Pete's trucker hat dipped slightly, which Jason interpreted as assent.

Jason turned back to Maggie and smiled ever so gently. "Go on, Maggie."

"Well," Maggie said, glancing at her husband nervously, "he came into my cube after everyone had left. He told me I had to stay after to finish a project. I had to miss my bus. He unzipped his pants ... and took it out."

"Took what out?" Jason asked, shooting Pete a warning look.

"His ... his penis," Maggie said, looking again at her husband fearfully.

"Goddamn it," Pete said under his breath. He couldn't or wouldn't look at Maggie. But he was capable of staring bloody murder at Jason.

Jason ignored him. "Was it erect?"

"Goddamn it!" Pete exploded. "What the hell kind of question is that? You some kind of pervert too? Asking my wife if it was 'e-rect'?" Pete was standing now, his legs pressed up against Jason's desk, his stomach distended over Jason's papers, and his sausage-like right index finger about two feet from Jason's face. Jason was a lanky six foot three and Pete outweighed him by at least seventy-five pounds, a substantial portion of which appeared to be muscle.

Jason wasn't concerned in the slightest. He'd seen this kind of alpha-male exhibition from aggrieved husbands before.

"Sit down, Pete," he said. "Sit down right now."

The Prick

Pete and Jason looked at each other. It took a few seconds, but Pete sat down.

Jason held Pete's eyes. "Now listen. Maggie has to be able to talk about what happened. If you file a lawsuit, she has to be able to say the words. She is going to have to tell the EEOC, she is going to have to tell defense attorneys in a deposition, and she is going to have to testify at trial. If you are really serious about going forward with this case, then you need to keep quiet. Do it now and forever or this is over."

Pete took a deep breath. He wanted the money. Jason could feel it. He wanted the money more than he wanted to make a show of avenging his wife's lost honor.

Jason turned his attention back to the purported victim. He wasn't sure he was buying it yet. He had heard worse, but why would Robert Spelkin III put all he had at risk for a potential liaison with the individual occupying the entire chair in front of him?

"Now, Maggie, was it erect?"

Pete exhaled loudly but said nothing.

"Yes ..."

"Okay, what happened next?"

"Well, he said that I wasn't done with the project until I took care of it, pointing ... you know. He had this big smile when he said it, like it was some big joke."

"Then what happened?"

"I turned around in my chair real quick and tried to just look at my computer. He didn't say anything. I was just hoping, you know, he would go away. But then, I ... felt it."

"Felt it?"

Maggie, bright red and huffing, looked down at her lap. Pete still wouldn't look at her.

"It was ... on my shoulder, against my neck."

4

The Prick

Jason glanced at Pete. His fists were clenched, the muscles in his arms visibly pulsating. He was staring at the wall like he was about to punch a hole through it. Jason hoped he wouldn't. They had made him pay a deposit.

"And then what?"

Maggie looked over at Pete, who continued to menace the wall. He wasn't much of a comfort to his wife, this Pete Moxley.

"And then what, Maggie?"

"I told him to stop."

"What exactly did you say?"

"I said, 'Stop, I can't.'"

"Goddammit," Pete said.

"You said 'I can't'?"

"Yes."

Jason was writing quickly to get it all down. There was still something off about it. How could Spelkin have been so stupid?

"Then what happened?"

"He said of course I could. He said nobody would know. He said he knew that I wanted to, that he had known for a while. He was leaning over me and breathing on me but I wouldn't turn around. I could smell drink on him."

Bingo. Jason fought off a big grin. That was it. Alcohol. Destroyer of men.

"He had been drinking?"

Maggie nodded, dabbing her eyes. "Uh-huh. They had just won a big settlement and he had been at the bar or club upstairs. He told me ..." She looked again at Pete.

"Just say it," Pete said, eyes still averted.

"He told me to put it ... in my mouth."

"Goddammit," Pete said.

"When he said that to you, to put it in your mouth, was it still pressed against you?"

5

The Prick

Maggie swallowed. "Yes."

He wrote it down. "Against your neck?"

"Yes."

"And you could smell the alcohol?"

"Uh-huh."

"All right, so then what?"

The words rushed out quickly, like a dam had broken. "I said I can't and I got up and ran to the ladies' room. He made like he was trying to grab me but he didn't. I don't think he followed me. Or, I know he didn't follow me. I waited in the ladies' room for about twenty minutes and then I went back to my desk. I couldn't leave. I didn't have my bag. When I got back, he was in his office. I could see the light on at the end of the hall. The door was cracked open. I tried to be really quiet so he wouldn't hear me. I got my bag and left."

"This all happened last week?"

"Yes, on Wednesday. I took Thursday off, said I was sick, and when I went in on Friday, he wasn't there. He was in Detroit."

"Was anybody else there when all of this happened?"

"No, they'd left. I think maybe the cleaning crew was in the building but they weren't around. Maybe I heard the vacuums somewhere in the other parts of the office."

Jason wrote down on his yellow pad: "Cleaners— interviews."

"Have you told anybody else about this?"

"My sister."

"When?"

"That night, on the phone."

"How long was the conversation?"

"Hours."

Jason wrote: "Sister— phone records—interview."

"Anybody else?"

6

The Prick

"No."

"All right," Jason said, looking over his notes, "had he ever done anything like this before?"

Maggie shook her head. "Nothing like this. I mean, he looks, you know, you can feel him looking at you. A lot of the girls talk about it."

"Who talks about it?" Jason asked. He wrote down the names. "Is there anything else you think I should know?"

Maggie looked right at him. It was one of the few times she had made actual eye contact throughout the ordeal. Jason saw some anger flash in her eyes.

"He was laughing."

"What?"

"When I ran away, to the ladies' room, I could hear him laughing."

Jason wrote it down. Laughing. That was good.

Jason described to the Moxleys what kind of claims Maggie could bring and put his contingency fee agreement in front of them. Maggie signed where he pointed, her teardrops leaving sad little circular watermarks on the page.

Jason managed a poker face. Finally.

The Prick

Chapter 2

Tuesday, April 2nd
Atlanta Offices of Levitt, Bennett & Taylor, LLP

"She's lying. The goddamn bitch is lying!" Robert Spelkin III pounded on the conference room table with an open palm, which immediately began to throb. His chest was heaving, and he was sweating so much that he could feel his shirt sticking to him. He looked around the table, daring someone to challenge him.

The conference room was on the fortieth floor of the Bank of America building in downtown Atlanta, with large bay windows facing north. Through them you could see Midtown, the buildings in Buckhead up Peachtree Road in northern Atlanta, and on a clear day you could see the Blue Ridge Mountains, which started in North Georgia and ran all the way through Virginia.

It was on this view that all eyes save Robert Spelkin's were uncomfortably focused.

Present were James (call me Jimmy) Peters, the bovine and placid managing partner of the Atlanta office, David Nichols, a rainmaker, and Ned Burroughs, one of the firm's in-house counsel, who had flown in that morning from Washington, DC. Robert had always thought Burroughs looked like an aardvark with glasses.

Peters had received, by FedEx, a demand letter from the Law Offices of Jason M. Hunter, Esq., which was, according to their quick research, a low-budget one-man operation on Ponce de Leon Avenue in Midtown. Burroughs had put out a few feelers, but nobody seemed to know much about Hunter or have litigation experience against him.

All four men had a copy of the letter, which consisted of nearly three pages of salacious and tawdry accusations about Robert's conduct, culminating in the claim that Robert had "pulled his erect penis out of his pants, put it against Mrs. Moxley's neck, and then demanded that she put it in her mouth." Humiliation washed over Robert each time he saw one of the others glance down at the pages. Humiliation, rage, and terror.

The letter also contained a monetary demand. In exchange for an immediate payment of two million dollars— five hundred thousand of which would go toward front pay for Mrs. Moxley's resignation and one million five hundred thousand for pain and suffering and punitive damages— Hunter was prepared to settle his client's claims quietly with a full release and confidentiality agreement.

"We know that she's full of shit," David said, turning from the window with a glance that told him to keep it together. "She's obviously just looking for a payout. We're all on your side."

Robert exhaled. David was a good man. One of his closest allies in the Atlanta office. "I'm sorry," he said to them all. "I'm just so pissed about this fucking bullshit. I swear to God I'll move for sanctions if this hack dares to bring this trash into court."

"I think," Peters said softly, "that it's in everyone's best interests that these allegations never make it to court."

"You can't mean you're actually thinking about paying her!"

"Please keep your voice down, Robert," said Burroughs.

The Prick

He was right of course. Anybody could be passing by. Because aardvarkedly bookish Burroughs, the in-house counsel, was present, their communications were arguably privileged, but that privilege didn't extend to words that could be heard by anyone in the hallway.

Robert attempted another deep breath. He had to get control of himself, exercise some self-discipline. He could feel himself sweating profusely into his tailored blue suit—his lucky suit—as he had been doing since Peters and David had come into his office the afternoon before, shut the door, and showed him the letter. He was probably red, too. He was always red when he got worked up.

"Sorry."

A moment passed. It was not a comfortable moment.

Burroughs cleared his throat. "Obviously this thing has the potential to be explosive," he said, glancing back and forth between Robert and Peters. David was mostly there for moral support. "At this point, containment and silence are key. Nobody in this room is to speak a word about this to anyone. Only in-house and Hal Stairs have been alerted. If we can make this go away quietly with a quick payout, that's what we'll do. This Hunter has represented in the letter that no Charge has yet been filed with the EEOC, no Complaint has been filed in court, and Hunter hasn't yet had any contact with the media. What we need to do is set up a meeting with him fast."

"Do we have a number we're willing to give?" Peters asked.

"Jesus Christ," Robert said quietly, "I just can't believe this. This did not fucking happen."

Burroughs turned and fixed on Robert.

"Any of it?"

Robert felt himself flush anew with anger. He extended his meaty arm and held the letter as close to Burroughs's narrow face as he could reach. "Not a goddamn word of this fucking thing is true."

"All right, then," Burroughs said, looking away. Robert put the letter down and continued to glare.

"We'll start at twenty-five thousand with immediate separation and no rehire," Burroughs said, turning to Peters, "and see how serious this guy is. If he doesn't go for it, we're going to retain outside counsel."

"Jesus Christ," Robert said.

"It's the smart move, Robert," David said. "It's exactly what we'd advise our clients to do. Who are we thinking of?" David asked Burroughs.

"Someone we know with extreme discretion, obviously," Burroughs said. "Someone with credibility with the local federal judges."

The suit was likely to arise in part under Title VII, the federal law prohibiting sexual harassment and discrimination, and accordingly would be brought in federal court, specifically the United States District Court for the Northern District of Georgia, Atlanta Division. It was downtown. You could see the building clearly from the firm's southern offices. Robert's office faced north, a better view reserved for the office's top earners.

"We're still weighing options," Burroughs said. "But let's not get ahead of ourselves. We still don't have any kind of read on this attorney. Guy might very well be a bottom-feeder who'll counter at forty K and settle quietly for twenty-seven five."

"Goddamn scumbag," Robert said.

"Yes," Burroughs said tersely, letting slip some impatience. Robert looked over at him, ready to unleash the full extent of his wrath on the nerdy marsupial if he took one step further. Burroughs was far below Robert in the firm's hierarchy and was therefore an entirely acceptable wrath recipient if the need or desire arose. Burroughs looked at Robert furtively and wrote something unintelligible on the pad in front of him.

"Go on," Robert said.

"Well, the more immediate problem is what to do about Moxley," Burroughs continued, shifting gears. "I understand that she came into work today?"

Robert nodded. "She was out again yesterday with no excuse. I haven't said a word to her today. Haven't even looked at her."

"Good. Obviously our chief concern at present is avoiding any retaliation, real or imagined. Until we figure out what to do with her, keep it that way. We're going to have to move her to another attorney and get you another assistant. Can you make that happen today, Jimmy? Quietly?"

"Yes."

Robert shook his head. "I can't fucking believe this. Have you guys ever gotten a good look at this woman? I wouldn't come onto her in a million years. If I was going to harass someone, no way it would be her."

Burroughs straightened in his chair and took a deep breath. "Robert," he said.

"Yeah?"

"Don't ever say anything like that ever again."

Robert crumpled the demand letter in his hand and walked out of the room.

*****

Jason had typed up the demand letter the moment the Moxleys left his office. First thing Monday morning, he FedExed it to James Peters, whom he'd found grinning on the website for Levitt, Bennett & Taylor, LLP, which website claimed that Levitt represented Fortune 500 companies across the country and had over twenty-five offices in the US and abroad. Deep pockets.

After sending the demand letter, Jason immediately calendared in Outlook the deadline for Mrs. Moxley to file a Charge with the Equal Employment Opportunity Commission, or "EEOC." The EEOC is the federal administrative agency charged with enforcing federal employment statutes, such as Title VII. In Georgia, the deadline to file a Charge with the EEOC is 180 days from the date of the incident. If you don't file a Charge with the EEOC within the required time frame, you can't file a Title VII claim. It doesn't matter if every day you came into work your boss hit you with a flying tackle and humped you while naked and screaming racial epithets. No timely EEOC Charge, no Title VII claim.

This wasn't only going to be a Title VII claim—maybe he wouldn't bring a Title VII claim at all—but he wanted the option. And he also wanted to sic the EEOC on Levitt to see what would happen.

If Moxley was telling the truth, this was a good case. It would be Jason's second good case since going out on his own just a year earlier. Jason had started working for an employment defense firm almost immediately upon graduating from Vanderbilt University law school in 2009, before he'd even passed the bar. For the next seven years, he had slogged it out as a junior defense lawyer for corporations, mostly large Fortune 500, but a few smaller local companies as well. Jason had defended American retail giants, pharmaceutical companies, manufacturers, and automobile companies against claims like Moxley's, claims for harassment, discrimination, retaliation, claims alleging disability discrimination, pregnancy discrimination, race discrimination, sex discrimination, national origin discrimination, and religious discrimination, including, Jason's favorite, a claim that a supervisor was "hexing" a subordinate.

When Jason finally got sick of it, sick of all the document review, sick of billing hours, sick of faceless and thankless businesses, sick of threatening, convincing, cajoling, and begging corporations to do what they were supposed to do, sick of the incessantly required sycophancy, he quit. Walking out the door, he felt like a freed and pardoned ex-con.

And when he set up shop in the little rented space on Ponce de Leon, an east-west thoroughfare in the center of Atlanta, he was filled with optimism. Sure that the next headline-grabbing millionaire-minting case was nothing more than a phone call away. The right plaintiff, the right defendant, the right egregious corporate action.

But so far he didn't have much business or income. While a reasonably steady stream of people came in his door, the vast majority of them had nothing resembling a case. One woman claimed that her supervisor was vindictively putting plants in his office that he knew she was allergic to. Another claimed that everyone at work thought she was a drug abuser because she was sniffling a lot. Nobody had ever accused her of using, but she could tell by the way they looked at her that they were accusing her in their minds. An older man who worked for a department store told Jason that he had been fired due to his age and that the company had invented a reason for termination by claiming that he'd stolen batteries off the shelf. When Jason asked, he admitted that he had been stealing batteries, a lot of batteries, in fact, but there was no way to prove it. In one very unpleasant in-person potential client interview, a woman who worked in retail claimed she was discriminated against when her boss requested that she change her pants after she had visibly menstruated through them. Jason politely declined to represent these people. They were always surprised and sometimes angry. Here or there, he would take on a case that initially sounded good but didn't withstand even a little scrutiny. A lot of people lied to him straight-faced. When he pushed on those lies a little, they caved in.

So far, Jason had taken seven real cases and settled three of them. He'd netted $34,500 after expenses. The year before he quit defending corporations, he had made $165,000 with a $40,000 bonus.

Thus, a year in, Jason was still answering his own phone, sending his own letters and bills, and checking his own citations. He was, perhaps most regrettably, still renting an office far too close to the Clermont Lounge, an establishment in the basement of an abandoned hotel specializing in nonconformist strippers. One of them was (in)famous for smashing beer cans between her massive breasts. She had a Wikipedia page.

The payments on the business loan Jason had taken out to start the firm were becoming harder and harder to make. In a few months, he wouldn't be able to pay them. Jason obsessively looked at his freefalling bank account daily as if vigilance could stop what was happening. The voice in his head that had told him he was making a big mistake when he'd quit had grown louder and more persistent.

The Moxley Case was thus very important to the Law Offices of Jason Hunter, Esq. In a day, it had become the firm's biggest asset.

*****

David Nichols sat on the dark leather couch in Robert Spelkin III's expansive corner office, sinking back with his arms up on the top edge. He put his feet up on the coffee table.

"Well?" David said.

The Prick

David was a ruthless litigator. Clients loved him because he unleashed hell on their behalf. Attorneys respected him, although he was sometimes accused of being willing to do anything to win, which was close to accurate. Robert had never known David to intentionally break a rule, procedural or ethical, but he'd seen him flirt with the ethical boundaries more often than most attorneys were comfortable doing. Sheer aggression pervaded David's litigation teams, and everything he touched was saturated with it. David was who you wanted on your side when you were up against it. And Robert was presently up against it.

"Who does that little bastard Burroughs think he's lecturing?" Robert spat. "I pay his goddamn salary."

David sighed. "Don't be a child, Robert. You know he's right. You've put us all at risk with this shit."

Robert flushed for what must have been the tenth time that day. He could feel his temperature rising.

"Sit down, Robert."

Robert considered.

"Robert."

Robert sat. He hated capitulating to anything as a matter of principle, but he was inclined to be more receptive given the circumstances. He just barely outranked David in the firm's hierarchy. Robert brought in about eighteen million a year in firm revenue, David sixteen at last count.

David took his feet off the table and dropped his elbows to his knees, leaning forward. "Well?" he asked again.

"Well what?"

"Well what the fuck, Robert! How could you be so stupid? And with that revolting blob out there? I figured you for better taste."

Robert forced himself to take a second before responding. He reminded himself that David was important, that David was on his side.

The Prick

"I didn't fucking do it."

"Come on."

"I swear to Christ. I didn't fucking go anywhere near that lying bitch."

"Who are you kidding? I know how loaded you were that night. We must have put down a whole bottle of Scotch upstairs. I was hung over for practically the next three days. I told you to go home when we left. Why the hell did you even come back down to the office?"

The day in question, March 21st, had been a big day for them both. After two and a half years of hardcore litigation, tens of depositions, hundreds of thousands of documents produced, an avalanche of motions and responses, and sanctions threatened on both sides, their opponent, Allen Investment Group, had surrendered.

Back in 2014, Allen had been formed by ten investment bankers and financial advisors who had left Robert's client, multinational bank RSK, NA, literally under cover of darkness, to start up their own competing hedge fund and brokerage house. The most senior of the advisors, Randolph Allen, Jr., had orchestrated the coup and led the group of turncoats out the door on a Friday night. He had incorporated the investment group in Delaware the week before and had been having secret meetings with the rest of the turncoats at RSK's Atlanta office for weeks before he struck the blow, securing hushed oral agreements from his partners and subordinate employees to leave with him if and when he bolted.

RSK General Counsel Rinku Sinati woke Robert up at 2:30 a.m., frantic. By 3:45, David was awake, as were five associates, two paralegals, and one legal assistant. 5:00 a.m. found them all in the office on a Saturday. The legal assistant brought coffee and bagels. The team worked around the clock all weekend to prepare an emergency motion for a temporary restraining order to be filed in federal court on Monday. An assistant general counsel flew down Saturday morning to "help" the team, which consisted mostly of looking over everyone's shoulder, sawing already frayed nerves, and generally getting in the way.

The emergency motion for temporary restraining order was filed at 9:00 a.m. Monday morning. Allen Investment Group hired a well-known white shoe firm out of New York. Both sides declared war. And the fees flowed. All told, Robert and his team racked up 7.5 million dollars due to the protracted discovery disputes and motion practice. Everything was a fight—which meant more hours billed and more revenue. The 7.5 million wasn't the kicker, though. The kicker was that Robert and David had negotiated a contract with RSK that allowed the firm a share of any recovery against Allen Investment Group in exchange for a reduced hourly rate. To be specific, in exchange for reducing partner rates from $750 to $550 an hour and associate rates from $425 to $350 an hour, the firm was promised 25 percent of the take from any settlement or judgment against Allen.

On March 20th, Allen had settled for 57.5 million dollars. On March 21st, the agreements were signed and the money was wired. The firm's coffers swelled by $14,375,000 in one day, on top of the $7.5 million Robert and David had already brought in.

They were the best damn lawyers on the planet. They were invincible.

And so they had taken the whole team upstairs to celebrate. On the top floor of their building was the Peachtree Club, to which Robert and David both belonged. The highlight was a long bar featuring huge windows overlooking Atlanta. Robert and David, slapping backs and high on world domination, declared open bar for their

18

associates and everyone else there, then declared open season on Peachtree's extraordinary selection of Scotch. They sat next to each other, surrounded by their adoring fans, ordered with gleeful and glutinous abandon, and told the waitress to keep coming back if she knew what was good for her. It was 3:30 in the afternoon when the madness began.

"I went back to the office because I had to make sure that I got a filing out," Robert said. "That cow was finalizing it for me."

"Bullshit," David said. "You could barely walk. There's no way you should have gone near any filing. More dangerous than trying to drive a car."

"Which, as I recall, you did."

"So the fuck what? I didn't get caught. I didn't rub my dick against a toll booth attendant on the way home."

Robert didn't laugh. "Listen to me, David. I did not do this."

"Okay," David said. "If that's what you're sticking with. You better hope she's got nothing corroborative. This could be a massive shit storm. Not just at work, you know."

"I know that. This Hunter cocksucker better take the settlement and get out quick. He's playing fast and loose with my life here. I will rip his fucking throat out."

The Prick

Chapter 3

Tuesday, April 2nd
The Moxley House
Norcross, Georgia

The Moxleys had a little house in Norcross that BB&T bank mostly owned. In the last couple years it had depreciated in value, which Pete blamed on President Obama loudly and frequently. The main room was the living room, which adjoined the "cozy" kitchen, adorned with linoleum flooring and fake wooden cabinets. There was a little front yard and a hundred-square-foot fenced-in backyard where they let the dog prowl during the day. The front yard boasted two bushes that had been dispiritedly decorated with one string of Christmas lights, still up from two years prior. There was one car in the short driveway, Pete's Dodge pickup. He dropped Maggie off at the bus station on the way to work in the morning and picked her up again at night, often reeking of beer.

Most weeknights after dinner, Pete watched TV in the living room with the lights off, whatever was on, and drank Keystone Lights in the blue glow while Maggie did sudokus or talked to her sister at the small, wooden kitchen table that badly mismatched the cabinets. Maggie's sister, Kate, had married (much) better than Maggie and lived in Dunwoody. Maggie cringed whenever Kate set foot in her kitchen and surveyed the clashing furniture and appliances.

The Prick

Maggie had recently graduated to moderate-level sudoku. Little sudoku packets only cost a dollar.

Tonight, Pete had apparently landed upon *Two and a Half Men*. Maggie heard him open a new Keystone, his fourth or fifth. There was a punch line and canned laughter came out of the speakers. Pete didn't join in. "This fucking show sucks," he advised, making no move for the remote resting on his stomach.

Maggie had called her sister, but there'd been no answer. Probably out to a nice dinner, although it was late now. She'd left a message asking Kate if she wouldn't mind talking to the lawyer, then placed the phone on the table next to her sudoku so she wouldn't miss it when it rang. She found herself looking at it in between filling in boxes. It was getting so late now.

A commercial blasted from the living room. "You hear from that fucking lawyer yet?" Pete shouted over it.

"Not since yesterday morning."

"Goddamn pervert," Pete said. "He looked like he was fourteen years old. Guy don't know shit. I think maybe we should look at the yellow pages or sump'in."

"But you said Russell recommended him."

"Russell fell off a goddamn ladder and broke his elbow. Too stupid to stay on a ladder. That's what I said at work today, too. Too stupid to stay on a ladder." Pete snorted. "Everybody laughed."

Maggie didn't respond.

"Not hard to prove a guy fell off a ladder."

"I like him," Maggie said quietly.

"Huh, I'm sure you do."

Maggie said nothing. She didn't want to go down this road. Not again.

"I'm sure you wouldn't mind staying after to help him with a little *project*."

The Prick

Maggie could feel the tears starting to well up. "Please don't."

"Yessir, wouldn't mind helping him out with that *extra* hours work." Pete laughed caustically, tilting the Keystone.

"Stop it, Pete!"

The show came back on and Pete quieted down. Maggie looked at the phone, which stayed mute.

Then, fresh out of beer, Pete lumbered into the kitchen. "Yessir," he said. "Yessir." He grabbed another one from the refrigerator, slammed the door shut, looked down at her, and scoffed, shaking his head. "My own goddamn wife. Staying after hours with the big shots ... Fuckin' disgrace." He turned and walked back to the living room. "Like some kind of desperate housewives shit."

"That's not what happened."

"Oh, I know what happened," Pete said. "I know."

Maggie went back to her sudoku and her phone vigil. She heard the crack of the can opening in living room.

"Fuckin' whore," Pete said.

*****

The Spelkin House
Buckhead

Robert arrived home at 7:30, an hour later than normal for a day he wasn't at trial. His house was a large stone expanse that looked like the spawn of a Tudor/castle coupling. Robert had plucked it off the market freshly built for just over five million a few years ago. He pulled his black Mercedes down the long driveway to the right of the house and into the attached garage. His wife, Mary, had managed, for once, to park her Range Rover to the left of the garage instead of dead center. Not endowed with spatial reasoning, she'd backed the SUV directly into their neighbor's mailbox across the street the week before. It still hadn't been fixed, and Robert smiled at the remnants on the way in. For whatever reason, the pile of rubble was one of the only things that cheered Robert up during this waking nightmare. He loved that goddamn smashed mailbox.

He left his briefcase in the trunk, as there was no chance of getting any work done with Moxley's prodigious weight hanging over his head like an obese sword of Damocles. Opening the interior door between the garage and the house, he sighed, totally exhausted. Being in fight-or-flight mode every waking hour took it out of him. And now he was to face the fresh hell of pretending that nothing was wrong until his wife fell asleep.

"Hello?" he called out, stepping into the kitchen. The television in the kids' playroom upstairs was blaring. Meant he had missed dinner.

The kitchen opened up onto the sunken living room, where his wife was reading on one of the pristine white couches, her back to him. Next to her on the edge of the side table, a glass of red wine loomed precariously over the cream-colored carpet. "You didn't call," she said.

"I know, I'm sorry. Got tied up."

"We had an agreement. If you're not going to be home by 6:30, you call."

She didn't trust him, his wife. Not for a while. And it often seemed that she didn't much like him either. There had been an impenetrable, icy, barrier between them for over a year.

"I know, I'm sorry."

She shook her head disapprovingly at her book. "There's pasta in the fridge."

"Thanks."

The Prick

He took his tie and jacket off, flung them on top of one of the two couches, and leaned over to give Mary a kiss on the cheek. She didn't look up at him, or acknowledge the affection, but she didn't pull away as she sometimes did. All in all, a decent reaction.

"How's your day?" he said.

"Fine. Don't think you're leaving your clothes down here."

"Of course not, dear. That would be unthinkable," he said, rubbing her shoulders.

A half smile, quickly suppressed. "And what kept you from dinner with your family—again?" The tone was accusatory. There was a deep wellspring of anger toward him that she could tap into at any time, upon any or no provocation.

What had kept him from dinner with his family, again, was the furious drafting of a threatening response to Hunter's demand letter, which, he knew, would likely be toned down and edited by numerous attorneys if sent at all. "Client control issues," he said. "We're trying to work with Zeneca Pharmaceuticals on understanding their document retention obligations."

"Is that as boring as it sounds?"

"You bet."

"There's pasta in the fridge," she repeated.

Robert got a beer from the kitchen and tore the cellophane off the bowl of cold pasta. "This microwaveable?"

"Yes. Just three minutes on eight. There's also no need for you to feel that you have to eat the whole thing."

"Daddy!" His five-year-old daughter, Sarah, vaulted off the stairs and ran toward him at a dead sprint.

He laughed. "Careful, honey."

The Prick

She bounded into the kitchen and hit his legs with a bear hug. His daughter, sunny, pure, loved him without limitation. She didn't see any of his flaws. She didn't remember any of his failings. Of course, to be fair, she didn't know what his flaws or failings were. Not yet.

Robert picked up his daughter. Out of the corner of his eye, he could see his wife defrosting slightly at the scene. It was temporary, he knew. She would re-frost as soon as she remembered what he'd done. They hadn't had sex in 402 days.

"How was your day today, darling?" he asked Sarah. "Pretty stressful?"

"Bobby won't let me play Xbox," Sarah whined.

"Well that's very good of him," Robert said. "He knows that Xbox is no good for you and that you should be practicing piano."

"Piano's boring."

"What a thing for Buckhead's finest pianist to say. Your fans will be horrified." He set her down. "Go get your recital homework and we'll work on it together."

She scampered off, and the microwave sounded. He grabbed the pasta and the Heineken and sat down at the kitchen table. His wife was watching him.

"Robert."

"Yes, dear?" he replied cautiously.

"Get a napkin."

"You got it," he said, immediately in compliance via the roll on the counter.

He set upon the pasta and beer at intervals. His daughter returned, still moving at a brisk sprint, dragged a chair next to him, and laid out her beginner's piano notebook on the wooden table. As he asked her about her favorite song and downed the pasta while his wife looked on semi-approvingly, as he dimly heard his son waging war against

The Prick

aliens upstairs, a singular thought cycled in his head: I could lose all this.

He had come close to losing it over a year ago when his wife had found the incriminating emails on his laptop. If she found out about the accusations, it would be over. He'd lost the benefit of the doubt in the infidelity department.

I could lose all this.

The Prick

Chapter 4

Thursday April 4th
The Peachtree Club Executive Conference Room

Ned Burroughs called Jason Hunter directly and arranged the meeting. Their conversation lasted all of thirty seconds, and only logistical details were exchanged. Ned wanted to give nothing away and, he suspected, neither did Hunter.

Ned did nothing without a plan and he had this one all worked out and choreographed. He had detailed the game plan in writing (with headers and bullet points) and run it by his boss, William "Will" not "Bill," Simmons, the firm's General Counsel. Simmons told him that it was fine as game plans go but his real task was to keep Spelkin under control and on message. Ned well knew that he had no control whatsoever over Spelkin, the raging and enraged megalomaniac, but he didn't want to admit that to Simmons. So instead he responded, "Yes, of course," as if it was the most natural thing in the world.

And he sat down with all of his key players prior to the meeting and explained with great pains and in great detail what should and should not be said to Hunter and who should say it. To wit, and in deference to his omnipotence, Spelkin would take the lead. He would tell Hunter without a hint of anger or perturbation, that while he understood that, as a *young, solo* litigator, the temptation was to take *any* case that came in the door—and believe *any* allegation that was made—this case had no factual support whatsoever. He would look Hunter squarely in the eye and explain that all of the disgusting and insulting allegations in Hunter's demand letter were ridiculous and completely fallacious and that it would be a tremendous waste of Hunter's time, money, and reputation to go any further with this farce. Above all, his emotional range would be limited to indignation.

Nichols would take over and explain to Hunter the firm's full backing of Robert, the success rate for Title VII sexual harassment cases in the Eleventh Circuit, and the slow and tremendously painful road, which would take years, before Hunter even had a shot at getting to the jury. Even then, Nichols would assure Hunter, the case had no shot at getting to a jury—not only would Moxley end up paying the defense costs, there was a strong likelihood that she would also end up paying the defense's attorneys' fees as well, as the case was nothing short of frivolous.

Enter Ned, who would hit Hunter with the lowball offer, which he would characterize as "generous," given the complete lack of merit in the case, and would demand an immediate resignation by Moxley, a full release of all claims, a confidentiality clause, and a no-rehire provision. Twenty-five thousand in one lump-sum payment to walk away and never say anything again. If Moxley and Hunter had executed a standard contingency-fee agreement, it would net Hunter between eight and ten thousand dollars.

The four men got to the conference room fifteen minutes before the meeting. Coffee and water, but no pastries, were set out. They were in the largest of the four conference rooms at the Peachtree Club.

Spelkin, seated between Ned and David, rubbed his eyes with his fingertips. He did not look well. Ned tried to watch

The Prick

him without being obvious and silently extolled him to keep it together.

Spelkin slammed his hand down on the table. Not a good sign. "This case isn't worth whatever we're paying for this conference room," he said.

"It's complimentary with our membership," Nichols said.

"Well, there you go. It's worth less than nothing."

"Maybe he'll be reasonable and we can end this today," Peters said.

"Let's hope," Ned said. He had brought a draft settlement agreement in a slightly-too-stylish black briefcase that he'd hidden under the table.

Not that settlement was likely to happen today. This was just going to be an opening salvo of threats that would hopefully quash any expectation Hunter had for big money, the starting point of grinding him down to settle somewhere south of $50,000.

After a few minutes, an anonymous Peachtree City Club employee appeared at the door. "Mr. Hunter is here," she said. He was early.

"Thank you," Nichols said. "Please show him in."

Moments later, Jason Hunter himself, the antichrist, walked briskly into the room.

Ned watched Spelkin slowly get out of his chair and shake Hunter's outstretched hand. "Robert Spelkin."

"Pleasure to meet you, Robert," Hunter replied, looking him in the eye. The rest of the men shook hands as well, civil but unmistakably cold.

Spelkin gestured toward a chair. "Have a seat."

"Thanks." Jason nodded to the pot on the other side of the room. "Mind if I grab some of that coffee?"

The Prick

"Sure, I'll pour you a cup," said Ned, quickly getting up to do so before Spelkin could do it. Spelkin walked around the table and closed the door.

As Ned delivered the coffee, Spelkin returned to his seat and gave Hunter his practiced dead-eye stare, usually reserved for hostile adverse witnesses. Hunter smiled back. Ned studied him. He did not appear overly intimidated by the assembled legal firepower.

Peters cleared his throat. "Well, thank you for coming in, Jason. You find it okay?"

"Sure, no problem," Hunter replied. "I actually used to work right down the street."

"With a plaintiff's outfit?" Nichols asked.

"No, up until I went out on my own, I did defense work for years. I was at Pendleton."

Ned exchanged a quick look with Peters. Pendleton was a good firm—actually, a competitor—although not necessarily a peer.

"And how long have you been on your own?" Spelkin asked.

"Just over a year."

"Had any trials yet?"

"Not since I started the firm. You know how many of these cases settle."

"Yes," Spelkin said. "Too many of our clients settle meritless cases just to avoid all the litigation costs."

Peters cleared his throat again, but it was Nichols who interjected, "Which brings us to today, Jason. Obviously, we received your demand letter. The only reason we're here today is to avoid the costs of litigation if you, or somebody else, were to pursue these ridiculous allegations. I understand that you only have your client's word to go on, but you may have some serious problems if you file a

The Prick

Complaint without factual basis, especially here in the Northern District."

Hunter nodded. "Having worked in defense, I know that all allegations made against any client are always ridiculous." He took out a yellow legal pad and pen from his briefcase. "So I take it that Robert denies what Mrs. Moxley says?"

"You're goddamn right I deny it," Spelkin thundered. "I would never go near ... that woman ... or any other woman in the office. I'm married. I have kids. This whole thing is just complete bullshit. It's .... it's fabrication, is what it is. She's just looking for a payday. And I think you, *Jason*, know that."

Hunter made some notes. Spelkin eyed his moving hand.

"Should we bring in a court reporter?" he asked sarcastically.

Ned tried not to wince. The denial had been planned. The swearing, overly hostile tone, extortion accusations, and unbridled aggression had not. In fact, he recalled actively discouraging same. Egotistical fuck had no self-control.

"Probably not necessary ... yet," Hunter said, not looking up. He made additional notes, taking his time. "Why do you think she's making this story up, seemingly out of the blue?"

"I have no idea," Spelkin said, his voice more even. "Maybe tired of her job and looking for a golden parachute out. How should I know? You're the one who took the case."

Hunter continued to write on his pad. Ned fiddled with his pen and glanced around the room. Nichols was alert, eyeing Hunter. Peters, as usual, gave one the impression that no synapses were firing.

Hunter finished writing, put his pen down, and reestablished eye contact with Spelkin. "So you never touched her sexually or made any sexual propositions to her?"

31

The Prick

Nichols laughed. "Objection, compound," he said. "You know this isn't a deposition, right? He already told you he didn't do anything of the sort. He denies everything. The firm denies everything."

"That's fine, Mr. Nichols. I'm just trying to get an understanding of what happened so I can figure out how to proceed. If Mr. Spelkin wants to take the Fifth here, that's fine. It can wait until the deposition."

"I am not fucking taking the fucking Fifth! None of this shit happened!"

Hunter raised his eyebrows. "Never?"

Spelkin looked at Hunter like he was trying to extinguish his existence through sheer force of will. "Never."

"What about on March 21st? Had you been drinking?"

"All right, that's it." Ned put his hand up like a police officer stopping traffic. "No more. You aren't going to subject Robert to cross-examination. We're here to make you an offer. In exchange for a full release of all claims, a confidentiality and nondisclosure agreement, Mrs. Moxley's immediate resignation, and a no-rehire clause, we'll pay her a severance of twenty-five thousand with customary payroll taxes, which we believe is very generous given the strength of the case."

Hunter smiled broadly. He wrote $25,000 at the top of his legal pad, in numbers big enough for everyone across the table to see. He put his pad and pen in his briefcase and stood.

"Listen, gentlemen, I'm not going to respond to that number. We all know it's a joke. If you want to make a real offer, you know how to reach me."

"In six months, you'll wish you'd taken that money and run," Spelkin spat out.

The Prick

"Maybe," Hunter said, "but I don't think so. I think in six months you'll wish you'd come to the table with a number that isn't insulting."

"You better be very careful, kid." Spelkin said. "This is my life you're playing with."

"Then you should take it more seriously," Hunter said. "Tomorrow afternoon, I'm taking Mrs. Moxley with me to the EEOC to file a Charge."

"She's supposed to be working tomorrow," Spelkin said.

"Surely you're not interfering with Mrs. Moxley's federally protected right to initiate a claim with the EEOC?"

"No," Peters said, coming to. "Of course not."

"Good," Hunter said, his hand on the door handle. "If you get me a real number by tomorrow morning, then I'll try to persuade my client to hold off on filing the Charge to see if we can resolve this thing. She may not, though. She's very upset."

Spelkin shook his big head. "Unbelievable. Just fucking unbelievable."

"We'll discuss this," Ned said. "Can you give us until next week?"

"No," Hunter said. "I hear a real number tomorrow or the Charge is filed. Then you have to not only contend with me, but explain things to the EEOC."

"We will be more than happy to do that," Spelkin said.

"We'll discuss it and get back to you," Ned corrected.

"Fine," Hunter said, looking at him, not Spelkin. "I look forward to hearing from you."

*****

Jason turned the handle and walked out. Down the hallway lined with portraits of former presidents of the Peachtree Club, past the posh restaurant and bar with the big views, around the front desk with the blankly smiling receptionist, and into the elevator, Jason Hunter was

33

smiling. This was real. They were scared. In that moment, he loved Maggie Moxley as much as he had ever loved anyone.

*****

Before Ned's afternoon flight back to D.C., he, Spelkin, and Nichols went to lunch at Morton's in downtown Atlanta. Peters had begged off in favor of a supposed client lunch. They quickly ordered and got down to business.

"He goes through with filing and the firm will immediately hire outside counsel," Ned announced, slicing a piece of his $40 steak with satisfaction. He clearly couldn't manage Spelkin. Someone more senior might be able to persuade him to keep his mouth shut.

The meeting with Hunter had not gone well, at all. Hunter hadn't even blinked. Spelkin had come off as a defensive blowhard and nearly threatened Hunter personally. The worst possible thing to do, for settlement purposes, was to tie the ego of the plaintiff's attorney to the case. Unless there was some strategic advantage, you didn't make it personal. Spelkin should know that.

"We obviously aren't going to bid against ourselves and send him a new offer tomorrow morning, right?" asked Nichols, who was moving aggressively through a rare T-bone.

"I'll have to speak with Will on that when I get back. My recommendation will be not to move from twenty-five thousand until Hunter's at least reduced his demand. We may want to raise the response a bit to show that we're willing to negotiate."

"Under normal circumstances, I would withdraw the settlement offer entirely," Spelkin piped up. "Let that arrogant little bastard explain to the client how he made thousands disappear."

The Prick

"Well ..."

Spelkin held up his hand. "In this case, however, I think we should go up to fifty K. At least delay the filing of the EEOC Charge and see if this fucker will talk in good faith."

Ned and Nichols exchanged a look, which, unfortunately, Spelkin caught.

"I'm not going to say this again," Spelkin said. "And I shouldn't have to. I did not fucking do this."

"We know that," Ned said, thinking the exact opposite. "I just—"

"That's a weak fucking move," Nichols said. "You know that, Robert. What would you say to a client who suggested bidding against himself? You need to be objective here, keep your emotions out of it."

"How am I supposed to be objective? This gets out and I am in a fucking shit storm at home. You know that, David." Spelkin turned to Ned. "Put yourself in my shoes. I need the firm to make this go away."

"Not two hours ago, you didn't want to pay a cent," Nichols said. "I believe you said the case is worth less than nothing. Now you want to up the ante to fifty?"

"Think about what happens if she files a Charge with the EEOC," Spelkin said. "Think of what happens if the EEOC takes it seriously and investigates. What happens if they come around wanting to do interviews with the other receptionists? How soon before this bullshit spreads around town? How soon before it gets around to Mary's friends?"

Ned noticed for the first time that Spelkin wasn't eating. He had carved the porterhouse up but it was just sitting on his plate in untouched squares.

"Okay. You know this is just going to whet the kid's appetite, right?" Nichols said.

The Prick

"I don't care," Spelkin said. "I need this to quietly go away. We need to squash this before anybody else hears about it." He looked right at Ned. "Make it go away."

Accustomed to seeing nothing but anger and condescension from Spelkin since this started, Ned was startled by the abrupt change. He was actually pleading. Ned nodded and looked away, embarrassed by the drop of the macho veneer, gratified to learn that the great Robert Spelkin III was in fact human and acknowledged the presence of mortal danger.

*****

"Jesus. Robert fucking Spelkin."

Jason grinned and took a sip of Weihenstephaner. He had a standing rendezvous with his old law school friend Mark Brunnell at Bookhouse Pub every Thursday happy hour, and it'd been a while since there'd been anything good to report.

"Yep. You should have seen them, circling the wagons around him. There must have been a collective net worth of fifty million across the table from me. At the goddamn Peachtree Club. David Nichols was there, too."

"Wow," Brunnell said. "You're pissing on a hornet's nest here. You know that, right? These are the big boys." Brunnell worked in commercial litigation defense and ran in some of the same circles, or at least was in the orbit of Spelkin's circles.

"I know."

"You keep this case and you may not be able to go back to defense work in this city."

Jason took a big gulp of his beer. Brunnell was right.

"Who says I want to go back? I may be able to pay back most of my loan with the money that's going to come rolling in on this one."

"You actually think he did it?"

The Prick

"Yeah. She's pretty convincing, and he thinks he owns the world. Thinks he's untouchable," Jason said. "You should have seen him today. He all but threatened me if I brought suit."

"It's hard to believe he'd be dumb enough to try to fuck someone in the office. Seems like he'd have more sense. Take it outside."

"When nature calls," Jason said. "He had an irresistible urge to point it in someone's direction. Sexual harassment will always be around unless we're all neutered. Men have been trying to compel female contact with their junks for thousands of years and will continue to do so long after we're gone."

Brunnell shook his head. "Men are such pigs."

"I tell you what my biggest problem is, if we ever get to a jury," Jason said. "The victim's pretty damn unattractive. It adds another level of persuasion. I have to convince the jury that Spelkin's a bad guy, that he would cheat on his wife, and that he'd risk life and career to put his dick on a woman that no man with viable options would go after."

Brunnell laughed. "Speaking of that, you want to go to the Clermont after this?"

"No way," Jason said. "I'm never going back there ever again."

"That's what I thought. You need to be more open-minded."

Jason shook his head. "I need this money, Brunnell," Jason said, raising his hand in the direction of the waitress for another beer. "If this thing works out, I may even be able to avoid bankruptcy."

The Prick

Chapter 5

Friday, April 5th
The Law Offices of Jason Hunter, Esq.

Jason rolled into his office around 10:15, bagel and coffee in hand. His pounding headache begrudgingly subsided while he checked his email, talked with Brunnell on Gchat, and meandered through Facebook for about an hour. As of 11:45, there was no word from Levitt, Bennett & Taylor, LLP.

"Very surprising," he said aloud.

He'd called the Moxleys at home before going to Bookhouse the night before, to tell them about the meeting and the $25000 offer. He had agreed with Pete Moxley's assessment that the offer was "fuckin' bullshit," consoled an upset Maggie Moxley—who was particularly offended that they expected her to resign—and assured both that the $25,000 was just the jumping-off point for negotiations. He'd told Maggie he would pick her up at work the next day to go to the EEOC. She was going to file unless the number was too good not to jump on immediately.

Jason cycled through a Facebook album of one of his ex-girlfriends, who'd apparently photographed every quarter minute of a debaucherous bachelorette party to Vegas, and watched the clock on the bottom right of his screen. 11:57 a.m., 11:58 a.m. Had he misread the situation? Was Spelkin really innocent? Was Moxley pathological? He couldn't go back on his word and counter the $25,000 now. He would look weak. Given the disparities in age and experience between Jason and the others at the Peachtree Club conference table, he had to maintain an air of self-assurance and at least the outward appearance of a backbone.

11:59 a.m. All right, they were going to play hardball. Jason came to the end of the bachelorette pictorial, which featured several blurred images from what seemed to be the end of the night. It was time to call Moxley, inform her of the bad news, assure her that everything would work out, likely try to quiet her crying, and draft a Complaint. Jason picked up the phone and started dialing.

Then the little manila envelope icon popped up on his screen. Twelve noon on the dot. It was an email from Ned Burroughs, copying Peters and somebody named Will Simmons. The subject of the email was CONFIDENTIAL SETTLEMENT COMMUNICATION. The subtext was capitulation.

Mr. Hunter:

In exchange for your agreement to delay the filing of the EEOC Charge, and in a good faith attempt to settle this action in lieu of unnecessary expenditure of attorneys' fees and costs, Levitt will agree to pay to Mrs. Moxley a lump sum payment of thirty-seven thousand, five hundred dollars ($37,500.00), less applicable payroll taxes, provided that Mrs. Moxley (i) execute a full release of any and all claims against Levitt, Bennett & Taylor, LLP, and Mr. Spelkin; (ii) immediately resign her employment; (iii) agree to a no re-hire clause; and (iv) agree to a confidentiality and nondisclosure agreement.

This is in no way any admission by Levitt regarding any of Mrs. Moxley's false allegations, which allegations Levitt denies in their entirety. Please be advised that, should Mrs. Moxley decide to pursue any action related to these false claims, Levitt will vigorously defend the action and will seek costs and attorneys' fees when it is dismissed.

Please confirm that you will delay filing the EEOC Charge, as we agreed, to permit the parties to continue to pursue resolution of this matter. If Mrs. Moxley agrees to the above terms, I will send you a draft settlement agreement for her to execute.

Regards,

Ned Burroughs

Jason smiled and dialed the number.

"Maggie, hi, this is Jason Hunter. How are you?"

"Fine. Did we hear anything?" She was whispering and Jason could barely make out what she was saying. He had called her on her cell phone but she was clearly at the office.

"Yes. They just bid against themselves. They're up to $37,500. They're scared, Maggie."

"Do ... do they still want me to leave?"

"Yes. That's pretty standard in these situations."

"But I need my job."

"I know. Whatever amount we get will be enough to hold you over until you can find a new one. Maybe something closer to home."

"Okay. Do you think we should take the offer?"

Jason closed his eyes and shook his head. Jesus. "No. This is just a starting point. And it's still low. Now we put the pressure on them. We'll go down to the EEOC this afternoon."

"Okay. Can you call Pete?"

Fuck. "Sure I can."

"He said he wanted to know everything that's going on."

"I'll give him a call, and I'll pick you up at your office at 2:30. Can you meet me in the parking lot?"

"Okay."

"All right, see you then. This is good news, Maggie."

"Okay."

Jason turned his attention back to Mr. Burroughs.

Ned,

Thank you for your email. While I'm sure this was simply a misunderstanding, I never agreed to delay the filing of the EEOC Charge if Levitt raised its offer from one unreasonable number to another slightly less unreasonable number. I agreed to attempt to persuade Mrs. Moxley to delay the filing of the EEOC Charge if I received a real number this morning. I did not. We will be filing the EEOC Charge today. I trust that Mrs. Moxley will be excused from work this afternoon in order to participate in the federally protected EEOC investigative process.

You should be hearing from the EEOC soon. Please ensure that there is no retaliation against Mrs. Moxley.

Please also note that Levitt is formally on notice of pending litigation, giving rise to an immediate and ongoing duty to preserve any and all discoverable documents and other material that is potentially relevant to this action, including, but not limited to, all electronically stored information, or "ESI." I will be seeking all relevant ESI immediately upon the filing of this action.

The Prick

Sincerely,
Jason Hunter

Jason reread the email twice, smiling to himself, and hit "send." Now the husband.

"This is Pete."

"Pete, Jason Hunter. Maggie asked me to call you and give you an update."

"Give me a minute."

Jason heard some commotion in the background, followed by Pete calling someone a "friggin' retard" and telling someone else he was on break. After about two minutes, Pete came back on the line.

"You still there?"

"I'm here."

"How much they offer?"

"Well, they came back at thirty-seven five. But that's—"

"Buuuulllllshit. You sure they know we're serious?"

"Yes, I'm sure. That's just a starting point. This process may take a while. I'm taking Maggie to the EEOC this afternoon. That will send a message."

"You didn't already send a message in your meeting yesterday? How much that meeting cost me?"

"I did and the meeting didn't cost you anything. Remember how I explained the contingency fee agreement?"

"Uh-huh. So when do we get some of this money?"

"No money until we actually reach an agreement. As I explained, if they don't come to the table and we have to litigate, it may take years."

"Fuck that. You sure you told them cocksuckers how serious this shit is?"

"Yes. I'll let you see the Complaint I put together."

The Prick

"Uh-huh. They still want her to leave her job? She needs that job."

"Right now they do."

"Better give us a lot of fuckin' money then."

"That's the general idea. There are no guarantees."

"Make sure to let me know how she does today," Pete said. "You want me to come?"

Jason flashed back to an EEOC mediation from his defense days. The plaintiff, a white woman who was claiming violations of the Americans with Disabilities Act, had brought her backwoods husband—who was wearing a Confederate flag T-shirt. While the EEOC mediator, a black woman, never mentioned the shirt, the mediation had gone quite well for the company Jason was defending.

"No, I'll handle it."

"Get it done," Pete said. "Them bastards got all the money in the world." He hung up.

"Prick," Jason said into the dial tone. Wife gets sexually molested and he thinks it's his lottery ticket. And that he's somehow in charge.

The Prick

Chapter 6

Friday, April 5th
The Atlanta Office of the EEOC

Ryan Sparks sighed and rebooted his ancient computer, which had frozen again. Third time today. He kicked it and then looked up at his doorway to make sure nobody had seen him. He had been with the EEOC for two and a half years—which he calculated was roughly 30 years after the agency had acquired the computer—and worked in the downtown location of the Atlanta branch. Small, and windowless, Ryan's interior office was packed with hundreds of case files that lined the walls and filled the cheap bookcases.

Ryan made just under thirty-five thousand dollars a year and worked from 8:00 to 5:30, Monday through Friday. He had 157 open Charges against 150 different employers. He couldn't hope to keep them all in his mind at once. The stacks of cases ringing his desk had grown higher in the past six months. Budget cutbacks had delayed the hiring of new investigators when there were resignations, but thankfully the office hadn't yet experienced any layoffs. Meanwhile, the volume of Charges they handled was at a record level. More alleged discrimination and harassment than ever before in the agency's history. Even after two and half years, Ryan thought most of the allegations were true. And if they weren't, well ... the corporations got away with enough. He was a people's champion, one of the very few.

A "people's champion," of course, was not what the EEOC professed to be. The EEOC was supposedly an independent and neutral government agency tasked with ascertaining whether an illegal employment action had in fact occurred, then taking whatever action was necessary to right the wrong. The EEOC was empowered, through its in-house attorneys, to file suit against employers, but only if an EEOC investigator had first engaged in a "neutral" investigation that led the investigator to conclude that there was cause to believe there had been discrimination, and that the employer thereafter didn't resolve the action through the conciliation process. The EEOC was supposed to take sides, in other words, only after the neutral investigation revealed that the employee's allegations had merit.

So Ryan's job, as formally described, was to intake written Charges of Discrimination from persons who felt they had been wronged, assist in the drafting of the Charge of Discrimination if necessary, send the Charge to the employer, and request information and a "position statement." In this position statement, presumably following an internal investigation into the matter, the employer was expected to describe its version of the challenged events and employment practices and justify the alleged adverse employment action that had befallen the employee.

Ryan had never seen a position statement that didn't deny each and every allegation of discrimination, harassment, retaliation, or wrongful treatment. According to corporate America, nothing bad ever happened. All was well.

Ryan was sending a follow-up email to a large poultry plant in rural Georgia, seeking documents regarding a claim of systemic discrimination against Hispanics when his phone rang. It was the front desk.

"This is Ryan."

"There's an attorney here to see you. He's with his client and wants to file a Charge."

"I'm not on Charge filing today."

"I know, but he asked for you specifically."

"What's his name?"

"Jason Hunter."

He laughed. "All right, I'll be around."

Ryan had met Hunter years earlier, on one of his first investigations. They'd wrangled with each other on three separate Charges filed against a grocery store chain by African-American plaintiffs alleging discrimination in promotions. Their earlier interactions had been largely testosterone-fueled shouting matches over the phone, but as the Charges progressed and the issues became more defined, the blustering lost steam, and the two found themselves speaking civilly to each other, perhaps more out of mutual exhaustion than anything else. Over time, they developed a good relationship, even an affable one. While Ryan and Hunter remained adversaries throughout what would turn out to be a grueling series of investigations, they fought only on the issues that needed fighting rather than every single possible point of contention that could be manufactured. Ryan, who experienced wide ranges of competency and forthrightness in the attorneys defending the corporations he investigated, came to respect Hunter. Smart, hardworking, and, for a defense attorney, honest. Probably as honest as he could be without getting fired.

The respect seemed to be mutual. Whenever Hunter had a client who needed to file a claim, he always asked for Ryan.

The Prick

When Ryan got up to the reception area, Hunter was speaking in low tones to a middle-aged woman.

"Jason."

Hunter turned around with a broad grin. "Good to see you, Ryan," he said, extending a big hand. "Ryan Sparks, meet Maggie Moxley."

"Hello, Mrs. Moxley."

"Oh, hello. Nice to meet you."

"Ryan is an investigator with the EEOC," Hunter explained. "Ryan, Maggie needs to file a Charge."

"Okay, why don't we move this discussion to my office," Ryan said, gesturing behind him to the hallway. Hunter pulled him quickly aside as Moxley moved to comply.

"You're going to like this one," Hunter said, nodding at his slow-moving client and grinning. "This one is a gift."

Ryan grinned back.

Chapter 7

Friday, April 5th
Washington D.C. Offices of Levitt, Bennett & Taylor, LLP

"Does this guy know what the fuck he's doing?"

Will Simmons, the firm's General Counsel and a former United States magistrate judge, slurped coffee at his huge mahogany desk. His back was to Ned, who'd been summoned to Simmons's office to discuss the Spelkin Situation a few hours after they received the disappointing (frightening) response from Hunter. Simmons reviewed the Hunter email on his forty-inch flat screen monitor. Ned had never seen a bigger monitor—the email was almost legible from eight feet away.

Although Burroughs had recommended to Simmons, in a three-page internal and confidential memorandum, that Levitt not come off the twenty-five thousand offer until they received at least some counter from Hunter, Burroughs had received a terse email instruction from Simmons at 11:55 a.m. to raise the offer to $37,500.00.

"Hard to tell." Ned responded. "Hunter is relatively junior, but he comes from Pendleton. Opened up his own shop about a year ago. Haven't been able to get much intel on him from the Atlanta office."

All of that had of course been in the memo, but it was unlikely that Simmons had read the memo.

"Well, it appears that he won't even fucking make a counteroffer to the thirty-seven five. And now he's gone and brought the EEOC into this mess. But I don't care what the great and powerful Robert Spelkin wants, I'm not bidding against myself a second time."

"We shouldn't have done it the first time," Ned said. "It just emboldened the guy." Perhaps a bit risky to criticize the boss's decision, but he was annoyed that his advice had been brushed aside.

"I know. I read your memo. Gave me heartburn to up the number. Spelkin called and asked me as a 'personal favor,'" Simmons said, making air quotes. He finally turned from the IMAX to face Ned.

"You think he did it?"

"Probably," Ned said. "He's pretty defensive for a guy with nothing to hide. And then there's the flip-flop. First he's making all these threats and saying the firm shouldn't offer a dime, and then he's making personal phone calls over my head to ask for an increase in our offer. Not exactly the behavior of an innocent man."

Simmons nodded slowly, closed his eyes, and massaged his temples. "What are we doing about this woman in the meantime, Moxley?"

"She's been transferred to a different attorney—I can get the name. Another legal assistant, male, has been temporarily assigned to Spelkin."

"This is a bad situation," Simmons said. "It's always worse when they're current employees. I almost want to fire her and take our lumps just to get her out of there."

"There'd be no way of getting around the retaliation Complaint. Even if Spelkin didn't do it and Hunter can't prove anything, he'd have us in the crosshairs if we termed her now."

"I know. I just wish this Hunter character seemed a bit more willing to negotiate. The guy won't move off two fucking million? Title VII punitive damages are capped at three hundred thousand."

"I don't know what he's thinking," Ned said. "Of course, he knows what this would do to Spelkin personally if it got out. There are other extralegal damages he's counting on."

"Well, if we aren't going to settle this thing early, and we aren't going to term her or get her to agree to resign, then we need to do an internal investigation." Simmons put his elbows on the desk. "She didn't exactly contact Human Resources, but she did have Hunter alert the Managing Partner that the harassment had taken place. We can hold off another week at the most. Soon, though, we have to start."

"That could get really messy."

"I know," Simmons said. "Is there any way we can get rid of her? Any legitimate reason that would hold up?"

They stared at each other for a moment, each fully cognizant that Simmons had just baldly suggested retaliation. Ned swallowed, visions of future depositions in his head. Their conversation was arguably privileged. But it was also arguably not.

"Moxley's been with the firm about five years," Ned answered cautiously. "Her performance evals are all largely the same. Bottom line, entirely competent at what she does. Has never been on a performance improvement plan, hasn't been disciplined."

"Goddammit," Simmons said, pressing his palms against his eyes. He looked as though he were self-administering a full head massage.

"We might be able to do it as a larger layoff," Ned suggested. "Maybe ten percent of the clerical staff in Atlanta? Then staff back up in six months. Would give Peters a chance to get rid of some of his dead weight."

The Prick

"Peters gets rid of dead weight and he'll get rid of Peters," Simmons said. "Interesting. Let me think on that. Right now, however, we need to figure out who to pull in from HR if we decide to pull the trigger on the investigation. And we need to retain outside counsel."

"Agreed," Ned said, inwardly rejoicing. His involvement in this mess, he hoped, was about to become exceedingly tangential. "Who do you have in mind?"

Simmons put his palms down on the desk and grinned wolfishly. "I was thinking maybe Rebecca Trent."

"Jesus. You think that's necessary?"

"Yes. It's time to let this Hunter kid know the fight he's in for if he keeps playing hardball on this thing."

Ned smiled.

*****

Personal Residence of Rebecca Trent, Esq.
Brookhaven, Georgia

Rebecca Trent allowed herself one drink a week. A double shot of Maker's on the rocks every Friday evening. When she wasn't traveling, she normally took it before the babysitter was set to leave. A bracer before consecutive hours enduring the family. The evening of Friday, April 5th, found Rebecca in her preferred position, lounging on the second-story deck in her favorite oversized cushioned wicker chair, feet up on the table, bourbon handy. The deck overlooked the large and lush backyard, where she could see the high school-aged babysitter chasing her screaming three-year-old around. She smiled at the scene. The babysitter wasn't long for this house. She was filling out and Rebecca had noticed her husband looking her over, thinking he was being subtle about it. Rebecca would make sure the next one was a dog. Although her husband knew better. One

51

slip up and Rebecca would call the police and leave him with nothing.

She was taking a good deep sip when her cell phone rang. It was a DC area code.

"Rebecca Trent," she answered briskly.

"Evening, Rebecca. Will Simmons."

A surprise. "Hey, Will. Long time no see."

"Yep. Ever since the fast food case wrapped up."

Simmons and Rebecca had worked together in a putative gender discrimination class action. Simmons, who represented the franchisor, had brought Rebecca in to represent the franchisee. She'd demolished the named plaintiff in deposition, effectively ending the case.

"So what's going on? You got another class action for me?"

"No, we've got ... well, we've got a bit of a situation in our Atlanta office. Very delicate situation in fact. I was hoping you might agree to help us out."

"What type of situation?"

"It has been alleged—" Simmons cleared his throat. "It has been *alleged* that one of our partners sexually harassed his legal assistant. Obviously this is highly confidential ... and potentially very damaging."

"I see," said Rebecca. "Let me guess: David Nichols."

Simmons actually laughed at that. "It's not Nichols, but I won't tell you the name until you're formally retained."

"Fair enough. Who's the accuser?"

"Her name is Margaret Moxley," Simmons said. "She's been in our Atlanta office for six years. Never before filed a Complaint against anyone, as far as we can tell. I very much doubt you've ever run across her."

"Gotta check."

"Of course."

"So what is it that Mrs. Moxley is alleging, exactly?"

Simmons cleared his throat again. "We will fill you in completely when you're formally retained."

"You got allergies, Will?"

"What? No, why?"

"Never mind. I actually have some bandwidth to take on something new. I would want to bring on a senior associate for this. Standard rates. Seven hundred an hour for me, four forty for the associate."

"That's fine."

Rebecca smiled. She liked clients who didn't blink. "I'm assuming this is going to be a bad one, or you wouldn't have called me."

More throat clearing. "Yes."

"All right. I'll run the conflicts check right away and send you the standard retainer letter."

"Thanks. Talk to you soon."

"Have a good weekend."

Rebecca hung up the phone. "Finally some fun again."

She drained the remaining half inch of Maker's in one gulp and dialed the number for her right hand, Maria Chan. As always, Maria answered on the first ring.

"Hi, Rebecca," she said in her perky soprano.

"You still at the office?" Rebecca asked, knowing the answer.

"Yes, just working on the Salons appeal."

"Good. Do me a favor. Run a quick conflicts check for Margaret Moxley, legal assistant at Levitt. Potential adverse party."

"Okay, will do!"

"Let me know the results tonight."

"Not a problem!"

"You have room on your plate for another case? Individual?"

"Sure, of course!"

The Prick

"All right. Just send me an email when you get the results in. It clears, you'll be on the case with me."

"Okay!"

Rebecca hung up. "Hey, Jennifer!" she shouted. "Bring Jeffrey in and get him washed up for dinner."

"Okay, Mrs. Trent," the little slut replied.

Alone on the back deck, Rebecca nodded, satisfied.

Chapter 8

Wednesday, April 10th
Atlanta Offices of Levitt, Bennett & Taylor, LLP

Jimmy Peters never worked more than five days a week and on most weeks only made it into the office two or three. He lived well north of the city, Atlanta traffic was among the worst in the nation, and there were only so many Nelson DeMille books that he could listen to on CD. So a few days a week, Jimmy would "work from home," which meant sporadically responding to email while watching the Golf Channel in his underwear. As the Managing Partner of the Atlanta office, he had a modest but steady stream of money coming in from old established clients (originally inherited from his father) on cases that he rarely had to deal with personally. He was given "origination credit" because his long-term relationships with the clients brought the cases in, and origination credit was all that really mattered to an equity partner. The end result was that he did about fifteen hours of actual work per week, did so when it suited him, and took home about half a million a year.

The average associate at Levitt billed about 2,100 hours a year, the average non-equity partner about 2,000, and the average equity partner about 1,700. Jimmy billed just over eight hundred. He made sure, however, to religiously log thousands of "non-billable" hours per year, mostly allocated to the amorphous "Management" billing code, which Jimmy privately interpreted to encompass nearly everything he did while awake. Really, all he had to do was manage the office, which was full of control-freak attorneys who wouldn't listen to him about anything important anyway. As for the staff, there was an Office Manager for that.

Jimmy had become lazy and complacent, both in body and mind. And he knew it. And he didn't give a solitary damn. He had figured out a loophole, and that made him smart.

But this Spelkin Situation was really putting a hurt on his loophole. All kinds of firm dignitaries had been calling his office line with disturbing frequency, including Hal Stairs, the firm's Managing Partner, and Will Simmons, the firm's General Counsel. Both seemingly expected him to be in his office, or at least within shouting distance, literally every weekday. Worse yet, when they reached him, they seemed to expect him to be fully aware of what was going on. He was also, at least judging from Simmons's tone, expected to be able to control the actions of such firm juggernauts as Robert Spelkin III, and David Fucking Nichols.

And so Jimmy was in his office the morning of Wednesday, April 13th, when the Charge came in. Although the EEOC had steadfastly refused to acknowledge the existence of email well into the twenty-first century, demanding communications be sent to them by standard US Mail and fax, the newer and younger investigators were beginning to buck the trend and take advantage of late '90s technology.

"Fuck," Jimmy said when the Charge popped up in his inbox, subject line "Margaret Moxley, Charge No. 2016-071312."

"Fuck," Jimmy said when he saw who the investigator was. Ryan Sparks was a very bad draw. Sparks, who had found Cause on the last two Charges of Discrimination that Jimmy had handled against the EEOC (through an associate, of course), had taken the liberty of emailing the Charge to Jimmy personally.

Jimmy opened the PDF and read the facts section.

I. Charging Party, Margaret Moxley, is employed by Respondent as a Legal Assistant in its Atlanta office. Charging Party has held the position of Legal Assistant for approximately five years. Respondent is an international law firm with over 25 locations and over 500 employees.

II. Charging Party was formerly the Legal Assistant for equity partner Robert Spelkin III.

III. On or about March 21, Mr. Spelkin instructed Charging Party that she had to stay late to finish a work assignment. Complying with her direct supervisor's instructions, Charging Party was working on the assignment after normal work hours at her desk when Mr. Spelkin came into her work area, exposed his erect penis to Charging Party, pointed at it, and told Charging Party that it was her "assignment." Charging Party immediately turned around and tried to ignore Mr. Spelkin and resume working on her computer. Mr. Spelkin then approached Charging

Party, and with her back to him, forcibly put his erect penis against her neck and told Charging Party to "put it in [her] mouth." When Charging Party tried to pull away and told Mr. Spelkin, "Stop" and "I can't," Mr. Spelkin kept trying to put his erect penis close to her face and told Charging Party, "I know you want to" and said "nobody will know."

IV. Charging party proceeded to get up from her chair and run to the ladies' room. Mr. Spelkin tried to physically impede Charging Party from leaving her cubicle and tried to grab her physically.

V. After approximately twenty minutes in the ladies' room, Charging Party went back to her desk to collect her belongings and left the building.

VI. On April 1, Charging Party reported Mr. Spelkin's conduct to James Peters *[Fuck!]*, the Managing Partner of the Atlanta office of Respondent, by and through her attorney. To date, Peters has taken no action to address the sexual assault other than to transfer Charging Party to another attorney.

VII. Charging Party alleges that Respondent has violated, *inter alia*,

The Prick

Title VII of the Civil Rights Act of 1964,
42 U.S.C. § 2000(e) *et seq.*, which
prohibits sexual harassment.

Jimmy felt his blood pressure rising and his beleaguered heart thumping. He forced himself to take deep breaths—it was dangerous for a man of his age and weight to have such a sudden spike in beats per minute. Hunter and Sparks had named him in the Charge! It was so unfair! They'd basically made him Spelkin's accomplice, complicit in the cocknecking. He had nothing to do with it!

The email requested documents relating to any firm policies regarding harassment, any complaints regarding harassment in the Atlanta office or Robert Spelkin, and "all documents evidencing or related to Levitt's investigation of Charging Party's formal complaint of sexual harassment by her supervisor." Finally, Sparks requested immediate dates for onsite interviews of Spelkin, Jimmy, Nichols, and legal assistants Patricia Hayes and Jessica Rossi. Patty Hayes was a middle-aged woman who had been in the office for as long as Jimmy could remember. He vaguely recalled seeing her eating lunch with Moxley in the break room on the forty-seventh floor. Jessica Rossi was an attractive and, he believed, single woman in her thirties. Jimmy didn't get the connection to Rossi. He'd never seen her with Moxley. Then again, Rossi used to assist David Nichols.

Jimmy shook his head, feeling incredibly sorry for himself. They had no right to drag him into this thing.

He forwarded the email, with the attached Charge, to Stairs, Simmons and Burroughs, changing the subject line to PRIVILEGED AND CONFIDENTIAL and writing, "Just received this. Have dealt with this investigator before. Please call me to discuss."

The Prick

Jimmy sighed. At least his blood pressure had come back down. But this was getting exponentially worse. He wouldn't want to be in the room when Spelkin found out. Once the onsite investigation started there would be no keeping it quiet.

*****

Every weekday at noon, Maggie had lunch with her best friends at work, who were also her best friends, period. She ate her sandwich, drank her apple juice, gossiped for exactly twenty-five minutes, and left with enough time to get back to her desk by 12:30. Under normal circumstances, lunch was her favorite part of the day.

But lately, after *IT* had happened, lunchtime had been torture. Maggie was filled with a vague sense of guilt all the time. After she'd met with the attorney it had gotten worse, and now that she'd actually filed a Charge, it had become intolerable.

She was paranoid. She involuntarily analyzed every comment, every look, every action to assess what it meant about that person's knowledge or opinion (if they knew) about what had happened with Robert.

Maggie looked at her watch. 11:59 a.m. She could hear Marcia Henderson coming around her cube, wheezing. Marcia always wheezed a little because she was well over three hundred pounds. Maggie secretly viewed Marcia as a precautionary warning and, even though it made her feel bad, she thought about Marcia when she contemplated dessert, or seconds. A wheezing, gracious, sweet disincentive.

Marcia paused at Maggie's desk and caught her breath. "You ready for lunch, sweetie?"

"Sure."

The Prick

"You awright, darling? You been awful quiet this week," Marcia said. Maggie nodded without saying anything and Marcia took the lead. Marcia always led or followed because it was impossible to walk next to her in the hallway. The two stopped at Patty Hayes's desk, which was on the way to the break room. Trina Stewart and Debbie Marsh would come from the other side of the building.

"You ready?" Marcia asked Patty.

"S'pose so," Patty said, smiling at Maggie. Was that a knowing smile? The caravan, grown by a third, got ambling again.

"You girls see the news today?" Patty always knew the news today.

"No," Marcia said, maintaining pole position. "Been working on this brief all morning. Robert put so much red ink on that kid's draft I have to stop and wonder why he didn't just start from scratch."

"Well," Patty said, "the police arrested a man for sittin' on his porch naked, touchin' himself when the mail lady came by." She burst out laughing, as did Marcia in front. Maggie almost threw up. They knew. They definitely knew.

"'Parently it wasn't even the first time he done it!" Patty managed to get out, still stricken with laughter behind Maggie.

How could Patty be so cruel? Maggie had thought Patty was her friend.

They reached the break room and took turns at the fridge. They had the room to themselves today. Trina and Debbie promptly joined them. Trina, the best looking of the bunch, was tall, blonde, stylish, and looked thirty-five at forty-seven. Debbie was small and mousy. Maggie always felt—even in the good times—that Debbie kind of picked on her. Marcia and Patty were still laughing when the two walked in.

The Prick

"What y'all laughing about?" asked Debbie.

"Wieners!" Marcia burst out. With that, Patty, who was by the sink trying to wash her hands, laughed so hard it seemed like she was having epileptic convulsions.

Lunch in hand, Maggie sat down at the nearest table, feeling faint. She grabbed on to the table edge to support herself.

"Whose wieners?" Trina asked, laughing along.

"Patty's just telling us the news," Marcia said, sitting down next to Maggie. She lopped over both sides of the chair. "Man got 'rested for pulling on his thing when the mail lady showed up."

To be casual, Maggie tried to start eating her sandwich. Ham and cheese. She couldn't taste it.

"Men!" Debbie exclaimed, looking at Maggie and shaking her head in faux exasperation. "They just don't know what to do with those things, do they Maggie?"

Maggie spit up her sandwich.

"Oh, Lord!" said Patty. The girls rushed for napkins.

The Prick

Chapter 9

Rebecca sat in her corner office overlooking the High Museum, Atlanta's halfhearted response to the Met. Her office was satisfyingly huge, likely the biggest in the building. The firm's offices had been built to specifications, her specifications, and she had specified that her office should be over three times the size of a standard associate's. A massive oak desk in the center of the room overflowed with stacks of papers from various cases. She was six two, and associates joked when they thought she was out of earshot—or not reading their emails—that she needed the square footage to house her long legs. But Rebecca found her height to be a distinct advantage. Especially with men. It made them uneasy.

Rebecca was quite busy, despite what she had told Will Simmons about her bandwidth. Five of the stacks were capped with yellow Post-it notes, indicating that they needed to be attended to immediately. In the far left corner of her desk, facing the chairs in front of her, stood a picture of her kids and another of her with the mayor and the other two named partners in her firm. Her walls were lined with diplomas, certificates, and awards, pictures with legal dignitaries, and, bloodily, in one corner, copies of checks from opposing counsel who had been ordered to pay fines as sanctions for misconduct in cases against her. Scalps.

Maria Chan also was in her office at the moment, on the edge of her chair, pen and legal pad at the ready. As always, she sat bolt upright, as if a steel pole had been grafted to her spine. Perhaps one had been. Rebecca never asked her anything personal.

The conflicts check on Moxley had cleared, not surprisingly, and Rebecca's debriefing had confirmed her instincts: this was a nasty case, potentially career-threatening for Robert Spelkin, one of Levitt's rainmakers, and a powder keg for Levitt itself. It was going to be a lot of fun. Spelkin had managed to clamp his balls in a vice and needed Rebecca to get him out of it. She would do it, and she wouldn't forget it, or let Spelkin. Not ever. Rebecca smiled. Spelkin was a hell of a business generator and even a pretty decent litigator, but he had the same weaknesses and incredible lapses in judgment as any other man.

Now all she had to do was run roughshod over the insignificant dipshit who'd stumbled over Robert's prick. She would beat this Hunter character into submission and settle the whole thing for about $50,000, which would be a gift to Levitt.

"What's this dipshit's phone number?"

Chan quickly supplied it. The phone rang a couple of times while Rebecca read ajc.com.

"Jason Hunter."

"Jason," Rebecca said. "Rebecca Trent."

A pause.

"Okay ... What can I do for you, Ms. Trent?"

"You can withdraw this bullshit Charge."

Hunter laughed. "You'll have to be more specific."

"The Charge you just helped Margaret Moxley file against Levitt. There's no substance to it."

The Prick

"I assume you've been retained by Levitt and aren't just taking an interest in the case as a concerned citizen?"

Rebecca smiled. "That's right. All further communications with Levitt go through me. No more letters to Jimmy Peters, got it?"

"He wasn't that responsive anyway. Let me save you some time, Ms. Trent. I have no intention of withdrawing or dismissing anything and am very much looking forward to filing the Complaint. My client is a victim of sexual assault by an equity partner of Levitt, who is frankly lucky he hasn't been arrested. My client is irreparably damaged emotionally, and your client has hundreds of millions of dollars. No, I think I'll wait and see what a jury thinks about all this."

"Quite a torrent. Let me save *you* some money and embarrassment, Jason. You file this Complaint, without any factual support, sign your name to it, it's a violation of Rule 11. Given the outrageous nature of these bullshit claims, my client will insist that we go after Moxley—and you—for sanctions, including attorneys' fees. You don't want to go down this road."

To Rebecca's surprise, Hunter didn't miss a beat.

"You file a Rule 11 motion and you'll have another one coming back at you the same day, I can assure you. In fact, I'll take the liberty of drafting one right now. Let me spell something out for you, Ms. Trent. These scare tactics are not going to work on me. I worked in defense for over half a decade. I know the routine. And let me tell you something else. This is the only case I'm seriously working on right now. This one case. I'm going to be working on it around the clock. How many cases do you have?"

He hung up.

Rebecca looked at Chan. "What do you think?" The "what do you think" rhetorical exercise made Chan exceedingly nervous, and so Rebecca did it whenever she remembered to.

The Prick

"I ... I don't know. He seemed to realize he's got some leverage."

"Are you kidding? He doesn't have any leverage. He just told us he's got no income coming in from any other cases. I'm sure he doesn't have any help. We'll bury him. And the little prick was caught off guard—you couldn't tell?"

"No, you're right. He was. And he did say—"

"We'll go talk to Spelkin tomorrow. Get his side of the story. I want the position statement on my desk by Monday. We also need to make sure that they're doing the right thing over there with Moxley. They need to at least make a good show of an investigation."

Chan was writing furiously. Rebecca leaned back in her chair and put her feet on her desk, her hands behind her head.

"Dipshit hung up on me," she said, amused. He clearly didn't know who she was. But he would find out.

"Yes, I can't believe it."

"You think he did it?"

"Robert Spelkin?"

"That's who the case is about, isn't it?"

"Yes—I don't know. It'll be interesting to see what he says tomorrow when—"

"He did it. They always do it. Don't let him convince you otherwise."

Chan nodded and attacked her pad again. Was she writing, "they always do it"?

"All right. Call Jimmy Peters and tell him to set up a meeting with us and Spelkin tomorrow afternoon."

"What time?"

Rebecca checked her Outlook calendar. "Any time after two. Tell him we want to meet with Spelkin alone."

"Okay."

"Thanks," Rebecca said pointedly. Chan scurried from the room.

The Prick

Chapter 10

Wednesday, April 10th
Atlanta Offices of Levitt, Bennett & Taylor, LLP

He hadn't gotten a fucking thing done all day. Not one goddamn fucking thing. This Moxley cataclysm was a mobile mental roadblock that stopped him in his tracks whenever he tried to focus on something else. All because of that fucking lying, fat, immaterial cow.

Robert glared out of his office and down the hall in Moxley's general direction. He had pivoted his chair somewhat to allow himself optimal glaring perspective. So far today she hadn't dared round his corner, at least while he was in the office. She had actually waddled past yesterday. The gall! The fucking gall to dare come that close to him. He was a goddamn giant. She was a meaningless speck. If not for the sheer physical space she gelatinously occupied in the universe, she might go unnoticed entirely. How dare she? When she walked by his office, he had to physically restrain himself from getting up and— confronting her? Hitting her? He didn't know.

Fifty years ago this wouldn't have been tolerated. Back then a man didn't have to sit on his hands; back then a man could defend his honor. Or something like that. Goddamn bitch.

Robert turned back to an appellate brief that an associate had drafted. Legally it was all there but stylistically it was dogshit and would have to be completely rewritten. If only he could force his consciousness to read two sentences consecutively without shifting back to—

His phone rang. "James Peters" appeared on the caller ID.

"Now what?" he barked.

"Um, hello, Robert. I wonder if you would come down to my office for a talk."

"I'm right in the middle of a brief."

"Okay, well, I guess I can just tell you over the phone."

"Tell me what? I have actual work to do."

"The thing is, Moxley filed her Charge with the EEOC."

Robert slammed the phone down, and threw the appellate brief against the double-paned window. The secretary immediately outside his office, Jessica something, poked her head up over the top of her little secretarial cube.

"It's fine," he told her. "Call Eric to get me a rewrite of this Rexco appellate brief first thing tomorrow. It reads like it's written by a first-year law student." Jessica something, who wasn't Robert or Eric's secretary, nodded quickly and ducked back down.

Robert got up and stormed down the hall to Peters's office. Moxley's cube was thankfully not on the way. Peters's door was closed and Robert ripped it open to find Peters at his desk, trying to call him again, a perplexed look on his face.

"Hello, Robert."

"Let me see it."

Peters gestured to a chair in front of his desk and Robert sat. Peters handed him a printout of the Charge.

Robert read it and felt himself reddening, his skin burning.

"Jesus fucking Christ," he said. It was a gut shot.

"Ryan Sparks is the investigator."

The Prick

Robert dropped the Charge to his lap and stared at Peters. "You can't be serious. How is that possible? That's a conflict of interest!"

"I'm not sure—"

"It's a goddamn conflict of interest!" Robert shouted, standing up. "I just had two Charges against Sparks last year. I accused him of misconduct in the investigation, for Chrissake! I reported him to the EEOC director!"

"I don't know if that—"

"He can't investigate me!"

"Robert, please calm down. Maybe we can get someone else put on the case."

"This cannot happen." Robert sat down again. "I mean, this just gets more unbelievable every day."

"I know," Peters said. "I'm sorry. Listen, Sparks wants to do an onsite. He wants to talk to—"

"Absolutely not! We cannot allow that!" Robert was standing again. He could feel the blood vessels pounding against the sides of his head. "Get Simmons on the phone!"

"Well—"

"I want Simmons in on this. We need to stop this."

"We've retained outside counsel, Robert."

"What? Who?"

"Rebecca Trent."

Robert's eyes got very wide. "I assume that you're joking. Please tell me you're joking."

"She's one of the best litigators in the city. At a relatively small firm."

"I've known her for twenty years! She's a competitor! She knows everyone in town!"

"I know that, but we need someone who can contain this thing. She's who Simmons wanted, and I agree. I'm sure she'll exercise complete discretion."

The Prick

"You didn't even think to ask me before making the decision?"

"It was Simmons's call."

"This is getting out of control." Robert shook his head. "All right, get her on the phone, then. We need to quash this onsite right away."

"They want to come meet with you tomorrow, actually."

"Who is 'they,' Jimmy?" Robert's annoyance at Peters's continual lack of specificity formed a distracting pocket in his waves of rage and fear.

"Trent, and an associate, a Maria Chan."

"When?"

"Sometime after two, whatever works for you."

"Whatever works for me. How gracious."

Robert got up and walked slowly back to his office. His humiliation was spreading all over town, into the ears of people who mattered. People like Rebecca Trent. Peters was right, though. Trent was a good call. She would crush Hunter. The onsite! The onsite had to be stopped at all costs. It would be the end of him. There'd be no keeping the gossip from spreading and multiplying like a virus.

Robert got back to his office and found Eric Fuller waiting outside in the hall, visibly nervous. Eric was a fourth-year associate, skinny and awkward, single, and probably into Star Trek or Dungeons and Dragons or some shit.

"Do you want to talk about the Rexco brief?" Eric queried shakily.

"You mean that brief?" Robert pointed to the pile of papers on the floor by the wall. Eric's eyes bulged absurdly at the sight of it.

"Was that your best effort?" Robert asked, brushing by Eric and into his office. Eric followed him in.

The Prick

"Yes, I mean ..." Eric hung by the edge of the doorway. "I have a lot on my plate right now, and I—"

"Let me tell you something." Robert slammed himself down in his chair. "When I was your age and I was an associate and I had an assignment from a partner, I made sure it was my best effort before I submitted it to him. Do you know why?" Robert turned away from Eric and looked at his computer.

"Yes, I mean—"

"It's because I didn't want to waste his fucking time."

Silence.

"I want a complete rewrite by tomorrow morning, and I want it written above a middle school reading level. Try pulling some other briefs off the system to see how it's done. There are plenty of examples. Do you know how to find briefs on the system? Have your assistant help you."

"Okay." Eric sounded like he was going to cry.

"I expect to see marked improvement in tomorrow's draft." Robert said, looking over his shoulder. Eric nodded and turned to go.

"Where are you going?"

"Back to my office?"

"Don't leave your dogshit on my floor," Robert said, pointing to the pile of papers.

Eric dropped his head and walked over to the window to where the nearly sixty pages were lying in a heap. Robert eyed him with pure malevolence as he crouched down to gather them up in silence. Papers collected, he turned to leave, eyes on the floor.

"Have a good night," Robert said.

*****

David Nichols watched as Spelkin retreated back down the hallway with his tail between his legs. Nichols didn't have a corner office like Spelkin, but he did enjoy a nice big office with a westward view. Nobody who walked in the door could accuse him of not being important.

This whole thing was pretty amusing, frankly. The great and powerful Robert Spelkin III had gotten his dick caught in the door, or, more perfectly, in or around the person of a fat married woman. And now the wolves were descending upon him. Persuading a man to risk everything for an experience that isn't even likely to be all that enjoyable was one of alcohol's more impressive tricks.

If he was going to be honest with himself, the whole Spelkin Situation made Nichols feel better about himself and his own personal Situation. He was divorced from a wonderful woman who had turned (arguably with his assistance) into a jealous shrew. She lived in Los Angeles, where she had moved with his daughter and a substantial percentage of his money. The divorce had come after his wife caught him cheating twice in an approximate five-year period, although the ratio of discovered to actual infidelity hadn't been high. He'd spent so much time staring at his bank statement and denouncing himself for lack of self-control. Watching another man with everything throw it away in sacrifice to the baser instincts was somewhat cathartic. What Nichols had done was the most normal thing in the world, merely an instinct that most of them—he guessed—acted on. His former mother-in-law shouldn't look at him like he was a monster, and neither should his former wife. Find another kind of man out there. Try it.

He picked up his office phone and dialed Peters's line.

"Hello?" Peters answered. Nichols wasn't sure if Peters realized that his phone had caller ID on it. He always sounded genuinely curious as to who was on the other end of the line.

"It's David."

"Oh, hello."

The Prick

"Now what?"

"What?"

"I saw Spelkin storm down to your office and walk back after a few minutes as if somebody had run over his dog. Hunter demanding chemical castration now or something?"

"No, it's the EEOC. She filed a Charge. They want an onsite."

"Well that's certainly not going to be pleasant." Nichols smiled. "Who do they want to talk to?"

Shuffling papers. "Robert, obviously. Me. Your name's on the list. And some of the administrative people."

"Probably that unattractive lunch group I sometimes see taking up space in the break room."

"A few of them, I believe." Peters said. Nichols was pretty sure Peters didn't know who he was referring to. He was almost never in the office.

"So who did we get? Who's the investigator?"

"Ryan Sparks."

Nichols laughed out loud. No wonder Spelkin had looked like the sky was falling. It was. "Sparks hates Robert," he told Peters. "Robert reported him to the regional director last year—said he was exceeding his investigatory powers and was acting as an unlicensed plaintiff's attorney instead of a neutral party, as I recall. It's all Robert talked about for a week."

"Robert said it was a conflict of interest."

"Good luck with that one. The EEOC isn't likely to take Roberts's side over Sparks's. In fact, I remember the director not being very amused with Robert's accusations. Probably best not to bark up that tree again."

"Yes," Peters said. "I expect outside counsel will make that decision."

"We have outside counsel on this? Since when?" Nichols put his feet up on his desk and stared at the windows of the

The Prick

Westin on the other side of Peachtree. For as close as he was to the glass hotel, you'd think he would see more women changing or getting out of the shower or whatever.

"I think she was formally retained today, actually."

"Who is 'she'?" Peters always talked like a civilian.

"Rebecca Trent."

Nichols laughed. "You're kidding me, right?"

"No, it was Simmons's call."

"Wow." Nichols would have paid to see Spelkin's reaction. "How did Robert take that news?"

"Not well."

"I would think not."

"She's coming over to meet with Robert tomorrow," Peters said. "She may want to stop by and talk to you, too."

"I'm at Ms. Trent's disposal." That would certainly be entertaining. "You know, I was under the impression that Robert persuaded Simmons to up the settlement offer. Hunter still went ahead and filed the Charge?"

"Apparently so. I wasn't copied on the email, but what I gathered from Simmons, Hunter wasn't too impressed with the amount."

"How much did we offer?"

"Thirty-seven, I believe."

Amateurs. "Jesus," Nichols said. "If you're going to bid against yourself, at least make a meaningful change. This kid obviously knows he's got his hands on something here. He's not going to go away quietly for an extra twelve thousand."

"It was Simmons's call."

Peters had apparently adopted "it was Simmons's call" as his mantra. He couldn't push this thing far enough away from himself. It wouldn't work, though. The mess was on his plate and he was going to have to eat it.

The Prick

"Yes, I'm sure," Nichols said. "So Trent tomorrow, and then when's the onsite?"

"Robert wants to oppose it."

Nichols laughed loudly. "I imagine he does. Unfortunately, the EEOC's ability to conduct onsites doesn't only apply in situations where the subject matter isn't embarrassing for the powers that be."

"I guess that will be up to Trent to decide with Simmons. Whether to oppose it, I mean."

"There'll be no keeping a lid on this once the EEOC comes to town," Nichols said. "I expect Robert came to the same conclusion."

"He certainly didn't like the idea."

Nichols laughed. "All right. Thanks Jimmy."

Nichols hung up and shook his head in disapproval at the Westin. The only people he ever saw in the rooms with any regularity were the sub-five-foot cleaning crew. One time last week there was a woman, but she just sat there, fully clothed, watching TV and texting.

There was nothing good to do, so he got up and strolled down the hall to comfort his good friend Robert.

The Prick

Chapter 11

Thursday, April 11th
Atlanta Offices of Levitt, Bennett & Taylor, LLP

"Did you do it?"

Rebecca Trent had spent the morning conducting largely useless interviews with Peters and Nichols, although Maria Chan had somehow managed to develop roughly twenty pages of handwritten notes. Now she and Chan were seated in the two thick and padded oak chairs in front of Robert Spelkin's desk. The accused sat behind the desk, bright red and agitated. Rebecca noticed perspiration at his temples. They had been talking for ten minutes.

"No." Spelkin said firmly, like a person who had been preparing to say it.

"Well, then, what the fuck, Robert? This kind of thing doesn't spring up out of nowhere."

"I have no idea," Spelkin said. "The whole thing is a fabrication. She obviously just wants a large sum of money for a retirement package. The woman must be pathological." He glanced with obvious irritation at Chan, who was furiously taking notes. Trent wasn't writing anything. She didn't even have a pen out.

"So she just woke up one day and decided, 'Today's the day I'm going to accuse my boss of forcibly putting his dick on my neck'?" Chan stopped writing and looked at Rebecca, wide-eyed.

The Prick

"You seem to be shocking your associate, Rebecca," Spelkin said. Chan's eyes immediately sought the refuge of her notepad.

"Answer the question."

"I already have. None of this happened. That woman's delusional and twisted motivations for making up the lie are irrelevant."

"You know the game," Rebecca said, reclining back in the chair and shaking her head in frustration. "We're here to help you. We're on your side. If you're hiding things from me, I can't effectively plan out the defense strategy. You're only hurting yourself."

"You're right. I do know the game. Lectures aren't required. Save them for the car ride home with Ms. Chan here."

"Fine. Tell me what happened that night."

"From what I can remember," Spelkin said, "the whole team was upstairs celebrating a big settlement. At the Peachtree Club. I told Moxley she shouldn't leave until she got the revisions done on a brief for a non-compete case. I wanted to get it filed that night. Anyway, I came back downstairs to read it over again, assuming that she would be done with it, and found her still slowly putting the changes in, down at her desk." Spelkin gestured in the general direction of Moxley's cubicle. "She's just about the slowest assistant I've ever worked with. So when I got back down I was a little frustrated, and I told her that we'd just have to wait and file the brief the next day and that she should leave for the night. I may have been a little harsh with her, but I never so much as touched her."

"That's it?"

"That's it."

"About what time did you come back downstairs?"

"Six thirty? Seven?"

"You don't remember?"

"No."

"Did you send any emails when you got back downstairs?"

"I don't remember. I don't think so."

"Have you checked?"

"No."

"Can you check now?"

Spelkin glanced at his screen. "What was the date?"

Rebecca rolled her eyes at Chan. "March 21st."

"I don't see any I sent past 3:30 p.m.," Spelkin said. "My last one was notifying the client that we had confirmed receipt of the settlement funds."

"Did you make any calls when you got back downstairs?"

"I may have called my wife."

"From your office line or cell phone?"

"Office line."

"What time did you leave to go home?"

"I, ah ... didn't go home."

Rebecca sat upright. "What do you mean?"

"I slept here," Spelkin admitted, gesturing toward the oversized leather couch behind Rebecca and Chan. They both turned to look at it.

"Why?" Rebecca asked. Things were coming into focus.

"I, um, I had been drinking. Celebrating, you know."

Rebecca nodded. "How much did you have?"

Spelkin grimaced. "I'm not entirely sure. We were all sharing a bottle of scotch."

"What kind?"

Spelkin looked surprised. "McClellan, I believe. Eighteen-year."

"Very nice," Rebecca said. "How many people split the bottle?"

The Prick

"Well, Nichols was there. And a bunch of associates. People kind of came and went, you know."

"Which associates?"

Chan wrote down the names.

"This a typical thing for you? Drinking too much upstairs and then sleeping in your office instead of going home?"

"It only happened once before. Years ago."

"Uh-huh," Rebecca said. "You wear the same thing the next day?"

"I went downstairs in the morning and bought a new shirt and a suit off the rack at Brooks Brothers. I wore it out of the store."

"Did anybody see you walking down in your suit from the previous day?"

"I don't think so. I got out of the office and went to a diner before anybody came in. And then I went from the diner to Brooks Brothers."

"Okay," Rebecca said. "Who else knows that you slept in your office?"

"My wife, obviously. And David."

"Was David here, or did you tell him?"

"I told him."

"Was anybody else around when you told Moxley to go home?"

"No. I don't think so."

"No or you don't think so?"

"No."

"All right, so this is the story you want me to go with. You came down to a deserted office after drinking an unknown quantity of scotch to find your assistant working by herself on a brief that you wanted to file that night, decided you didn't want to file the brief after all, sent her home without laying a finger—or anything else—on her, called the missus to tell her you weren't going to make it

79

home, and then curled up innocently on the couch in your office as a responsible citizen who would never drive under the influence. That's the story we're going with?"

Spelkin glared. "That's what happened."

"And you're comfortable that story will hold up to cross-examination?"

"Yes."

"All right," Rebecca said. "Anything else you want us to know?"

"No. But I want you to stop this EEOC persecution. Get Sparks off the Charge due to a conflict of interest and stop this goddamn onsite they have planned."

"What's the conflict with Sparks?"

"I reported him to the EEOC director for acting unethically and exceeding his authority to question employees of a client outside of my presence," Spelkin said. "He kept calling them to schedule interviews outside of the plant without even alerting me first. Trying to get statements from them. It was ridiculous. The guy thinks he's a plaintiff's attorney."

"Was he contacting managerial employees or non-managerial?" Rebecca asked.

"Non-managerial," Spelkin admitted. "But he didn't even let me know he was doing it. The client was furious."

"What did the director say?"

"That she would look into it. I never got a substantive response from her. But Sparks stayed on the case. He found "No Cause" a few weeks later, so the whole thing kind of just went away. He hates me, though. I know it."

Rebecca raised her eyebrows. "So that's your conflict?"

"Yes, goddammit," Spelkin yelled. "The EEOC is supposed to be neutral. How can they be neutral when the investigator has previously been accused of misconduct by the alleged harasser?"

The Prick

"Okay," Rebecca said. "You may have a point there."

"You're goddamn right I do."

"And what's your reason for stopping the onsite?"

Spelkin glanced at Chan. "Can I speak with you privately, Rebecca?"

Well, this was interesting. Rebecca told Chan to step outside for a minute.

Spelkin leaned forward, elbows on the desk, took a deep breath, and stared directly into Rebecca's eyes. "Have you met my wife?"

"I don't think so."

"Her name is Mary and she's a wonderful woman. We have two kids, a boy and a girl."

Rebecca smiled thinly and Spelkin continued. "Over a year ago, seems like a lifetime ago, I was, ah, unfaithful. It was a dumb thing. Didn't mean anything. But she caught me —read my email and found the proof, you know. I was caught red handed."

"Uh-huh."

"Anyway, things were really rough. I slept in the guest room for a long time and there was even some talk of divorce. But she got over it, and I was allowed to, you know, move back into our bedroom."

"I see."

"Yes. The point is that I'm not entirely sure that I'll be given the benefit of the doubt on this one if Mary hears about it. Despite the fact that I'm completely innocent. And if the EEOC is allowed to come in here and broadcast all of this bullshit to every secretary, paralegal, and attorney they can get their hands on, word will get around the city in about an hour. There'll be no keeping it from Mary."

"You don't think you should tell her up front?"

"No," Spelkin said. "Not yet. There's still a chance we can settle this thing before it gets out. Nothing's been filed in

The Prick

court. I think I can count on Nichols and Peters to keep their mouths shut."

"Sure, fine, Robert. But I don't think this one's going to settle early. I think we're in for a fight before it's over."

"That little bastard still hasn't come off two fucking million?"

"No," Rebecca said. "And there is no sign that he's going to soon. We may have to depose Moxley to make him see the light."

"Jesus Christ." Spelkin put his head in his hands.

"I would tell your wife now."

"Can we offer the fucker something he would think twice about passing up? Something in the high five figures?"

"No," Rebecca said. "One time bidding against ourselves is already too much. We move up again and you're basically admitting guilt. You know that."

"I just can't fucking believe this." Spelkin buried his head in his hands. "How can this be happening?"

"We'll do whatever we can," Rebecca said.

"What if I contributed to the settlement personally?"

"No." Rebecca's stomach turned a little. Spelkin was panicking. Pathetic. If there was one thing she couldn't stand it was weakness.

"We'll be in touch," Rebecca said, walking out. She collected Chan, who was standing in the hall, and the two walked in silence to the elevator bank. Rebecca waited until the elevator doors closed before speaking. Her ears popped as they made the forty-five-floor descent.

"What do you think?" she asked Chan.

"I'm not sure. I—"

"We don't settle this thing early and he's fucked." Trent said, thinking Chan's thoughts for her.

The Prick

Chapter 12

Thursday, April 11th
Trent, Ellis & Fitzpatrick, LLP

"What the fuck are you saying?" Rebecca yelled into her speakerphone. "You fucking fired her?"

Jimmy Peters had called a few hours after she left Spelkin's office. He was speaking slowly between Rebecca's curses, attempting to communicate fully his colossal fuck-up.

"It's a layoff, Rebecca. And not yet. She and the others will be informed tomorrow."

Rebecca muted the call. "Get Maria around here now!" She switched off mute. "I can only assume you are fucking joking. That this is some kind of terrible fucking late April Fools' joke."

"No, it's just an operational decision. Just part of a ten percent staff layoff in the Atlanta office. Nothing to do with the Charge, or her allegations. She will, of course, be offered severance."

"Of course. You actually expect me to believe that this is a layoff? You expect the EEOC to believe that? The jury?"

"I, ah, well ... it's just an operational decision."

"Yes, Jimmy, you mentioned that. What, were you given a script to use?"

Silence.

"Goddammit. Don't do this. You're giving her an airtight retaliation claim. It's a gift to Hunter."

Maria Chan ran into Rebecca's office, pen and pad in hand and out of breath.

"Maria's just joined us, Jimmy," Rebecca said. "Maria, Jimmy was just explaining to me the firm's decision to fire Maggie Moxley." Chan's jaw dropped.

"Layoff," came Peters's voice over the speakerphone. "It's just a layoff."

"So it's just a coincidence that she's caught up in a layoff the same month she files a Charge accusing one of your rainmakers of putting his dick on her neck and the EEOC wants to do a full investigation."

"Ah, yes, just one of those things, you know?"

"Just one of those things like you're going to retaliate against a charging party?"

"No, of course not. And she might sign the severance, you know. The agreement has a release of all her claims in it."

"Genius. So you were just going to sneak that by Hunter and have her sign without involvement from an attorney who's actively representing her in her claims against the company? That may actually be one of the examples that the bar uses in the rules defining unethical conduct."

"Well, no....she'd be able to consult him, of course."

"And how much is the severance you are offering?"

"Two months' pay."

"Which works out to what, seven or eight thousand before taxes?"

Silence. Peters obviously didn't know what it worked out to.

"So you think," Rebecca continued, "that despite the fact that Hunter has already turned down $37,500, firing his client will appease him and get him to settle for much less, despite the fact that he now has a rock-solid retaliation claim. That's the prevailing thought over at Levitt?"

Silence. And then the speakerphone said, "It's not my call, Rebecca."

Some honesty. "Whose call is it?"

"Word came down from Washington."

"When?"

"Today."

"When was the decision made?"

"I don't know," Peters said.

"Is the Atlanta office over budget?"

"Yes."

"Has there been a slowdown in work at the Atlanta office?"

"Well, we did just settle a big case—"

"You're kidding me, right? The big case that Spelkin settled when this thing allegedly happened?"

"It was a lot of work that's gone away now."

"Unbelievable. Are there layoffs in other offices?"

"I don't know."

"Who's affected in the Atlanta office besides Moxley?"

"Three legal assistants, one paralegal, and one office services worker."

"And that works out to ten percent of the office staff?"

"Roughly," Peters said.

"All right. let me be very clear on this right now. I do not approve of this purported layoff, and I sure as shit don't recommend it. Clearly, the decision was made before, and without, consulting me. I'm going to have Maria send over a letter memorializing the fact that I was not consulted regarding Mrs. Moxley's termination, I do not recommend Mrs. Moxley's termination, and, in fact, my advice is not to terminate Mrs. Moxley. Got that?"

"Yes." Peters said. His sigh was audible.

The Prick

"If I were you, I wouldn't let them put me in this position, Jimmy. You do this, you're positioning yourself directly in the crosshairs. And they will come after you."

Another sigh. "It's been decided," he said. "It's purely operational."

"Practice that line, Jimmy. I recommend you make it more convincing."

Rebecca hung up and stared at Chan. "Fuck," she said. "Type up that fucking letter immediately. I want it sent tonight. I'm not going to be the one left holding the bag on this impending disaster."

The Prick

Chapter 13

Thursday, April 11th
Bookhouse Pub

Brunnell was getting drunk. And he kept talking about it. "I'm getting so drunk tonight," he said, for example.

"So you mentioned," Jason said. "Any particular reason?"

"Because I'm sick of my goddamn boss and I'm sick of my goddamn job." Brunnell raised a hand to the waitress for another one. "And I'm going to call in sick tomorrow."

"Yeah? What's wrong with you?"

"Swine flu."

"I hear that's going around," Jason said. "So was there some kind of last straw today or something?"

"Not really. Just more of the same—he thinks I'm his bitch."

"Aren't you his bitch?"

"Not officially. He orders me around like I'm his secretary. I have a law degree!" Brunnell said at an abnormally high volume and pitch. He and Jason were beginning to get concerned looks from other beer drinkers, who, as a demographic, don't easily concern.

"That's a great pickup line, dude. You tried screaming at girls that you have a juris doctorate?"

The Prick

Brunnell took a huge swig. "No need for pickup lines, man. I've got the best girl in the world!" Brunnell raised his arms to the sky in celebration.

Some of the other patrons at a nearby table were beginning to actively stare. In their defense, it was just past 8:00 on a weeknight. "I'll have what he's having, right?" Jason said to them. They turned away.

"So Nikki's become the best girl in the world?"

"She was always the best girl in the world," Brunnell assured him. "I just was too stupid to realize it."

"And how did you finally see the light?"

"She seems really into me, man. We've been having sex a lot lately."

"Sounds enchanting."

"Not just missionary."

"There are positions other than missionary?"

"We like to experiment. The other night we had sex on her balcony."

"I'm sure the neighbors very much enjoyed the sight of your body writhing passionately."

"She let me bend her over the rail."

"I've always said you can get anything you want as long as you ask nicely."

"It was great, man," Brunnell concluded happily. "Great." The beer arrived and he drank immediately, pouring about half the pint down his throat.

"Why don't you quit?"

"Drinking? No way. It's the only way I can get drunk."

"Your job," Jason said. "Why don't you quit your job?"

"And do what?"

"I don't know. Something else. Go out on your own."

"It doesn't seem to be all that easy. Seeing you start your firm has made me think that's not the way to go."

The Prick

"Thanks a lot," Jason said. "It's just tough in the beginning, until you get your first big score. Like this new case against Levitt."

"Think so?" Brunnell asked. "I'm not sure. Do you have the bankroll to fight for years against a big law firm?"

"They'll cave. There's no way Spelkin wants to litigate this thing, and there's no way they're comfortable with her still working there. She's a walking retaliation case."

"I hope so, for your sake." Brunnell drained the rest of the beer.

"They'll cave," Jason repeated, assuring himself. "The payday is coming."

"Yeah," Brunnell said. "I'm not so sure."

The Prick

Chapter 14

Friday, April 12th
The Law Offices of Jason Hunter, Esq.

They'd fired her. Jason could not believe it. It was more incredible to him than Spelkin drunkenly rubbing his piece on a flabby, middle-aged woman and demanding fellatio in the first goddamn place.

The ruthlessness of the move didn't surprise him. Dispassionate amoral behavior was the exclusive province of corporations and sociopaths. It was the stupidity, the brash stupidity of it. Levitt was an ultra-sophisticated defendant, a top international law firm that had hired arguably the smartest and inarguably the most aggressive outside counsel in the city. How could they just hand him a slam-dunk retaliation case like this? What the hell was Trent thinking?

Maybe the intention was merely to inflict the Moxleys upon him. If that was the plan, it was working. Maggie was sitting in his office, sobbing. Pete had called in and was on the speakerphone, shouting self-indulgently. Jason wished that Pete's carpet mill wasn't so lenient with breaks, as he tried to craft a tone and combination of words that might settle the Moxley duo down.

Deciding that Pete's shouting was the more irritating sound—and wasn't aiding Maggie's crying—Jason elected to start there. He tuned back into Pete, who was in the middle of threatening graphic physical harm to Robert Spelkin if Maggie was not immediately rehired, "...and with a raise!"

"Listen, this was an incredibly stupid and unquestionably illegal maneuver by Levitt. However, they're not going to rehire her unless a court makes them, and you are not going to go near Spelkin or any other Levitt partner or employee. We're going to figure this out."

"We need that fucking money," Pete growled.

It was not difficult for Jason to sense the danger here. He had to defuse Pete's anger without becoming the target of it. "I know," he said. "Remember, I'm completely on your side on this thing. They shouldn't have done it. It was illegal. But we need to carefully think out our next steps."

"We don't have that income, we can't live," said Pete. "Whatcha gonna do about that?"

Was this Levitt's plan? Was Trent trying to apply financial pressure to force him into a lowball settlement?

"Maggie is going to have to try to find another job."

"Yeah, right. How's she gonna do that? In this economy?"

"She has to try," Jason said. "She has to do what's called mitigating her damages. She has to look for work."

"The fuck?" Pete said. "Mitigrate her damages?"

"Yes, miti*gate*."

Maggie was still a flushed, sobbing mess in the chair to the right of his desk. She would at least be able to present a credible picture of emotional distress. His representation of Maggie Moxley was threatening to tap the office supply of Kleenex.

"Well, what the fuck does that mean?" asked Pete.

"It means that she has to look for another job," Jason said again. "Look, I know this seems like a bad thing, and a hard thing, and it is. But the silver lining here is that they've just given Maggie another claim—a retaliation claim. That carries with it the possibility of recovering all of the wages she's now losing because they fired her. In order to claim all of those lost wages, however, Maggie needs to be able to show that she was looking for other work."

"We might lose the house," Maggie said.

Fuck. If this was some kind of depletion-of-resources strategy by Trent, it might actually work.

"Can you front us some money?" asked Pete. "A loan against the lawsuit?"

And there it was. "No," Jason said. "Unfortunately, I can't. Even if I had the money, which I don't, it wouldn't be ethical. The rules don't allow it."

"Not ethical to help somebody out so they don't lose their damn house?" Pete asked.

Jason winced. "Yes. I could get in trouble."

"Uh-huh," Pete said. "And you ain't got the money."

"It wouldn't matter if I did."

"Uh-huh."

This was not a productive subject. "What exactly did they say, Maggie?"

"Mr. Jensen, he called me and told me to come into his office. He told me he was sorry, but that it was a layoff."

"What?"

"Yeah, he said it was a layoff. He said me and some of the other girls, and one paralegal, we had to get laid off."

So this was how they were going to try to explain it. The smokescreen. "Did he say who else was being laid off?"

"No, he said it was confidential."

"And who is Mr. Jensen? What's his first name?"

"Arthur," Maggie said. "He's the Office Manager."

"All right. Did they offer you any severance?"

Maggie reached for her big purse, pulled out a crumpled packet and handed it to him.

"You didn't sign anything did you?" Jason asked.

The Prick

Maggie shook her head.

"Jesus Christ, Maggie, you signed the fucking paper?" Pete shouted.

"No, she didn't sign it, Pete."

"Jesus fucking Christ!"

"All right," Jason said, looking at the severance agreement. They're offering you two months' severance in exchange for," Jason flipped through the pages, "a full release of all claims, known or unknown, and an agreement not to sue."

"They said I had three weeks to sign," Maggie said. "Should I do it?"

It was a test of willpower for Jason not to yell at her. "No, Maggie. You should definitely *not* sign it. They've already offered you more money than two months' severance. This is just a standard agreement that they give to everyone who's terminated. They were probably hoping that you were just going to sign it. Which is in itself unethical."

"What a fuckin' s'prise." Pete said.

"Agreed."

"Well, what the hell do we do now?" Pete said. Maggie was staring at him with moist blue eyes, dabbing at them with a ball of Kleenex.

"Now we hit them back."

The Prick

Chapter 15

Friday, April 12th
Atlanta Offices of Levitt, Bennett & Taylor, LLP

Arthur Jensen always told everyone that this was the part of the job that he hated. He even told himself that. "This is the part of the job that I hate," he would mutter to himself as he gathered the necessary documents and filled out the termination forms.

Donald Jeffries was the last victim of the day. A paralegal. Arthur looked around to see if he had any tissues left in his office. The men didn't normally cry, but that was the thing about changing people's lives. You never knew what their reaction would be. Mostly hurt and anger, some grief. Every once in a while, relief?

The legal assistants he had canned earlier had cried like he'd told them the world was ending. One threatened a lawsuit. But that was normal. It hadn't fazed him one bit. "It didn't even faze me one bit," Arthur said aloud.

He picked up the phone and dialed Don Jeffries's extension. Jeffries, a tall, willowy man with stringy blond hair, was a strange one. Bathing didn't seem to be a regular thing for him. Mostly kept to himself, or so Arthur was told. Arthur kept to himself, for that matter. Regardless, Jeffries was gone. "He'll have to keep to himself somewhere else," Arthur said, chuckling softly.

The Prick

"Hello?" Jeffries answered on the second ring. He had a high, cartoonish voice.

"Hi, Don, would you come see me in my office?"

"Okay. Sounds serious." It was like talking to a cartoon mouse.

"Just come on over to my office and we'll discuss it."

"Am I in trouble?"

"We'll talk about it when you get here."

Arthur pushed around the papers on his desk and waited —his heart was thumping.

Jeffries appeared in his doorframe about thirty seconds later. "What's going on?" He was pale. At the sight of the terrified prey, Arthur felt confidence swell up inside him.

"Come in and close the door, Don."

Jeffries complied and sat in the chair in front of Arthur's desk. Arthur noticed he was on the edge of his seat, absurdly so. He only had about an inch of contact with the chair.

"Listen, Don, we're letting you go. It's purely budgetary and—"

Arthur wasn't ready for what happened. Jeffries grabbed the chair he was perched on and spun around to face the wall. He slowly raised his hands to his head and started pulling at his stringy blond hair. Softly at first. "No, no, no, no, no, no."

"Don? Don, it's—it's okay. What—"

The hair pulling became faster and harder. God. He was ripping his goddamn hair out.

"No, no, no, no, no, no, no, no."

"Stop it, Don. Don't do that."

Faster, harder. Clumps were coming out now, big clumps. Blood streamed down Jeffries's scalp to his neck and blue-checkered shirt.

"No, no, no, no, no, no, no, no, no ..."

The Prick

Arthur had the phone in his hand again and stood safely behind his desk. "Security! Right away! Don! Stop it!"

Jeffries turned his head around in the chair, his scalp bleeding and hair in his hands, and made eye contact with Arthur. His eyes were wild, animalistic. It was terrifying, Arthur would say later.

"Stop," Arthur pleaded. "Security is coming."

"I'm going to die," the cartoon mouse said. "Now I am going to die."

Arthur stared at him. "You don't ..."

Don turned back to the wall. The ripping began again.

"What am I supposed to do? What am I going to do now?"

Security pounded on the door. "Everything okay?"

"Get in here!" Arthur shouted.

Carl from downstairs burst through. He stopped short and stared at Don, who didn't seem to have registered his entrance.

"What?" Carl asked in disbelief at the scene. Clumps of bloody hair were on Arthur's floor.

"Stop him!" Arthur commanded.

Carl turned to stare at Arthur. "How?"

"Grab his arms! Call for help!"

Carl lifted his radio. "I'll call the cops."

*****

David Nichols hopped into the elevator, wondering what the hell the police were doing in the lobby. Maybe Moxley was pressing criminal charges, he thought, smiling. He looked at his watch. Still time to catch a quick nine, possibly, if the traffic wasn't too bad. Then hit the restaurant at the club, see what was going on.

When the doors opened at the first floor, his phone rang. He looked at the number and grinned.

The Prick

"Well, hello. To what do I owe the pleasure?" he said, walking through the busy marble great hall of the building. The top of the hall was a glass pyramid. Natural light flooded the space, warm yellow-orange of late afternoon.

"You fucking bastard!" Jessica shouted into his ear. "How could you?"

David stopped dead in his tracks. "How could I what?"

"Oh, like you don't know."

"I don't know what?"

"They fired me today, David."

"What?" he shouted. People around him stared briefly, then kept it moving.

"You expect me to believe you weren't behind it? What is it, David, you're tired of me? Or are you worried that people might find out?"

David went to a corner of the lobby and tried to conceal himself behind a potted tree. He lowered his voice. "Jess, I don't know what you're talking about. This is the first I'm hearing about this."

"Like they would fire your assistant without talking to you first. What kind of an idiot do you really take me for?"

She technically wasn't his assistant anymore, but this was no time for technicalities.

"I don't ... That's not at all what ... I'm sure it's just some mistake."

She laughed. "You're right about that. I still have the text messages. And the emails. And the voicemails. I kept them all. Big, *big* mistake, David."

"Jess, be reasonable. I didn't do this and I didn't know anything about it. Nothing has happened that we can't fix."

"Fix how? Hire me back? After they fired me? Beg for my dick-sucking job back?"

Oh shit. "Jess, come on."

97

The Prick

"Wait till they find out, David. Wait till they find out what we did in your office. In the conference room. Wait till they find out I was under your desk when people came in your office. That I had your cock in my mouth when you were on the phone with clients. They're going to find out about all of it, David."

"Jess, I..."

"I saved everything."

"I know you're upset, but you're blaming the wrong man. I didn't even know this was happening."

"They humiliated me today. How do you think I feel?"

"I know, I'm sorry. We'll work something out. I can get you another job."

She scoffed. "You're going to have to do a lot better than that. Maybe I'll give Maggie Moxley's lawyer a call."

David called her no less than seven times after she hung up and got sent to voicemail each time. He found Peters's number in his phone.

"Hello?" Peters answered. He sounded like he had been sleeping.

"Where are you?" David shouted. "Where are you right now, you stupid, fat son of a bitch?"

The Prick

Chapter 16

Friday, April 12th
I-85

Jimmy Peters hadn't been sleeping. He had been driving home, trying to survive rush hour. That was before the all-powerful David Nichols had called him, insulted him three different ways for some unknown reason, and demanded that he turn around and meet him at his condo in Buckhead.

So Jimmy turned his SUV around at the next exit and headed back to the city. It took him forty-five minutes to get to Nichols's building, a soaring pillar on Peachtree.

Jimmy pulled a ticket and drove into the garage, looking for a spot with an empty space to the left so he could move his bulk out of the car without propelling the door into another car. It took him ten minutes to find such a spot.

The lobby had a doorman *and* a concierge-type person standing behind a desk. There was also some other functionary milling around with an indiscernible purpose.

"I'm here to see David Nichols," Jimmy told the man behind the desk. "I think he's on the top floor."

The concierge checked a notepad. "Jim Peters?" he asked.

"The very same," Jimmy said, with an ingratiating smile.

"Yes, sir, he said you would be coming by. It's the silver elevator down the hall to the left. Hit the penthouse button and then I will approve it."

The Prick

"Approve it?"

"Yes, sir."

Jimmy found the silver elevator down the hall and to the left and did as directed. The "PH" button didn't immediately light up. He hit it again. Then he heard a beep, and the button illuminated. Concierge came over the elevator intercom: "You're all set, sir." The door closed.

Jimmy took a deep breath as the ascent began. This was it. He was going to be fired. He didn't know what exactly he had done, or why it was going to be Nichols that fired him, but this was it. His apathy and growing incompetence had finally been noticed by someone who mattered. This whole goddamn Spelkin Situation had put the spotlight on him.

Smart not to do this in the office. They were always so fucking smart.

When he reached the top, Jimmy understood the reason for the security downstairs. The elevator opened up directly into Nichols's expansive condo. There was no clutter whatsoever, and it was apparent, even to Jimmy, that everything was top of the line. It was just the feel of it. Or maybe it was his impending doom that made Jimmy so sure that Nichols, the bloodsucker, was gorging himself. The marble, columned entranceway displayed an open kitchen that was all gleaming stainless steel and black marble, a dining room just beyond it with black oak furniture, and a living room to the left where black leather couches had a massive flat screen surrounded.

"Hello?" Jimmy called out.

"Outside!" came a shout.

"Where?"

"I'm outside, you fat fuck! Come in and turn right!"

Jimmy complied and saw what the voice was getting at. Down a hardwood floor hallway and on the other side of an open sliding glass door, Nichols was sitting among trees in a

The Prick

garden, his silver and white hair moving in the wind. Nobody seemed to be with him and he had no papers in his hand. In the sky garden overlooking the city, he looked like an Olympian god.

Jimmy didn't know exactly what to say to a man who was sitting in a garden hundreds of feet above street level.

Nichols turned. "Make yourself a drink and come on out," he said, showing Jimmy a glass of what looked like whiskey or scotch.

"I, uh, don't drink."

"Jesus Christ," Nichols said. "I guess it's a good thing. Keeps your mind sharp. Just come on out, then."

Through the trees on the balcony you could see Peachtree Street meandering from Buckhead to Midtown to Downtown. Nichols was apparently contemplating this view. It was striking, Jimmy had to admit. He lowered himself into a chair a few feet away. The wind wasn't too bad, because of the trees.

The two sat in silence for a while.

"How do you do this?" Jimmy asked finally.

"Do what?"

"Keep a garden up here."

"Fuck if I know," Nichols said. "It was here when I bought the place. And the building has a gardener. I like it, don't you?"

"It's amazing," Jimmy said softly, more to himself than to Nichols.

Nichols nodded. "Jimmy," he said, "did you fucking fire Jessica Rossi today?"

"I—it was a reduction in force."

"So, yes, you fired Jessica Rossi today?"

"Well, yes, I mean Art, the Office Manager, fired her. Laid her off."

The Prick

Nichols turned to glare icily at Jimmy. "Art," he echoed, "*Art,* the Office Manager, fired Jessica Rossi today?"

"It was a reduction in force. Ten percent, give or take."

"Whose decision was it to fire Jessica Rossi?"

Shit. "Well, I guess it was mine," Jimmy said. "I, um, I just picked her."

Nichols took his feet off the chair and pivoted in Jimmy's direction. "What do you mean you just *picked* her?"

Jimmy swallowed. Nichols's eyes were burrowing into his head.

"They said I had to lay off ten percent and—

"Who said? Aren't you the Managing Partner of the fucking office?"

"Washington. Simmons and Burroughs said I had to lay off ten percent right away."

"Why her? Why in God's name did you pick her?"

"I, um, just pulled blindly from the files. I thought it was the fairest way."

Nichols's eyes narrowed. "What the fuck do you mean you just pulled blindly from the files?"

What Jimmy meant was that he had just pulled blindly from the files. He had asked Art the Office Manager to bring him all the personnel files with the full intention of reading through them and selecting employees with the lowest performance ratings. But there were too many of them, and it was tedious work, and all the scores seemed like they were going to be about the same. So Jimmy put the box of folders on his desk, closed his eyes, and picked.

"I mean, it was random, just random. I thought that was the fairest way to do it."

"Who else got the axe?"

"Tim Husser, Don Jeffries, the paralegal, Jessica, obviously, Sara Welks in Office Services, Alice Bentley, and, um, oh yeah, Maggie Moxley."

The Prick

Nichols eyes lit with understanding. "You fired Maggie Moxley?"

"Laid off, as part of the ten percent."

Nichols laughed. "Dumb fucking luck," he said. "You try to get rid of Moxley without having the balls to fire her outright and Jess gets caught up in the cover-up."

"What?"

"You know that this is basically the easiest retaliation case in the world that you've just given that little prick Hunter, right?" Nichols said, still laughing. "You've made everything so much worse, you goddamn slow-witted buffalo."

"The layoff had nothing to do with—"

"Yeah, sure," Nichols said. "And you know what? Not only did you just double down on the Moxley lawsuit, you just manufactured a brand new one."

Nichols sighed and leaned back in his chair.

"I've been fucking Jessica Rossi. For about six months now. She thinks I arranged for her to get fired to keep her quiet, stupid as that concept is."

Jimmy felt relief flow through him. He wasn't in trouble, Nichols was. Maybe he would have a drink after all.

"She's got all kinds of evidence—text messages, et cetera. Now, I'm not Robert. All of this was consensual."

Jimmy stared at him, trying not to smile.

Nichols regarded him incredulously. "Don't you get it? You've just created another lawsuit, trying to cover up for the original one. You dumb fucking bastard." He drained his glass and walked inside.

*****

Rebecca Trent sat down in her favorite chair on the back porch and put her whiskey down on the table beside her. The phone rang.

"Jimmy. Come to your senses, I hope?"

103

The Prick

"Ah, what?"

"I asked you if you were calling me to tell me that you had come to your senses and decided not to fire Moxley."

"No. Listen, Rebecca, we have a problem ..."

"No shit." Trent said. "I imagine Hunter is on the warpath?"

"Not, ah, well, you know David, right?" Trent could make out a gruff voice in the background yelling at Peters. "Of course, you do, well, ah..."

The Prick

Chapter 17

Monday, April 15th
Atlanta Offices of Levitt, Bennett & Taylor, LLP

Outside his office, in the hallway and down the many stories of the building, bottoming out on the bustling street, life went on. Inside his office, life was over. Everything was over. Robert Spelkin III sat at his desk with his head in his hands. He saw only black.

Lying flat before Robert, not quite touching his elbows, was today's issue of the *Daily Record*, a periodical circulated among Atlanta's legal community. His picture was on the cover. The end of his life was today's top story.

LEVITT PARTNER ROBERT SPELKIN III ACCUSED OF SEXUAL MOLESTATION

Former assistant alleges that Spelkin put his erect penis on her neck and demanded fellatio.

By George Hull

In a Complaint filed today in Fulton County Superior Court, Margaret Moxley, former legal assistant of Robert Spelkin III, alleges that, on March 21st, the high-profile litigator approached her at her desk after regular work hours and demanded that she perform fellatio on him in the office.

The Prick

Spelkin told Moxley, she alleges, that his genitalia was a "project" that she needed to complete before he would allow her to leave. Moxley claims that, when she refused Spelkin's sexual demands and turned away from him, he approached her from behind and forcibly put his erect penis against her neck. Moxley further claims that when she refused his sexual advances again, he expressly told her to "put it in her mouth."

When Moxley tried to escape, Spelkin tried to grab her to prevent her from leaving, the Complaint goes on to allege. Perhaps contributing to Spelkin's grossly unlawful behavior, the Complaint suggests, was the fact that he had been drinking heavily after a big settlement.

In her Complaint Moxley brings claims against Spelkin for civil assault and battery and intentional infliction of emotional distress and a claim against Levitt for negligent retention and supervision.

The defendant's illegal actions did not end that night, according to Moxley's attorney, Jason M. Hunter. "Mrs. Moxley filed a Charge with the EEOC about what happened. Almost immediately after she did so, Levitt fired her, claiming it was a layoff."

The real reason, according to Hunter, was retaliation for filing the EEOC Charge, giving rise to a separate cause of action for retaliation against Levitt. When asked whether he believed that Spelkin was behind the termination of Moxley, Hunter stated: "We will find that out in discovery, rest assured. It's hard to believe, however, that he did not know that his own legal assistant, who had made these claims against him to the EEOC, was set to be fired."

Hunter said that he intends to amend the Complaint to include Title VII sexual harassment and retaliation claims following the EEOC investigation, which is ongoing. "I am confident that the EEOC investigation will both confirm Mrs. Moxley's claims and shed light on the true motivation for her sudden termination."

Counsel for Levitt was not immediately available for comment.

The picture they'd used was from Levitt's website, the one where he was smiling broadly in his lucky suit. That smile, which he'd seen a thousand times before when running Internet searches on himself, seemed so sleazy in this context that Spelkin could hardly recognize it as his own.

Not that it mattered any longer. Concerns over publicity belonged to his former self in his former life. He'd made his mind up the instant he saw the headline. Still, must keep up appearances until it was time. He unburied his face and picked up the phone, kicking his feet up on the desk and trying to summon power and swagger from wherever they were hiding.

"I thought I might be hearing from you," Rebecca Trent said.

"I want his balls cut off."

"I thought you might. This is one of the worst media attacks I've seen."

"Whose fucking goddamn dick-brained idea was it to fire her? I know it wasn't yours."

"No, it wasn't."

"Then who?"

"You'll have to take that question to Jimmy."

"Fucking goddamn worthless pile of dogshit."

"Not entirely worthless. He seems to be taking the bullet for you, retaliation-wise, anyway. I'm not sure if he knows it or not, but that's what he's doing."

"And it's supposed to be some kind of layoff?"

"That's the official story."

"Jimmy's never been very good at thinking," Robert said.

"I honestly don't think it was his call. I think it came down from on high."

"Washington?"

"Yes."

"And let the chips fall where they may, I guess?"

"That seems to be the idea."

"They seem to have fallen on me."

"Yes, they have."

"You couldn't have tipped me off?"

"I was going to come tell you today in person and talk it through. It just happened Friday afternoon. I didn't know the little fucker was going to pull this circus stunt. Kid's got balls, you've got to hand it to him."

"I want them cut off."

"Yes, you said."

"So?"

"How do you recommend I do that?"

"With a blunt instrument, like you normally do."

"I don't see an opening yet."

"He libeled me."

"No, he didn't"

"Fine, the *Daily Record* libeled me. He defamed me."

"It didn't. He didn't. He was actually very careful not to, if you read it closely. All he did was state what the allegations are. All the *Daily Record* did was report what was in the Complaint, which is a publicly available document."

"And which was apparently provided to the *Daily Record* before it was filed."

"Come on, Robert."

"I want to bring a claim against him for defamation and demand an immediate retraction."

"That's not a good idea." Trent said. "He didn't actually publish it. There's some authority that he's responsible for what the reporter says if he feeds him the Complaint with the intention of getting him to publish it, but that's tricky. And, regardless, truth is a defense. You want a second lawsuit with this shit as the subject matter? Even if you win, you lose."

"File it anyway."

"I won't"

"You don't do it, I'll hire my own attorney who will," Robert said, his voice getting hot.

"That's not advisable. You know it."

"What I know is that you don't seem to have any control whatsoever over this fucking situation!" Robert hung up.

He dialed the next number.

"Robert, what can I do for you?"

"Liquidate everything."

"What?"

"Do it, Barry. Now. I don't care about losses or tax treatment. Liquidate everything now and put it in the BOA emergency account we set up last year. You know the one."

He dialed the next number. The receptionist at the front desk picked up. "Yes, Mr. Spelkin?"

"When Jimmy gets here, tell him I want to see him right away."

"Yes, sir."

He hung up. And smiled, just a little bit.

The Prick

*****

Jason set off for work around 8:00. Compulsive checking of email from his car at approximately 8:12, 8:18, 8:21, 8:32, 8:34, and 8:44 yielded a few junk emails and an inquiry from a client regarding a settlement check. When he got to his desk, just after 9:00, he had thirty-seven messages about the article and the case and, as he started to click through them, more stacked at the top every minute. They were coming in so fast it seemed like Outlook had some kind of virus. Most were from people at his old firm, attorneys, paralegals, and assistants; others were from law school classmates and other plaintiff's firms in town. All of them were congratulatory, as if he had already won the case. Jason spent about ten minutes rereading the article and responding to the more important people who'd emailed him before his phone rang.

"Here we go." Jason picked up.

"Hi, Rebecca," he said cheerfully.

"Hey kid, you really fucked this one up."

"How's that?"

"You had a case with some bite to it, despite the fact that your client is full of shit. And then, this weekend apparently, you completely fucked it up."

"Is that right?"

"Yep. Let me ask you, what did you think was the strongest part of your case?"

"The fact that Robert Spelkin drunkenly rubbed his dick on my client, demanded a blow job, and then fired her when she filed an EEOC claim. I think that part's pretty strong."

Trent laughed. "The green lawyers always think they're telling the truth, don't they? No, let me tell you what the strongest part of your case is—or was—since apparently you don't know. You had Robert Spelkin in a vice. Even if he denied the allegations, you could seriously damage his reputation, professionally and personally. The threat of that gave you leverage, and it was leverage you *could* have used to push me into a nice settlement for you and your client."

Jason didn't say anything.

"But this weekend," she continued, "you apparently decided to destroy that leverage. Robert and Levitt had something to lose. Now they've lost it. They have nothing to gain by early settlement. Might as well litigate and try to vindicate themselves. I hope you have income coming in from other places, kid, because this one is going the distance now."

"Levitt pushed us down this road when they decided to fire Mrs. Moxley in what may be the clearest case of retaliation I've ever even heard of," Jason said, "I assume you were behind the termination?"

Trent laughed. "You mean to tell me you blew the cover on this thing because you thought a budgetary layoff was some kind of vindictive action? You've got to do your homework before calling the press."

"I assume you'll accept service of the Complaint?"

"Of course," Trent said. "Just as an FYI, there may be a defamation Complaint filed against you personally today or tomorrow. I assume you'll accept service of that?"

"Sure," Jason said. "Or serve me. You know where I am." He hung up.

She was likely lying, bluffing, posturing, but Jason was drenched in sweat and his hands were shaking.

*****

Within a few minutes of delivering the sucker punch to Hunter, Rebecca Trent's phone rang.

"This is Ryan Sparks with the EEOC."

"What can I do for you, Mr. Sparks?"

The Prick

"I'm calling about the Moxley Charge against your client Levitt, Bennett and Taylor, LLP. I received your position statement and I want to set up a time to do the onsite. You didn't provide me with any dates."

"What did you have in mind?"

"How about Wednesday?"

"Which Wednesday?" Rebecca asked, pulling up her Outlook calendar.

"Wednesday the twentieth, this week."

"Two days from now?" Rebecca asked incredulously.

"Yes, are you available?"

"I am, but I don't know about the people you want to talk to. Remind me again who they are?"

"Robert Spelkin, David Nichols, Jessica Rossi, James Peters, Patricia Hayes."

Murderers' Row. "I don't know what their availability is."

"Check and get back to me. I would also remind your client that retaliation for participating in EEOC proceedings is prohibited."

Shit. "I already—"

"I would tell them again." Sparks said, and hung up on her.

That was the thing with federal agencies. They could interrupt you and then hang up on you. They didn't need you for anything. And they seemed to get off on it.

Chapter 18

Monday, April 15th
Trent, Ellis & Fitzpatrick, LLP

Rebecca spent the rest of her morning waging discovery warfare with a big, white-shoe New York firm who needed a lesson in who she was. She ate lunch at her desk—two bananas and a yogurt—and by 1:15 p.m. was able to turn back to the Spelkin fiasco.

"Get me the Moxley file!" she shouted out into the hall. A few seconds later her assistant Stephanie scooted in with file in hand. Rebecca shook her head disapprovingly at the file. "Call Maria around," she demanded, her tone betraying exasperation. Stephanie scooted out and a few minutes later Chan breathlessly appeared.

Rebecca filled Chan in about her conversations with Peters, Spelkin, Hunter, and Sparks, omitting only Spelkin's castration request. Chan had seen the *Daily Record* article, and so had everyone else. Luckily, it hadn't mentioned Trent or her firm.

"Let's call Simmons," Rebecca said, and dialed the number.

"What the hell is going on down there?" Simmons said.

"Nothing good. This is what happens when you willfully retaliate."

"Who else is in the room with you?" Simmons demanded.

The Prick

Trent raised her eyebrows. "My associate, Maria Chan."

"Anybody else on the line?"

"No."

The phone was silent for a few seconds. "We had to get her out of there."

"Any particular reason?"

"An office can't function like that. Attorneys can't work in a space where they're watching every word to make sure it can't be construed as retaliatory. The moment she filed that Charge, Moxley created a toxic working environment. Her retaliation claim isn't worth the everyday cost of that toxic working environment."

"Did Spelkin ask you to do it?"

"No, he didn't even know it was happening," Simmons said. "I imagine the whole thing came as quite a surprise."

"That's what he's expressing to me."

"And what? You didn't believe him?"

"About which part?"

Simmons laughed. "All right, fair enough. Tell me how bad this is."

"It's real bad," Rebecca said. "First, as you must know, you've given Moxley an airtight retaliation claim. Even if the underlying sexual assault claim is bullshit, the retaliation claim's not, and it carries damages of lost wages, as well as compensatory and punitives, capped under Title VII at 300,000. That says nothing of the bad press, which has apparently caused the EEOC to go on the warpath. The investigator's a real crusader; he wants an onsite this week. They may pick this up and sue the firm themselves."

"Bush league move, splashing this all over the front page."

"More like hardball. Say what you want about the kid, but the *Daily Record* article was a clear signal that he's not going to roll over. Somebody's going to have to talk Spelkin out of suing him personally for slander."

"What?"

"I assume you've seen the article?"

"Yes," Simmons said. "Hack job."

"It is. And there's likely to be another one just like it soon, maybe tomorrow."

"You mean the David Nichols thing," Simmons said, sounding exhausted.

"Yes, Will, the David Nichols thing," Rebecca said. "Tell me something—did you know?"

"Know what?"

"When you were constructing this cover-up layoff disaster, did you know that you were firing David Nichols's in-house mistress, this Jessica Rossi?"

"No. That one is all Jimmy Peters. Although I'm confident he didn't know what he was doing."

"What a surprise, Jimmy Peters not knowing what he's doing," Rebecca said. "He doesn't seem to be running too tight a ship over there. Is anyone in that office keeping their body parts to themselves?"

Simmons was silent.

"Anyway," Rebecca continued, "this Rossi woman threatened to go to Hunter."

"I heard."

"Which means the EEOC will also know about it soon."

"Fuck."

"I expect we'll also be getting another demand letter from Hunter soon, on behalf of Rossi."

"We should probably try to settle that one quick," Simmons said. "We can't let this get out."

"Hunter will know that, I'm sure," Rebecca said. "The funny thing about that situation is that it sounds like it was all consensual, at least from what Nichols tells me. Just two adults having voluntary intercourse, albeit in some embarrassing places for the firm. Rossi wouldn't have much in the way of a claim, or she didn't until Peters termed her."

"This layoff may not have been such a good idea."

Rebecca rolled her eyes.

"But I had to protect the office," Simmons said. "People —attorneys—can't work in that kind of environment."

No, Rebecca knew. Levitt didn't fire Maggie Moxley to protect the "working environment" or to save Robert Spelkin some well-deserved stress. They did it because they were Levitt and she was Maggie Moxley, and *fuck* Maggie Moxley.

The Prick

Chapter 19

Tuesday, April 16th
The Law Offices of Jason Hunter, Esq.

Now *this* was a sexual harassment plaintiff. Jessica Rossi was in Jason's office and, for the first time, he was embarrassed by the furnishings. He wanted to show her his car. Was there any plausible reason to? His eyes drifted to his cheap desk and then back up to Rossi, who was staring at him confidently. She was one of those women who knew it. Some of them knew it.

"All right, Ms. Rossi, I appreciate you coming in."

"Call me Jess." she said.

"Jess" had blonde hair and assertively filled out a tight cotton T-shirt. Despite his best efforts, Jason was having a hard time keeping his eyes in the professionally appropriate places. His pupils felt like they had weights pulling them down. It was too early in the morning to bombard him with this.

"Okay, Jess, how long did you work for Levitt?"

"Almost four years," she said. "I was in marketing before that, for a radio station."

"College?"

"Alabama." She smiled and brushed her hair off her face. "Roll tide."

"Right," Jason said, returning the smile. The problem with this sexual harassment plaintiff was that she didn't seem all that upset. Then again, he may have been overexposed to sobbing plaintiffs recently. Maybe (hopefully) a lot of them were like this one.

"When did you start working with David Nichols?"

"Right when I joined the firm. After I got done with the training. But he basically trained me on what he wanted me to do."

Jason let that one go. "Did he interview you?"

"Yes. Him and the Office Manager."

"Did you have any legal assistant experience at all prior to working at Levitt?"

"None," she said, smiling again. "But in my interview, David told me that experience wasn't required. He was right, I guess. It's not that hard."

"Right," Jason said, writing. "Did you work for Nichols continuously until your termination?"

"Almost. There was some reshuffling in the office at the beginning of the year. I was moved to another attorney. Two other attorneys, actually."

"Do you know why?"

"They said I could handle more work, and that I would get a raise."

"Do you know if Nichols requested it?"

"No, he was pissed off. But he didn't fight it. Probably because of how it would have looked."

"Would have looked?"

She paused and brushed her hair back again. "Yeah. Because, you know, by that time we were ..."

"Sleeping together?"

Rossi laughed. "That's such an innocent way of putting it. Yes, we were 'sleeping together' at that point." She used air quotes. Jason hated that.

"Okay, how would you characterize what you two were doing?" he asked with a touch of annoyance.

More laughter. "I would characterize what we were doing as fucking in his office. Fucking in the supply closet. Fucking in the conference room."

"So, "fucking," then?"

"That's what it was," she said. "No sense in making it all romantic. I gave him head when he was sitting at his desk on the phone with clients. It wasn't storybook."

Jesus. "How many times did you do that?"

"Give him head?"

"Under the desk at the office when he was talking to clients."

She laughed again. It wasn't exactly an injured laugh. It was more of a cackle. "A lot. He loved it. Called it 'multitasking.'"

Jason wrote the words "a lot" and "multitasking" on his legal pad.

"Is this something that happened every week?"

"Multiple times a week when he was in the office. I think he got off on the danger of it. Like, what do you call it, an adrenaline junkie?"

"Okay," Jason said. "Happen to remember which clients?"

She told him the names. They were big names. Big, embarrassing names.

"Do you know if, he, uh ..."

She smirked coyly at his obvious discomfort. "If he what?"

"Had problems concentrating on those calls?"

"Oh, I guarantee you he had problems concentrating," she said. Jason looked away and tried to mentally prohibit the flush.

"Any fallout from that?" he asked.

"In terms of?"

The Prick

"Mistakes? Problems with clients? Times he would ask clients for information they'd already given?"

She shifted in the chair. "Not that I know of. David, you know, David is very smooth. He can talk his way out of anything."

There was something about the way she said it. She was impressed with Nichols. People with charisma always had a certain aura, regardless of whatever else they were about.

"So how did things start?"

She smiled again. She would have to smile less. A lot less.

"He asked me to stay late to help him with a filing and—"

"You're kidding."

"What? Why? Oh, because that's how Robert came after Maggie, right," she said, laughing. "Never would have pictured those two together. No, that's how it happened. He asked me to stay late. He was in his office writing edits on drafts, and he would bring them around for me to put into the electronic versions, and I would print them out and bring them to him so we could review them at his desk. There was one edit that I couldn't read and I brought it into his office to ask him what it was. I was on his side of the desk, leaning over him, and he had this cologne on, and it just happened."

"What just happened?"

"We kissed, and, you know, it went from there. Never did find out what that word was."

"Who initiated it?"

"I don't know, it was mutual I guess."

Shit.

"I know what you're thinking," she said. "Why did I want to be with such an older man. It's hard to explain, but David is, I don't know, sexy."

The Prick

That had not been what Jason was thinking. The woman exuding raw sexuality in front of his desk was suffering from a relatively common misconception. Consensual sex between two adults didn't add up to a lawsuit, even if it was between a boss and a subordinate and even if it happened in the office. Nichols had certainly committed malpractice with the phone-head, and Jason was sure he had violated firm policies, but technically there was no claim. Unless …

"Why were you fired?"

She snorted. "So people wouldn't find out we were fucking, after the whole thing with Robert and Maggie blew up."

Bingo.

Jason nodded encouragingly. "What makes you think that?"

"Well, look at the timing." Now her voice had an edge to it. "Maggie and I, two women who were sexually involved with partners, get fired the exact same day, as some kind of 'layoff'? Come on."

"You think they saw you as a liability after Maggie came forward and did this to get rid of you?" Jason asked, leadingly.

"Yes, exactly."

This wasn't entirely plausible. If they hadn't just fired Maggie, Jason wouldn't have believed that Levitt would do such a thing, as the natural effect of terminating Rossi would be to send her running to an attorney's office. But Levitt had proved to be stupidly cutthroat with respect to sexual harassment plaintiffs.

"Of course, David denies it," she continued. "Says he had nothing to do with me being fired."

Jason scoffed. "You believe him?"

"Not for a second."

The Prick

"All right," Jason said. "Now what we have to expect is that David will deny that you ever had a relationship with him, and—"

"There's no chance of that," Rossi said. "I have evidence."

People threw that word around a little too loosely. "What evidence?"

She got up and came around to his side of the desk, taking her iPhone out of the tight front pocket of her jeans, and put it on the desk in front of Jason. "It's all on here."

It was. Standing over his left shoulder, she showed him a series of explicit and embarrassing texts *and* emails, as well as a history of late-night phone calls. A couple of the emails had pictures—of her—that Nichols had apparently taken. Jason fought the flush back again and didn't look at her as he cycled through images of her in lingerie and provocative poses. Despite the very many reactions the pictures were provoking, Jason mostly wondered how David Nichols could be so fucking reckless.

"Hotel room?" Jason pointed to a picture of her on what looked like a hotel bed.

"Yes," she said. "Sometimes we left work during the day and checked in at the downtown Ritz."

Jason nodded, keeping eyes straight down.

"We need to make a copy of all of this."

"Okay," she said, cheerfully.

"I've got a guy who does this kind of thing. Can you leave the phone with me and pick it up tomorrow?"

"Sure," she said, getting up to leave. "Need anything else from me?"

Yes. Jason put his contingency agreement in front of her and showed her where to sign, which she did without hesitation. He told her he would put together a demand letter and let her look at it before it went out. She was on board with everything.

It was a delight not having to seek the approval of a redneck husband on every decision.

As Jessica Rossi was leaving his office, Jason asked his standard close-out question. "Is there anything else you think I should know?"

"Well," she said, pausing with her hand on the door frame. "I'm not sure if this would be helpful or not, but if David tried to deny it, you know, deny that we were having sex, well, ah, his dick is very ... distinctive."

This was a new one. "Distinctive how?"

"It's ... huge. Like, huge." She put her hands up in the air to show the hugeness.

"All right." Not exactly the distinction he had been hoping for, but, hey, you played the hand you were dealt.

"Yeah," she said, shrugging. "Don't know if that's helpful or what, but anyway, there it is."

"There it is." Jason agreed.

The Prick

Chapter 20

Wednesday, April 24th
Atlanta Offices of Levitt, Bennett & Taylor, LLP

David Nichols was being interviewed/interrogated by EEOC investigator Ryan Sparks, which he (David) found amusing. They were in the big conference room where the first meeting about the Spelkin Situation took place. David could see his condo building looming over Buckhead in the distance. He smiled. $3.75 million and he had paid in cash, even after his ex had taken more than half of everything in the divorce. Not many people on the planet could do that.

Also present was the incredibly lanky Rebecca Trent, in one of her seemingly countless pantsuits. She was sprawled out in a chair, typing on her BlackBerry and ignoring everyone.

Sparks had taken a badge out and laid it on the table. It was gold and looked very official. If one didn't know better, one might assume that the person who possessed such an item could effectuate an arrest. David wondered if most witnesses were intimidated by the sight of it. In actuality, Sparks didn't even have the authority to compel David to participate in the interview. But if David refused, Sparks could file a subpoena action and try to persuade a court to order him to submit. That was an unpleasant process and it gave the wrong appearance, especially in front of one of the federal judges David appeared before with regularity. And so here David sat, being questioned by an amateur with an IQ that he estimated hovered right around 100.

David was under oath. The EEOC now insisted that all witnesses be sworn before the interview.

"And so you're telling me you don't know whether or not Mr. Spelkin drank more than one drink on March 21st?"

"What I'm telling you, Investigator Sparks, is that I lack sufficient recollection to give a sworn statement regarding the amount of alcohol consumed by Mr. Spelkin on any occasion, including March 21st. I'm not going to hazard a guess under oath." David leaned back in his chair and grinned. "Do you always keep your badge on the table during the entire interview?"

"So you did not observe Mr. Spelkin having more than one drink during the approximately three hours the two of you were at the bar at the Peachtree Club?" Sparks leaned over the table, elbows pressed against the oak, and glared at David. He looked to be about thirty-five, getting to the point of his life where he'd realize that he wouldn't amount to much of anything.

"It's not my practice to monitor the consumption of other people at the bar," David said. "I imagine that practice would get one disinvited to most parties." David threw Trent his best is-this-guy-serious expression. Trent just stared at him blankly and turned back to her BlackBerry.

"Did you ever observe Mr. Spelkin interacting with Mrs. Moxley?" Sparks asked. There was no missing the aggravation in his voice.

"During the years that she worked as his assistant? Yes."

"Did you ever see him touch her?"

"No."

"Did you ever talk with Mr. Spelkin about Mrs. Moxley?"

"During the years that she worked as his assistant? Yes."

"What did he say about her?"

The Prick

"Many things."

"Such as?"

"He would say things like, 'Maggie's putting my edits in the brief. She'll send it to you.'"

"Anything unrelated to work?"

"One year, I think we discussed what we should get our assistants for Christmas. I think I settled on a gift card. Impersonal, maybe, but then they can just get what they want, you know?"

Sparks's whole body lifted with his exasperated (and exaggerated) sigh. "Do you think this is a game, Mr. Nichols?"

Trent looked up. "He's just answering the questions you're asking him, Ryan."

Sparks nodded, looking very much like he wanted to let his fists do the asking.

"All right," he said. "Let me be more clear. Did Mr. Spelkin ever talk about Mrs. Moxley in a romantic or sexual way?"

"No."

"Are you aware of the allegations Mrs. Moxley made in her Charge?"

"Yes."

"Have you talked to Mr. Spelkin about the Charge?"

"Yes."

"Don't disclose any communications with Robert that were made in the presence of counsel," Trent warned, for Sparks's benefit.

"Okay," David said cheerfully, reclining even farther in his chair.

"Have you talked to Mr. Spelkin about the Charge outside the presence of counsel?"

"Yes."

"What did he say?"

The Prick

"She's lying."

Sparks nodded. He had stopped writing anything on the pad in front of him and was staring at David. "Anything else?"

"Only other variants on that theme."

"What?"

"She's lying," said David. "He says she's lying."

"Do you believe him?"

"Yes."

"So you think she's just making all this up?"

"Yes."

"Were you involved in her termination?"

"No."

"Suspicious timing, don't you think?"

"Come on, Ryan," Trent said.

"No," David answered.

Sparks nodded and, for the first time, grinned back at David.

"Do you know a Jessica Rossi?"

If Sparks had been hoping for a change in demeanor in David, a reddening, or a swallowing, or a nervous glance at Trent, he was disappointed. David's reaction betrayed nothing.

"Yes."

"Was she your assistant?"

"Yes."

"Did you have a sexual relationship with her?"

"In the last year, yes."

Sparks raised his eyebrows. He looked over at Trent, who didn't even seem to be paying attention. He wrote on his pad.

"Did you have sex with her in the office?"

"Which office?"

"Did you have sex with her in your office?"

"Yes."

"Did you have sex with her in other places in this building?"

"What other places?"

"Why don't you tell me the places that you and she had sex?"

"No."

"You won't answer the question?" Sparks asked, looking over at Trent, who continued to show more interest in whatever was going on with her BlackBerry.

"No. That's private."

"Your sexual relationship with your subordinate employee is private?"

"Yes," David said. "And although it should be obvious, my consensual sexual relationship has nothing whatsoever to do with Mrs. Moxley or her Charge."

"You're aware that Ms. Rossi was terminated the same day as Mrs. Moxley?"

"Yes. They were laid off, I understand."

"Did you have any involvement in Ms. Rossi's termination?"

"No."

"So they terminated your assistant without consulting you?" The tone of the question suggested that perhaps Sparks did not believe him.

"She wasn't my assistant when she was terminated," David told him.

"What?" Sparks seemed on the precipice of combustion.

"She wasn't my assistant when she was terminated."

Sparks was breathing deeply in a deliberate way, like someone telling himself to breathe deeply in order to stay calm.

"When did she stop being your assistant?" he asked.

The Prick

"Months earlier. You'll have to talk to the Office Manager to get the exact date. Art."

"Was that your decision—to have her stop reporting to you?"

David shook his head. "Some kind of office restructuring. Again, the Office Manager would be the one to talk to about all that. Art."

Sparks looked down at his notes for a good twenty seconds. David glanced over at Trent, who was thumbing furiously on her BlackBerry. Judging from her expression, all was not right with the world.

"Okay," Sparks finally said, after more deep breathing, "that's all the questions I have for you, Mr. Nichols. I'll be in touch if I have anything further. Ms. Trent, this brings us to Mr. Spelkin, I believe. Will the interview be—"

Jimmy Peters burst into the room as only an obese person can burst into a room: slowly and with noticeable effort. He also was breathing heavily but with a greater degree of urgency. They all stared at him.

"Sorry," Peters said, "to interrupt. We need to evacuate the building."

"What, why?" Sparks said. "I'm in the middle of interviews."

"I know," Peters said between oxygen-sucking gasps. "And I apologize. It's a former employee. He was just arrested in the lobby downstairs. He was carrying a gun, and ... he's claiming there's a bomb."

Trent put down her BlackBerry. "Seems we'll have to reschedule," she said.

*****

Where was he? Maria had checked all Levitt offices and all conference rooms on all four Levitt floors, had called Spelkin's office line, even though she had repeatedly checked his office in person, his home line, his cell phone, and his wife's cell phone (from the emergency contact list). She had checked the downstairs lobby, the coffee shop, the diner, the Brooks Brothers where he said he had gotten the suit, and had peered in windows of all retail businesses between the office and the diner and between the office and Brooks Brothers. She had emailed him, his assistant, Peters, Nichols (even though she knew he was in a meeting), his wife, and Ned Burroughs. She had asked male employees to check the men's rooms. They'd looked at her like she was crazy but they'd complied. She didn't tell them what it was about and thankfully they didn't ask. She had called her office to see if anyone had received a call, voicemail or email from him. Nobody had. She emailed Trent repeatedly to tell her she couldn't find Spelkin, even though it was her job to find Spelkin, and Spelkin was supposed to be interviewed after Nichols.

Trent had said, via response email: *That is unacceptable. Find him now!*

But she couldn't find him. He was nowhere to be found. Where was he? She got her notes out again and looked to see if he had said he would meet her somewhere in particular. But each time she looked at her notes, they told her that Spelkin would meet her in his office. But her notes were wrong. He was not in his office. Where was he?

She was doing another circuit of Spelkin's floor and refreshing her email every half second when one came in from Trent.

We dodged a bullet. Meet you downstairs. Locate Spelkin right fucking now.

The Prick

Chapter 21

Wednesday, April 24th
Crowne Plaza
New Orleans, Louisiana

The Crowne Plaza hotel in New Orleans was located at the intersection of Canal and Bourbon, just a few blocks from Harrah's Casino and right across the street from the drunken madness that was the touristy section of Bourbon. It was therefore perfect for Robert's purposes, which purposes consisted of doing whatever the goddamn fuck he wanted.

Robert had driven from Atlanta, drinking coffee with whiskey and blasting *Exile on Main Street* on repeat. The coffee had come from gas stations every hundred miles or so and the whiskey had come from his (former) desk. Coffee and gas were paid for in cash. Robert had become a cash operation. He went directly to the New Orleans airport, put his car in long-term parking, and took a taxi to the hotel. He had one suitcase full of clothes and another with over $200,000 in US currency, in hundreds. The hotel had demanded a credit card for the room but promised him that it wouldn't be charged unless he checked out. The initial reservation was for three weeks but he would leave whenever the goddamn fuck he wanted.

Robert showered and put on the lucky suit and lucky shirt that had been owned by the late Robert Spelkin III, his

131

former self. He opened his safe, retrieved five thousand, and took the elevator down to the lobby.

Across the street, the fracas was already underway. A brass band played just at the entrance to Bourbon Street and was surrounded mostly by tourist jerks drinking gigantic neon yardsticks with straws and locals eying the tourists. A mounted cop sat in the dead center of Canal Street, between the trolley lines, looming over the scene. Robert headed straight into the mess.

Around him groups of intoxicated people swarmed, most of them armed with the yardsticks or other neon drinks, some in the shape of grenades. The streets smelled strongly of vomit.

Robert picked a bar that opened up onto the street and sat in a chair facing Bourbon. As far as he could tell, he was the only patron in the bar wearing a suit. Groups of people cavorted by, seemingly oblivious to the retch-stench. Most were neon yardstick constituents. Some of them even had a beaded necklace that connected to the glass and allowed them to drink hands-free.

"Just you, honey?" a voice behind him inquired. Robert turned to see that it was a woman in her late forties with unwashed hair and a green-and-white striped shirt who had managed to so effectively sum up his new life.

"From here on out," Robert confirmed. "Tell me ... Jennifer," he said, finding her name tag, "what's in the long drink that seems to be all the rage on the street?"

"There are different kinds," she said. "But they all got different types of liquor in them and fruit juice or a cocktail mix."

"Multiple types of liquor in one drink?" Robert asked.

"Right," Jennifer said.

"They work?"

Jennifer made a confused face. "Work for what?"

The Prick

"They get you good and fucked up?"

The confusion cleared. This was apparently an oft-fielded question in a bar with no wall separating it from Bourbon Street. "Oh, yes, honey," she said. "If that's what you mean to do, that's the perfect drink to get."

"That is indeed what I mean to do," Robert said, putting his feet up on one of the unoccupied chairs at the table. "Give me the strongest one of those available and a po'boy, please."

Jennifer went off to do her work and Robert prepared to do his, which was, of course, complete mental annihilation. His brain was his enemy to the extent that it contained and presented him with memories of the former Robert Spelkin III, who, to be fair to the brain, was its former tenant and had left all sorts of belongings strewn around the place when he had exited. The memory cells were cancerous to the well-being of Robert Reinvented and he intended to blast them with murderous toxins so as to beat them into submission and surrender. Whatever collateral damage this inflicted to his body and to the other persons inhabiting his orbit was just that and could not be helped, much as an oncological treatment had follicular and immunosuppressant consequences.

Even on his inebriated drive from Atlanta to New Orleans, and even as he attempted to white-out thought with the Rolling Stones at jarring volume, the brain flashed Robert Spelkin III's memories and thoughts into his consciousness like an involuntary slideshow with him tied to the seat. His wife. His children. His parents. His cases. Even the dog. Who was going to walk the goddamn labradoodle in the morning? His little girl was going to grow up without—

Enough of *that*. *That* was exactly what the fuck he was talking about. And even though he had thrown Robert

The Prick

Spelkin III's BlackBerry out the window on I-20 at eighty-five miles per hour, he was still feeling phantom vibrations in his leg and thinking he had a call or an email. None of that was acceptable, not in the reinvention.

Jennifer mercifully arrived with the florescent drink and said something inconsequential about the po'boy. Robert took a minute to lovingly admire the tall glass. Then it began.

The Prick

Chapter 22

Wednesday, April 24th
The Moxley House

She was gaining weight, rapidly. This was the analysis of both the aluminum scale beneath the stained towels on the wall and Pete, although Pete was far more expressive about it. The scale did not tell her, for example, that if she kept sitting her fat ass around the house all day she would just keep getting fatter, although it did confirm this to be true.

Maggie supposed at times that she could tell Pete where to get off because by any measure Pete was more overweight than she was, and had been so for more than half a decade. But she knew where that would end up, and she knew that looks were more important for a woman than a man. Besides, he was the one with a job. And as he frequently bayed from his favorite chair in his living room, he was the only one in this house bringing in any damn money.

If she didn't get a job soon they were going to be in trouble. That was a fact. Pete did bring in money, but not as much as she had as a legal secretary for Levitt. The income disparity, before she'd been fired, had always been an uncomfortable issue for them. Part of the recent income-related aggression from Pete was revenge for her having made more money than him for so long. Or maybe it wasn't. What did she know. The point was that their joint income had been reduced by about 60 percent in one shot, and if she didn't find something soon, they wouldn't be able to cover the house payment and the payment for Pete's truck and the utilities and phone bill. The numbers only added up one way.

She didn't want to blame the lawyer, and she knew it (probably) wasn't *his* fault that she'd lost her job and her income and was gaining weight despite feeling sick to her stomach all the time. It wasn't his fault that she'd lost all of her friends at work and might lose her house to the bank, or that Pete—who'd left for the bar down the street an hour ago —made less eye contact with her than ever before. But how could he let her get fired like that? Didn't he say it would be illegal to fire her for signing that EEOC paper? Things had gotten worse—much, much worse—since Attorney Jason had started representing her. He was so nice, but maybe Pete was right about him. Maybe she should try to find a new lawyer, somebody older.

She walked into the bedroom and found the phone on the bed. She located Attorney Jason's card, which she kept in the drawer of the nightstand on her side of the bed, and dialed the number.

Someone answered on the third ring. Whoever picked up sounded like he was at a bar, based on the ambient noise. Maggie frowned at the phone. She had called Attorney Jason's office line.

"Who is this?" she asked the voice.

"That's normally the call recipient's question."

"Maybe I have the wrong number," Maggie said. "I was trying to call my attorney."

"Maggie?"

So it was him. Was he having some kind of office party? "Yes, it's me. Are you ... I was trying to call you at the office."

"Oh, yeah, sorry, most of the time when I'm not there I have calls forwarded to my cell phone. So I don't miss anything."

"Oh. Can you talk? It sounds like you're … at a bar."

"Sure, I can talk for a minute," Attorney Jason said. "Let me just try to find a quieter area."

Maggie waited.

"Okay," Attorney Jason said. "I walked to the corner of the room. Can you hear me okay? It's pretty loud in here."

"Um, yes."

"Great, what's up?"

What's up? Her life was falling apart and her lawyer was out at a bar. Maggie took a deep breath. "I was just wondering if there's any news on my case, if they want to settle, make a better settlement offer."

"Nothing new on the settlement front. It may take a while for them to put a real number on the table. You're probably going to have to have your deposition taken first."

"When will that be? I can do it this week."

Attorney Jason laughed. "That won't happen for months, unfortunately. They still have weeks to file their Answer to the Complaint, we don't even have the Title VII claims in yet, and there'll have to be a document exchange before any depositions are taken. It'll all probably happen much later this year, or even at the beginning of next year if there are extensions."

"Well can you maybe, you know, try to speed up the process somehow?" Maggie's voice cracked a little bit. "I can't find a job and we need the money."

There was a pause. Maggie heard someone shouting in the background.

"Look, Maggie, I'm sorry, I know you're in a tough situation. But I can't make the process go any faster—with a tough defendant these things go years. None of this is fair or right, but you're just going to have to be patient." There was more shouting in the background. "Listen, I have to go," Attorney Jason said. "I'll let you know as soon as I hear anything."

Maggie looked around the dingy bedroom and at Pete's clothes strewn around on the floor and felt the unmistakable onset of tears welling up inside of her. She pushed herself up and sat on the edge of the bed, feeling the rolls of fat stack up on her stomach. The push of the sobbing was stronger against the back of her eyes.

She looked down at her right hand, which was still gripping the phone so hard that it hurt. She felt like she was going to smash it. And then she did. Maggie Moxley hurled the phone at the wall, where it exploded all around the room in component pieces, some landing on Pete's old laundry. She stormed to the kitchen, yanked the yellow pages down from the fridge, and flipped to the Attorney section. She was going to do something about this. Here she was at home suffering and expanding, and everyone else who was *supposed* to be doing something was out drinking.

*****

"Sorry about that," Jason said, returning to the table and apologizing mainly in the direction of his "date," Lauren. Lauren was a friend of Nikki, Brunnell's girlfriend, and Nikki and Brunnell had expressed a hope that the double date they'd set up would evolve into a more permanent arrangement. This night, the first go at making that dream a reality, was regrettably in its beginning stages.

At least they were at a decent venue. Brick Store, a bar/pub in Decatur, had a massive beer list and tables made out of tree stump splices, if you could get them, which they had. Their table was in the corner of the room, near the front door but neatly tucked in a little alcove that gave them privacy about 80 percent of the way around.

"No problem," Lauren said, smiling and holding his gaze. Jason couldn't resolve whether he was attracted to her. She was pretty but bore a striking resemblance to a doe. It was disconcerting, and Jason had to keep forcibly ejecting the image of a deer from his mind. It wasn't a thought that he wanted to have, or was trying to have, but it kept popping up unbidden in the old consciousness and could not be expelled for long.

"Client?" Brunnell asked. His right hand was wrapped around a pint. His left was nowhere to be seen but looked to be, from the angle of his arm, wrapped around Nikki's ass.

"Yep," Jason said. "Needed a little handholding. Wants to know why she hasn't been paid already."

"So you're a, uh, prosecutor?" Lauren asked.

Jason tried to stifle a laugh while Brunnell smiled and Nikki looked bored. "No, prosecutors work in criminal law and are employed by the government to, you know, prosecute criminals. I handle civil lawsuits."

"Oh," Lauren said. Admittedly, nowhere really to go conversationally from there.

"I mostly handle employment lawsuits" he said. "Lawsuits by employees or former employees against companies."

Lauren's eyes brightened. "Oh! My father's company has a lot of those. Employees are always trying to make up claims against it—trying to get money out of him. He says all companies have to deal with frivolous lawsuits. Like, what was that case with the coffee? When the woman spilled coffee on herself and sued McDonald's?"

Brunnell and Jason exchanged a look.

"They have really good pretzels here." Brunnell shoved the menu across the table. "And they come with pimento cheese. It's a good combo."

The Prick

"I don't like pimento cheese!" Nikki said. "And it's really fattening."

Lauren nodded solemnly. "All cheese is."

"You know that woman had to get skin grafts," Jason said.

The girls stared at him. Brunnell sighed and leaned back in his chair.

"What?" Nikki said.

"The woman who spilled the coffee on herself. The coffee was so hot that she got third-degree burns. They had to take skin from other parts of her body."

Nikki made a face. "Ew, that's gross."

"But it's coffee, it's supposed to be hot," Lauren protested. "And didn't she dump on herself?"

"She spilled it on herself," Jason said, "but the coffee was around a hundred eighty degrees. You can't drink it at that temperature. And McDonald's had gotten hundreds of complaints about how hot it was and how other people had been burned."

"Well, I don't think people should get to sue for spilling things on themselves," Lauren said, forcing a laugh and looking at Nikki.

Jason shook his head. "The point is that McDonald's knew it was putting customers at risk for burns, because it had been happening all over the place, and they did nothing about it. They just didn't care. Now they don't serve it so hot. You might feel different if it happened to *you* and *you* needed skin grafts." Jason addressed this last part right to Lauren, realizing just after he said it that just maybe it was a bit over the top for what was supposed to be a first date.

Nikki rolled her eyes. Lauren was looking at the table in front of her.

"So, pretzels?" Brunnell asked.

Chapter 23

Thursday, April 25th
Atlanta Offices of Levitt, Bennett & Taylor, LLP

Rebecca Trent, Maria Chan, David Nichols, and Jimmy Peters were huddled in Peters's office with the door closed. Will Simmons and Ned Burroughs, in DC, were on the black speakerphone in the center of Peters's desk. Jimmy leaned back in his chair. Trent, Chan, and Nichols sat in visitors' chairs in front of his desk. Chan sat bolt upright while Nichols, utterly at ease, flipped a fountain pen in his right hand. Trent, as always, typed away on her BlackBerry.

"Okay," Jimmy began, directing his voice and eyes to the speakerphone, and clearing his throat. "We've got a bit of situation here."

"I assume," came Simmons's voice over the speakerphone, "that you're not referring to the Spelkin Situation, which has now morphed into the Spelkin and Nichols Situation, but some new goddamn situation?"

Jimmy looked at Trent for help, eyes a blue cocktail of panic and desperation. She didn't return eye contact and continued to type.

"Well it's ... related," Jimmy stammered, noting as he did that Nichols was struggling to suppress a smile. What was so goddamned funny? "Nobody has heard from Robert."

"What do you mean?"

The Prick

Trent looked up and jumped in. "Will, Robert hasn't shown up to work in at least six days. He blew off the EEOC interview, which we happened to luck out on because some wack job you all just fired in an attempt to cover up the retaliatory firing of Moxley made a bomb threat and showed up to the building with a gun. Nobody can reach Robert. His new assistant has no idea where he is and he isn't responding to emails. His phone goes straight to voicemail."

They all stared at the speakerphone for a few seconds. The room was very still, with the exception of Nichols flipping his pen.

"Have you tried calling his house?" the speakerphone eventually asked.

Chan shifted uncomfortably in her seat.

"Yes, we've called repeatedly. His wife hasn't seen him either. She said that if we get in touch with him to tell him that he'll be hearing from her divorce lawyer."

"Jesus," invoked the speakerphone.

"Yes," Trent said. "I don't know if he's holed up in a hotel somewhere with his phone off, or if he's left the country, or joined a cult. I have no clue where this guy is. If we don't hear from him by tomorrow, I recommend that we hire a private investigator."

"I would check the airports," Nichols said. "If I were him, I'd be fleeing the country with a checked bag full of cash."

"You're not too far off from being him, David. Should we have you turn in your passport?" Trent said.

Nichols laughed. "I'm not going anywhere, believe me. I'll have some research pulled but as far as I'm aware, it's still legal to have consensual sex in this country."

"All right," Simmons said, "get the private investigator. Do you have one who's discrete?"

"Yes," Trent said. "I'll call him today with instructions to start tomorrow if we don't hear anything."

"So as far as we know, Spelkin's just disappeared?" Simmons said.

"Totally incommunicado," Trent said.

"Good lord," Simmons said. "Just ... keep me updated, I guess,"

Trent nodded and looked at Chan, who had been scribbling since the call started.

Jimmy cleared his throat. "Uh, Will, there's something else ..."

Silence on the other end. Jimmy forged ahead. "Yeah, uh, we got another demand letter from Jason Hunter. It's about Jessica Rossi, who was ..." Jimmy looked at Nichols uneasily. Nichols just smiled at him. "Jessica Rossi was—"

"The secretary who David was sleeping with in the office without your knowledge and who you managed to fire along with Moxley, creating one more retaliation claim that we currently know about," Simmons finished for him, his words coming out of the speakerphone quick and hard like they were being punched on a typewriter.

"Uh, yes."

"Well?"

"Uh ..."

"I think he wants to know how much Hunter is demanding," Trent prompted.

"Oh, okay, well..." Jimmy stalled, while trying to find the demand letter. Trent watched him rifle through various papers on his desk. None of the disorderly scattered pages seemed to be yielding up the answer and Jimmy looked up at Trent for help. "Rebecca, do you—I don't seem to have the number, uh, directly accessible"

"Eight hundred and fifty thousand," Trent said loudly into the speakerphone.

"Yes, that's right!" Jimmy said, relieved. "Will, I was thinking," Jimmy began, "that we should respond by—"

The Prick

He was interrupted by the loud and resounding dial tone blaring from the speakerphone. Washington had hung up.

"Good meeting," Nichols observed. "Hey, Chan, can you send me those notes when you get them all typed up and proofread?"

The Prick

Chapter 24

Thursday, April 25th
The Law Offices of Jason Hunter, Esq.

"Because she was boring, she insulted my job, and she wasn't as attractive as you said she was, okay?" With that, Jason concluded his conversation with Brunnell, shut the car door, and unevenly made his way across the parking lot to his office, sadly wearing the same clothes he'd had on the day before but armed with a giant Krispy Kreme coffee spiked with what must have been the equivalent of six sugar packets. The lady at the drive-through window was in charge of the composition and he always let her off the leash.

Jason's car was still in a parking lot in Decatur somewhere. He had some idea where but wouldn't allocate the old 100 percent surety to it. Things had gotten a little out of hand after the whole McDonald's debate/rant. Brunnell had valiantly attempted to remedy the bad taste in the group's collective mouth by ordering many (more than several) rounds of drinks without asking if anybody wanted them when the previous round(s) were not yet drained. Each new drink made one (or at least Jason) feel compelled to quickly finish its predecessor as if falling behind on an assembly line.

All of the alcohol consumption led to Brunnell and Jason engaging in an in-depth and strangely emotional conversation regarding the strengths and weaknesses of

The Prick

their respective fantasy football teams while Nikki and Lauren dialoged about the strengths and weaknesses of various couples they knew. The competing conversations were on diagonals as Lauren was sitting between Brunnell and Jason, the words crossing streams in the center of the table, which exaggerated Jason's already blatant ignoring of his "date." Nikki and Brunnell tried to merge the conversations on a few occasions in the first few rounds, but Jason was having none of it, and Lauren, for her part, seemed equally unwilling to reengage.

That's how things went until about midnight, when Nikki and Lauren announced they were leaving. New drinks (four of them) had just arrived and Brunnell and Jason jointly decided, without consulting each other, that they were not going until that issue was addressed.

"Well, bye!" Lauren said to him, fake and enthusiastic in the high-pitched voice that girls use when they are being super sweet.

"Bye, nice to meet you, see you later!" Jason said, for some reason offering three separate independently acceptable send-offs and matching her tone (but not her pitch) as best he was able.

They walked out. Nikki, as he was to learn later, drove Brunnell's car to his house. He had no idea how Lauren got home.

"You didn't even ask for her number," Brunnell complained when they left.

"Didn't want it."

"Why?" Brunnell asked. "She's a nice girl, pretty, got a good body." He had started in on Nikki's drink first, which had an orange slice in it. "She teaches some classes at LA Fitness—you know she's got to be in shape."

"She had shitty taste in drinks," Jason said, examining the one she had abandoned. The Brick Store had glasses that matched every drink on the menu and this one purported to be a cider. "She got a cider."

"Some of those are good."

Jason drank the untouched cider and asked Brunnell about his job.

"It's okay, I guess." Brunnell said.

"Getting along better with the boss?"

"He treats me like a peon. I'm a peon!" he shouted, arms raised to the sky in frustration.

"It seems like whenever we go out for drinks, the rest of the bar stares at us," Jason said. "Any idea why that might be?"

"Pheromones."

At 1:45 a.m. they were warned that it was last call and made good on it, ordering up a couple Duvel Tripel Hops, boasting a 9.5 percent alcohol content, which pushed them right over the edge. As the lights were being flicked on and off, they were incoherently trying to negotiate a deal for the night's leftover pretzels as their waitress was (somewhat) good-naturedly trying to usher them out the door.

Stumbling out into the night, they spoke at top volume through Decatur Square, and as they passed the old courthouse their voices ricocheted off the gray building. Down the street, they walked through the drive-through of the McDonalds and hoofed it the remaining few blocks to Brunnell's house, on the other side of the train tracks that ran parallel to DeKalb Ave in Decatur, leaving a trail of french fries in their wake. Opening the door, they found Nikki passed out on the couch in the living room with a half-full bag of popcorn in her lap. Brunnell mostly woke her up and dragged her to the bedroom. Jason replaced her on the couch, which was where a crushing headache greeted him at 9:15 a.m. the next day.

The Prick

And so returning to the office around 10:30, as best he could work out, his balance sheet for the night held eight to ten beers of various alcohol contents, one cider, two Big Macs, the majority of a large fries, and some popcorn. He did not feel well. Numerous internal organs were reporting massive discontent.

"Hello, everyone!" he said as he opened the door to his empty office. He headed straight for the coffee machine and got it working on reinforcements. Sitting down at his desk with a groan, he was immediately greeted with a host of new emails. A few subject lines sent jolts to the nervous system. He clicked first on the one reading "Maggie Moxley" and his already queasy stomach dropped:

> Mr. Hunter,
>
> I received a call last night from Maggie Moxley, who I understand is a client of yours. I spoke with Mrs. Moxley this morning and she expressed to me that she may want to retain my services with respect to her case against Levitt. She did not indicate that she wanted to terminate your representation of her but rather that she wanted to be jointly represented by both of us. I explained to Mrs. Moxley that I would only undertake such representation if: (i) it was understood by her and by you that I was lead counsel, (ii) you agreed to the arrangement, and (iii) you agreed to modify the contingency fee agreement between your firm and Mrs. Moxley to provide for allocation of an appropriate percentage of fees to my firm.
>
> Mrs. Moxley asked me to reach out to you regarding these terms. Call at your convenience.
>
> Best,

The Prick

Richard L. Weston
Weston, Brenson & Alps, LLP
1600 Peachtree Street NE, Suite 1000
Atlanta, GA 30302

As Jason's stomach recovered from the shock, the remainder of his body pulsated with rage. What the fuck? Fingers were already dialing.

"Hello?"

"Maggie, this is Jason Hunter."

"Oh, hi." She sounded guilty.

"I just got an email from Richard Weston," Jason said.

Silence.

"He says that you called him, and that you want him to represent you."

"Uh, yes. Is that okay?"

Jason had to bite his lip for a few seconds.

"Maggie," he said, as calmly as he could, "what are you doing?"

"Well, you know, I just thought that you seemed really busy and I—I can't find a job, and Levitt doesn't seem to want to deal with us or to, you know, do the right thing, and I just thought—"

"I seemed really busy?" Jason said, arms thrown in the air with exasperation. "Maggie, since you came into my office a few weeks ago, the vast majority of my time has been spent on your case."

"Well, I don't know, maybe it would be good to get some extra help," she said, like an innocent lamb. "Mr. Weston seemed very interested in helping."

Jason fucking bet he did. A first-year could spot the zeroes before the decimal point on this case. "I don't need any extra help. I know this isn't going as fast as you want, but it's only been a few weeks. Remember how we talked about how these things normally take months or even years?" He paused, wondering why he had to keep explaining this concept to a goddamn *legal assistant*. "Is this something that you wanted or that Pete wanted?"

Maggie cleared her throat. "Pete doesn't know."

"Really?"

"Yeah," she said. "I was going to talk to him about it last night but he was down the street at the bar and I ... I just thought it might be good to get someone else, another lawyer, you know, on my case"

Oh. So that was it. He was being lumped together with the alcoholic, uncaring husband. Never pick up the phone in the bar again. Strike that, he thought as he put his throbbing head in his hands; never go to a bar again.

At least now he understood what the hell was going on. She had made an emotional decision and it was time to get the emotions flowing back in his favor.

"Maggie," he said, his voice lower and *so full of hurt*, "do you trust me?"

"Oh, yes, of course I do!"

"Do you trust that I'm working as hard as I can on your case, and that I'm going to get you the best result possible?"

"Yes, I do," she said. He caught a bit of sniffling.

"Do you still want me to be lead counsel for you on your case?"

Definite crying now. "Yes."

"Okay," Jason said. "I will reach out to Mr. Weston. Are you sure that you want him on the case?"

"I—I don't know."

"All right," Jason said, making a decision. "How about I tell him that you're willing to let him represent you, but that I'm lead counsel, and then he and I will work out fees?"

Maggie blew her nose loudly. "Whatever you want to do."

The Prick

"How about I offer him that, and see what he says," Jason said soothingly.

"Okay, whatever you want to do," she repeated. As mantras went, it was a good one.

"Let's try that."

"Okay. I'm ... so sorry."

Jason smiled weakly. "It's okay, Maggie, no harm done. Please just don't do anything like this again without talking to me first."

"Oh, no!" Maggie said, sounding horrified at the mere thought of doing the exact thing she had just done. "I wouldn't!"

"All right. I'll call Weston. And I'll let you know as soon as we hear anything from Levitt."

"Okay."

"Talk to you soon."

"Bye, Jas—Mr. Hunter. I'm sorry..."

"No problem, bye."

"Well, that was interesting," he said to himself. He pulled out the drawer where the Advil lived, took four, and washed them down with increasingly cold Krispy Kreme sugar-coffee. He could do with fewer fire drills on mornings like these.

The client element of the problem had been manipulated away. Now, however, he had to deal with Richard L. Weston, and with about a quarter of his brain cells reporting.

He knew who Weston was. He'd seen him at Labor and Employment functions in his defense days when he'd forced himself to go to such things. Easily recognizable due to his large mane of bright blond hair—which was quite obviously artificially maintained—Weston was a cantankerous elder statesman whose great prominence in Atlanta (and, truth be told, national) employment law circles almost justified his notorious ego. While Weston took a few plaintiffs' cases from time to time when it suited him, he'd made his name doing defense work. He'd been associated with some of the biggest cases in the country—fifteen or twenty years ago. More recently, the degree to which Weston's actual accomplishments matched his powerhouse reputation had greatly diminished. Jason hadn't seen his name associated with any big *actual current* cases in at least ten years. Nevertheless, he was on a first-name basis with most of the federal judges in Atlanta, and was frequently quoted opining *about* big cases (being handled by other lawyers), and thus remained a big, big name.

All of this partly explained why Weston felt entitled to email a nothing like Jason and tell him that he was now lead counsel on Jason's case.

Jason picked up the phone.

"Weston, Branson and Alps," a receptionist answered, cheerfully. "How may I direct your call?"

"Richard Weston, please."

"And who may I say is calling?"

"Jason Hunter."

"And what is this regarding?"

Weston trying to steal my biggest case and bankrupt me. "Maggie Moxley."

"Hold, please."

"Mr. Hunter?" a gruff voice said.

"Call me Jason."

"Jason, this is Richard Weston." Weston's growl sounded like an old grizzly bear awakened prematurely.

"Yes, hello, I'm calling, obviously, because I received your email regarding my client."

"Yes."

The Prick

"I spoke with her a few minutes ago. She and I agreed that we would be very happy to have you and your firm join me on the case."

Silence.

"With respect to your email, however, we won't agree that you are lead counsel if you come on."

Silence.

"I will be lead counsel."

Still no response.

"We can of course discuss what to do about the fee agreement," Jason pressed on. "I was thinking that we can put together a pro-rata agreement, whereby the ... uh ... contingency fee is split based on the number of hours that are put into the case. I've worked with—"

"I'll call you back." Weston hung up.

Grinning, Jason took the now-empty Styrofoam cup to the coffeepot in the corner of his windowless office and poured himself a full refill, black. Returning to his desk, he opened the second email that had piqued his interest, subject line "Jessica Rossi." It was from Ned Burroughs.

> Mr. Hunter,
>
> We are in receipt of your demand letter with respect to Ms. Rossi. Please advise whether your client would be amenable to early confidential mediation.
>
> It should go without saying, but our offer to mediate will be immediately withdrawn if you or your client issue any public statement whatsoever regarding the dispute.
>
> Ned Burroughs

The fluttering in Jason's stomach was positive this time, although as far as his stomach was concerned, any further activity was unwelcome. Jason called his favorite client.

The Prick

"Well if it isn't my attorney," Jessica Rossi answered, overtly flirtatious.

"Yep," Jason said. "Just got an email from Levitt's in-house counsel, Ned Burroughs. Wants to know if we want to mediate."

"That was fast."

"I'm guessing I don't need to explain what mediation is."

"No," she laughed, "you don't. So they want to settle quickly and quietly?"

"Looks that way. They threatened to call it off if we make any public statement."

"Guess you made an impression with that *Daily Record* article."

"Looks that way," Jason said. "My bet is they don't want to be on the cover again soon as defendants."

"Definitely not. I knew I picked the right attorney. So when is it?"

"I'll push for a date in the next month or so. Maybe we can get you paid by summer."

"Get *us* paid," she corrected.

The favorite-client competition was proving to be a runaway. "That's the idea. I'll let you know when we get a date locked down."

"Sounds good," Jessica said. "And then we'll have to celebrate."

Careful. "Deal. If we settle, dinner is on me."

"I'll buy the drinks," she said. "Talk to you soon."

As soon as he pushed the "End" button, the phone started ringing again. It was Maggie Moxley.

"Hi, Ja—Mr. Hunter."

"Jason's fine."

"What?"

"Never mind. What can I do for you?"

"Mr. Weston just called me."

The Prick

Son of a bitch! Jason's nails dug into the edge of his desk. "What did he say?"

"He asked me if I wanted you to lead ... lead my case."

"Be the lead attorney?"

"Uh-huh." The woman was actually crying again. Maybe she never stopped crying.

"And what did you say?"

"I told him yes. That you were the top attorney on the case."

Good girl. "All right, Maggie, thank you. Did he say anything else?"

"No, he got mad and hung up."

"A little gruff, isn't he?"

She sniffled. "Yes."

Well, it's your goddamned fault he's involved at all, he very much wanted to tell her. But, crazily, her knee-jerk emotional reaction of getting Weston in the game might actually work to their benefit if Weston accepted a secondary role. His name would give the case instant credibility and might shake up even Rebecca Trent.

"There's nothing for you to worry about," he assured her. "I'll deal with Weston and we'll move forward."

"Okay, thank you. I'm sorry..."

"Not a problem. Talk to you soon."

Jason clicked listlessly through espn.com. Weston called back just a few minutes later.

"Hello, Richard."

"Send me the proposed agreement and let's meet for lunch tomorrow."

"Ah ... okay."

"Goodbye," Weston spat out.

Jason hung up the phone, went into his bathroom, and threw up.

The Prick

Chapter 25

Thursday, April 25th
Crowne Plaza
New Orleans

It was the pain, the frankly unbelievable pain inside of his skull, that he noticed first. Facedown in a suit and tie, he was still wearing his shoes; that much was evident without active investigation. Smell of vomit was unmistakable and close by. There was something in his pockets. He felt with his hands. Hard circles. Somebody had put hard circles in his pockets. "What the fuck," Robert said into the pillow.

"What?" somebody said.

That was a person. Definitively a person. From what he could tell, the person was to his left. The pillow sandwiched his face; his eyes saw only white and he immediately closed them. The pain in his head counseled against moving the head one millimeter. That some individual seemed to be in the same bed as him, however, needed addressing. Carefully, he identified his left hand and brought it slowly up to the left side of his pillow. The hand brushed his hair, and he was thankful for the sensation because it confirmed that the movement had occurred. He took that hand, flattened it on the side of the pillow, and slowly pushed down, compressing it and freeing his left eye. Slowly, he opened the eye. There was a woman there. She was a few feet away from him and she was looking at him.

The Prick

"Are you okay?"

"Yes," his mouth said. "Where do you keep the pills?"

"The pills?" she asked, obstinately, like she didn't know exactly what he was talking about. He became angry with her.

"The pills. The pain pills."

"This is your hotel room."

She had him. There was no way to directly refute that at present.

"Why are we here? Why are you here?"

She snorted. "You serious?"

He one-eye blinked at her.

"You paid me to come back with you, you prick. You said you had a suite." She looked around. "This ain't no suite."

"I paid you?'

"Well, not yet. But you will," she said. "Bet yo' ass you will."

"For sex?" he asked, knowing the answer.

"You tried to fuck me with your suit on. You said it was your lucky suit."

Come to think of it, his dick was out of his pants. He could feel it through the zipper and against the sheets. This struck him as hysterically funny and he laughed into the pillow.

"What the fuck?" the prostitute said.

"It's not my suit. It's another man's suit."

"Huh. Get that shit dry cleaned before you give it back to him," the prostitute recommended. "You puked on your shoulder, after we stopped trying to do it."

He looked at his shoulder but didn't see anything. She could be lying.

"The other shoulder," Prostitute said. "You puked over the bed ... after you couldn't get it up." Prostitute laughed after she said that. It was a grating, horrible, chain-smoking laugh.

"Get out."

"Not until you pay me, muthafucka. You said you had money in the safe. Tell me the combination and I'll get it and go."

"How much?"

"Fi—six hundred."

She was trying to take advantage of him. She wasn't even good at it. "Five hundred," he said. "Not a penny more."

"Fine, limp dick, just pay me."

He reached again for his pockets, trying to feel out cash without moving his head. Had to get Prostitute out of the room. There was nothing paper in his pockets, just the circles.

"You don't have any cash. Open the safe." She was demanding things of him. Demanding the safe. It was becoming clear that this situation needed to be resolved before happiness could be had. His brain was being squeezed by a metal hand. In one slow movement, he rolled over. It probably took him a full five seconds—like, five one-one thousand, two one-thousand seconds—to roll over.

"Ughhhh."

"What did you drink last night?

He ignored her. The mystery of the circles was the item on his agenda. There were so many of them in his pockets. He reached in and clasped one of them with a slightly shaking right hand. He brought it up to his eye. It was a casino chip—from Harrah's. It was black. Five hundred dollars, it said.

"Hmm," he said. Prostitute was staring at him.

"Take this and get out," he said, tossing the chip in her lap. "Get the fuck out right now or I'm calling the police."

"The cops? For what?"

The Prick

"You drugged me."

"Muthafucka, I didn't drug no one."

"How's your reputation in town? Pretty credible?"

"Muthafucka."

"You have one minute," he advised her, looking around the room for the phone. There was one right next to him, on his side of the bed. He would concede, yes, it had some puke on it.

"I can't take this shit to the casino," she protested.

"Why?"

"They kicked us out, remember? You kept yelling 'I'm a phoenix, I'm a phoenix.' They called security."

"I was yelling that I was a phoenix?"

"Yes, goddammit. I can't go back there today."

He pulled another chip out of his pocket. It, too, was black. He tossed it to her. "For your trouble," he said. "Now get the fuck out."

She cursed at him and kept cursing at him, but she collected her stuff and he could tell she was happy. Once the horror had closed the door behind herself, he took all the chips out of his pockets and put them on the bed next to him. They made a pile. He found others in his suit jacket pockets and, upon further investigation, there was a $1,000 chip in his shirt pocket.

"Spoils of war," he said.

There was another phone over by the TV, but he wasn't up for it. He picked up the one by the bed and tried to wipe the vomit on the pillowcase. Some of the puke had hardened. It was on Robert Spelkin III's suit, too. Prostitute hadn't been lying about that. There was some phrase for that—"Honesty among whores"? That wasn't right. Regardless, she hadn't been lying about how he puked on the suit.

He dialed zero.

The Prick

"Front desk, how may I help you?"

"Room service."

"I'll transfer you."

It rang again and another hotel person answered.

"Room service."

"Yes. I'll have toast, four scrambled eggs, bacon, coffee, Bloody Marys, and extra-strength Excedrin."

"Excedrin?"

"Yes, a bottle."

"Uh, we don't have that, sir."

"Go pick it up. There's a CVS down the street."

"Uh ..."

"I'll give you a five hundred dollar tip. This is an emergency."

"Yes, sir, what else?"

"Do you have any of the hurricanes they have on Bourbon Street?"

"Yes, we have our own recipe. The bar isn't open yet, though, so—"

"Open it and bring up a batch of them. There's five hundred in it for you and your friends."

"Yes, sir."

"Do it quickly."

Robert looked around the room. The curtains covering the two windows were mercifully closed. There was a TV on a dresser and not much else. He might have to bring in some artwork. Spruce it up.

He looked down and saw that his dick was still out.

"I'll put that away before room service gets here," he said.

The Prick

Chapter 26

Thursday, April 25th
Midtown Atlanta

Weston walked with a cane after the surgery. His right leg was stiff, and it dragged. He dragged it with him now through the gray lot to his car, which he parked in a special reserved space instead of a handicapped spot. Decades ago, he had run marathons. Trained for them while acting as lead counsel on some of the largest and most important cases in the country. Cases that had shaped the landscape of the industry. Cases that people were still talking about, even now, when he qualified for handicapped parking.

He pulled his old silver Lexus out onto Peachtree without doing much due diligence regarding oncoming traffic and incited a few angry honks. The honks made him smile some, even though his knee hurt like hell.

He made a quick right into Ansley Park, not taking his foot off the accelerator for the turn. He cut through to Piedmont and made a sharp left into the Oak Club, where he luncheoned multiple times a week. They had invited him to join in the '80s. The vote on his membership had been unanimous. People understood that it was a big deal. And the people who didn't, well, there wasn't much to say about those people.

He wondered if Jason Hunter knew it was a big deal. He wondered if Jason Hunter knew what a privilege it was to be

The Prick

asked to go to lunch at the Oak Club. With Richard Weston, no less. That was the word for it, privilege. Not so long ago, in certain circles, it would have been the hottest ticket in town.

Probably not. The arrogant little upstart probably didn't even know that the Oak Club wasn't currently accepting new members. He probably thought it was just a regular club.

"Ha!" Weston said out loud.

The gall, the sheer gall of it, telling Richard Weston that he wasn't going to be lead counsel. Unimaginable during his prime. Of course, in his prime he didn't contact attorneys out of the blue, attempting to hijack their cases. They had come to him, in supplication, asking for his help. That wasn't the point, though, he thought as he swung the Lexus into the club's inauspicious entryway. The point was, didn't this punk know what a *privilege* it would be just to be associated with him?

Getting out of the car was as unpleasant as always. While the valet patiently held open the door and stared blankly into the middle distance, Weston had to gather himself and jerk his weight sideways to generate enough momentum to haul his right leg out the door.

"Goddammit." He snatched the ticket out of the valet's hand and barked, "I'll be out in an hour."

"Yes, sir."

Weston hobbled the familiar track into the restaurant. If it'd been dinner he would have brought a bottle of wine. Then again, he wouldn't waste a bottle on an insignificant speck like Hunter. Unless Hunter actually appreciated good wine. Weston snorted. Probably not. Hunter probably didn't have enough money in his little firm to front the corkage fees here, which were reasonable.

"Hello, Mr. Weston," the host said. "Good to see you again."

The Prick

"Hello. I have a reservation for two."

"Yes, sir. Mr. Hunter is already seated. Allow me to take you to your table."

Weston scanned the dining room. A teenager in a suit was waving at him. "Fine," he said. He'd been hoping to get to the table first so Hunter wouldn't see him limping. That's why he'd gotten there early, for fuck's sake.

Hunter at least rose to greet him. Weston shook the offered hand and sat. "Two bowls of the she-crab soup," Weston said to the host.

"Thanks," Hunter said, raising his eyebrows. "That a specialty here?"

Weston grunted in assent. "You'll like it."

Hunter nodded agreeably. "All right."

"Tell me about your practice"

"Well—"

"Hang on," Weston said. "Hello, George!"

George Ellington, passing by the table, was old money and also a member at East Lake. Weston was old money, too, if it mattered. His family could trace its ancestry back to the Mayflower and often did, with or without prompting. But Weston was also new money. While he'd had a large inheritance, he'd made even more money himself, with his own wits, so to speak. This permitted him to maintain a dual citizenship, accepted in the old-money crowd who looked down at the new money crowd, and accepted in the new-money crowd who congratulated themselves on their own successes. He was a self-made man who didn't need to be.

"Hello, Richard," Ellington said. "Been out enjoying this weather?"

"Got out yesterday. Played with Peter Chase."

"How'd you shoot?"

"Not bad for an old man."

The Prick

Ellington's laugh was obviously forced. "Well," he said, glancing a bit uneasily at Hunter, to whom he'd not been introduced, "I won't keep you. I'll line us up at East Lake sometime soon."

"Look forward to it," Weston said. Ellington glided away.

Weston turned back to Hunter. "You were saying?"

Hunter had on a small smile. "I opened doors last year after—"

"Dick!" Weston exclaimed. Dick Butler was Weston's frequent golf companion and had recently retired from a high-profile med mal defense firm in Buckhead. Weston rose from his chair to greet him. As Weston and Dick discussed the latest conditions on the course, the she-crab soup arrived. Weston noticed that Hunter started without him after briefly examining but foregoing the little glass of sherry that accompanied it. Amateur.

Tee time with Dick agreed upon for Saturday, Weston carefully lowered himself back into the chair. He grabbed the sherry and poured it in, lock, stock, and barrel.

"You don't take sherry?" he asked in a tone that suggested that not taking sherry was a grievous character flaw.

"Wasn't sure what it was. Thought maybe they had a lunch special, soup and a shot."

Weston grunted. "It's better with sherry," he said, accusingly.

"I'll know for tomorrow."

Weston eyed him. He couldn't tell. Was he being mocked? He had this look, Hunter. Like something amused him.

"I'm surprised you're interested in this case," Hunter said, breaking the silence. "Seems like small potatoes for you."

The Prick

Hmm. Maybe he did know something. Weston picked up his spoon and attacked the she-crab with vigor. "Read the *Daily Record* article and pulled the Complaint," Weston said, between slurps. "Seems good."

"It is. But don't you normally handle big class actions? Why do you want to come in on this small individual sex harassment case?"

Head bowed over the bowl, Weston raised his eyes. There was the truth and then there was what he was going to tell Hunter.

"We take small cases," Weston said. "As a matter of firm policy, when they're meritorious. Sometimes the single-plaintiff cases can be just as important."

Hunter nodded.

"We have a duty to represent people who have been victimized. And there's a sympathetic plaintiff here." Weston mopped up the bisque remains with bread.

"Got it," Hunter said. "Well, it will be nice to have you on board. Your name on the pleadings might make Rebecca Trent and Levitt take this thing a bit more seriously."

Weston nodded and ripped off another hunk of bread. This kid didn't entirely have his head up his ass.

The waiter took their orders, and Hunter said, "I imagine companies shake in their boots and ask who to make the check out to when they see that you've joined."

Weston laughed appreciatively. He was starting to like this Hunter. Of course Hunter didn't want to just hand over his best case. He was smart and aggressive. In fact, he reminded Weston of himself as a young man. Good looking, respectful, knew a good case when he saw it. "It makes them uncomfortable, to be sure."

"And the judges know," Hunter continued, "that if you lend your name to a case, it's got merit."

Weston smiled. "You play golf?"

The Prick

They agreed on Hunter's original pro-rata fee agreement, which Weston had to admit was fair. He didn't push any harder on the lead counsel angle, for now, so Hunter could maintain his young ego. If he absolutely insisted on being lead counsel at some point, Hunter would probably acquiesce. The kid had a head on his shoulders. They discussed (and Hunter even brought up) Weston's many successful campaigns in the '80s and '90s and the precedent he had helped create. It was clear that Hunter really knew his stuff, and he listened attentively to Weston as he lectured about it all. Smart to do that, to get the law straight from the warhorse's mouth. Weston even made suggestions about starting and maintaining a profitable law firm.

They talked about the case too—Weston's suggestions for it, and Rebecca Trent's defamation threat, which Weston assured Hunter was bogus. If the kid had been at all nervous about it, he wouldn't be now. It was just like Trent to try to intimidate a young attorney with something like that.

"She's a pill," Weston said. "And not very attractive."

The lunch was going so well that Weston suggested that they have an after-lunch drink. Hunter, who was proving to be quite agreeable, agreed. Weston ordered scotch and Hunter followed suit.

"You ever litigate against Spelkin?" Hunter asked.

Weston said that he had. But he didn't elaborate. Didn't tell the promising young man why it was Spelkin's status as a defendant that made him want the case so bad, why Weston had grinned from ear to ear all day when he'd seen the *Daily Record* story, and why he'd nearly jumped for joy, knee notwithstanding, when the plaintiff had called *him* out of nowhere and invited him to be on the case against Spelkin. Robert Spelkin III, who had humiliated him, exposed him as a legal dinosaur, and gotten him sanctioned.

The Prick

Who had cost him his biggest, most longstanding client, and his good name.

*****

He had been held overnight, but there was really no way to detain him past that. He'd made bail on the gun charge and the assault charge and they hadn't yet pressed charges on the bomb threat charge, although they certainly could.

Don Jeffries, who at this point was completely bald, having shaved his head to get rid of the remaining pockets of long strands, was in his bedroom in the basement of his mother's house in Dunwoody. He had his own shithole apartment in the city, but he stayed in his old room a lot. Especially on the weekends, when the other apartments in his building got loud. And especially when he was going through one of his emotional crises, into which category present circumstances fit unequivocally.

The gun hadn't even been loaded, his mother had first observed, and his attorney later pointed out to the judge.

"It wasn't even loaded," he said. He was sitting on the old musty, white fabric couch, looking at the TV, which was muted and tuned to a random channel. The silent images flashed and changed about once every six seconds at least. It was totally dark except for the flickering blue light. "It wasn't even loaded. It wasn't even loaded."

His mother had cried at the hearing when the prosecutor read the charges. She had tissues to her eyes. She brought tissues with her everywhere. "It wasn't even loaded," he said, remembering.

His lawyer had reiterated that point. "That doesn't preclude an assault claim, Your Honor," the prosecutor said. And he accused Don of waving the gun around at people in the lobby. "That fucker," Don whispered. "Trying to put me in jail."

The Prick

"I'll get him." There had to be some way to get them. There was a way to get all of them. They couldn't treat him like this. They couldn't all treat him like this.

"It's almost over," he said. He wasn't sure what he meant by that but he hoped it was true. Upstairs it was all quiet. His mother had gone to sleep hours ago.

Book Two

The Prick

Chapter 1

Friday, June 7th
Offices of Burner & Bass, LLP
Midtown Atlanta

Jason was very close to broke. There was no money coming in from anywhere. Nothing was happening in the Moxley case aside from what seemed like multiple daily phone calls with both Weston and Moxley. Telephonic hand-holding. The case was stalled and there was nothing he could do to jumpstart it until discovery got fully underway. The addition of Weston had raised a few eyebrows but hadn't generated a higher settlement offer, which Weston stated on numerous occasions that he just flat out could not believe. The man seemed to have a lot of spare time.

Other cases that Jason had hoped would settle had not. It was as if all of the defendants had gotten together and decided concertedly to put up a fight. A couple of new ones that initially looked promising turned to dust as soon as he learned more of the facts via acerbic and condescending correspondence from opposing counsel. The bottom line was that he could make rent on the office and pay utilities and Westlaw for two months with existing funds. He was already dodging calls from unnamed persons who were trying to collect sums owed for Internet advertising. "Dire" would be the right word to describe the situation.

The Prick

The glimmer of hope on the Law Offices of Jason Hunter's balance sheet was Jessica Rossi. Jason had finally managed to schedule the mediation for today, June 7th, working his way through minefields of conflicting dates for Levitt personnel and Rebecca Trent, who seemed to be incredibly busy literally all of the time. He'd pushed and pushed for an early date while trying to maintain the appearance, as best he could, of being very casual about it all. As if he could care less either way—they'd pay him now or when he won at trial in two years. Any hint of desperation and the number would drop precipitously. He had to puff up, like a terrified blowfish.

He had managed to secure Jeff Bass. One of the best employment mediators in the city, Bass was also a plaintiff's attorney. His hourly rate was $600 for mediations, which Jason didn't even want to think about, given that his firm would be on the hook for half of that if the case didn't settle.

Jason had been awake, involuntarily, since 5:15 a.m. He'd practiced his opening speech five or six times the night before and did so again in his boxers, pacing in the kitchen five more times that morning. He made coffee and watched SportsCenter while fidgeting on the couch until 7:15.

He'd been in the Promenade II building, where Bass's law firm and Trent's office were both located, since just before 8:00. Two hours early for a goddamn mediation, he kept saying to himself in self-disgust and pity. He got yet another coffee from the little fake-artisan coffee place in the building and bought some kind of biscuit thing that he had no ability to eat. Coffee in hand and biscuit on the table like a prop, he sat in an square imitation-leather chair in the lobby and read his notes again and again until he couldn't focus on the words anymore. His feet bounced in front of him and he checked multiple times (hopefully surreptitiously) to make sure he'd remembered to put on deodorant.

This went on for an excruciating forty-five minutes or so until Trent herself circled through the revolving doors. He had spotted her firm's brass nameplate on the middle bank of elevators. Very goddamn impressive. Trent proved resistant to his mental exhortations not to notice him looking unsettled and uncomfortable, like an uninvited salesman, in the boxy lobby chair. She waved at him. He gave a thin smile back and got up out of the chair, subtly (he hoped) wiping his right hand on his right leg to temporary de-clammify it. He wasn't altogether successful.

Trent didn't make a face or anything when she shook his hand.

"You're here early," she said, making it sound like a question.

"Heard great things about your building's coffee."

"Hmm. Is your client with you?"

"Not yet."

"You can come up to the office if you want," Trent offered, making him feel even more like a loiterer. Admittedly, the two security guys at the lobby desk had begun to eye him a little bit.

"I'm good," Jason said. "I'm meeting the client here. I'll see you up at Bass's office."

"Okay," she said, and walked off brusquely. Jason settled back down uneasily in the chair and waited, fingers drumming on the armrest.

At 9:35 a.m. Rossi showed up, very much looking the part. It was great to see her come through the sunlit glass like some goddamn watered-down Venus. Jason smiled as the two security guys blatantly checked her out.

She was wearing a tight-fitting long blue skirt and white blouse top thing, managing to look both professional and provocative. The perfect picture of the unwilling recipient of sexual advances in the modern American workplace. A woman who, try as she might, could not conceal her sexuality. He had given her no instruction on what to wear. She had conjured up this portrait all by herself.

"Am I late?" she asked, coming over to him.

"Not at all," Jason said. "We have a half hour until it starts. But we might as well go up."

They took the elevator to the ninth floor. The front façade of Burner & Bass, LLP, was all glass. The receptionist buzzed them in and directed them through a stylish, modern foyer and into a large conference room, offering coffee, tea, water, et cetera.

"Very modern," Rossi said. Jason hoped she wasn't internally comparing this office to his.

"Lot of overhead." Jason closed the door behind them. "You have any last-minute questions for me?"

"No." Rossi smiled. "I've heard all about mediations from David. I don't say anything and the attorneys yell at each other for about an hour until we're broken into separate rooms. Then the mediator carries numbers back and forth between us until everyone gets worn out and settles."

"It's nice having such a well-informed client," Jason said. "I may have to represent only former employees of law firms from here on out."

"That seems to be a big part of your practice already," Rossi said coyly, sipping her water.

Jason grinned. "Levitt is making it easy for me."

There was a knock at the door.

"Yes," Jason said.

In came Jeff Bass. Although he bore a fish's surname, he looked strikingly like a potato. His large oval head was nearly hairless, with white hair not going much farther north than his ears. Frameless glasses accentuated an already soft and harmless manner. The man clearly struggled with his weight and, while over six feet tall, still managed to look pudgy.

"I heard you were here and wanted to come by and say hello," Bass said pleasantly. He perspired pleasantness.

"Nice to see you again, Jeff." Jason extended his hand. "This is my client, Jessica Rossi."

Bass smiled just so affably at them both. "Nice to meet you, Ms. Rossi. I see you've both been offered beverages. This room will be your home for the day. The other side hasn't arrived yet, but, of course, they're in the building."

Bass settled into a chair at the large conference table and they sat down on the other side. "Jason," he said, "I assume you've already fully explained the mediation process to Ms. Rossi?"

"I didn't have to do much explaining. She worked at Levitt under David Nichols for years, so she knows the ins and outs of the process."

Christ, Jason thought, manage enough sexual references there?

Bass looked at him a bit quizzically. "Yes, of course. I have a little speech, but I'll give you the abridged version, Ms. Rossi. I am completely neutral. It may seem throughout the day that I'm arguing for the other side, but I'm not. It's my job to point out the weaknesses in both parties' cases so that both can be as realistic as possible about their chances, which always helps getting the case resolved."

"I understand," Rossi said.

"Great," Bass said, smiling again. He had a seemingly inexhaustible supply of smiles. "I, of course, want the case to settle because that's my job. But I have no monetary interest in that, as I get paid either way. At the end of the day, after both sides have exchanged a series of threats and ultimatums and I've figured out what they're willing to pay, it's going to be your decision, with the apt counsel of your attorney, whether to take whatever amount they put on the table."

"I understand," Rossi said.

"Wonderful," Bass said, pushing his way up out of his chair. He was wearing suspenders, Jason noticed absently, his heart racing. He couldn't remember being this nervous since his first year of practice. If today went south, the Law Offices of Jason Hunter might follow suit.

"I'll leave you to talk," Bass said, pushing through the door. "If you need anything, just let our receptionist know. Bathrooms are down the hall."

"He's nice," Rossi said. Jason looked her over. She didn't seem the slightest bit nervous, or even excited. Why the hell not?

"Yes. He's very good at this."

"You've used him before?"

"A few times, back when I was on the defense," Jason said. "Every one of the cases settled."

"Well, I'm not going cheap."

What the hell did that mean? If they put a good number on the table and she walked, Jason would bodily test the thickness of the glass separating him from open air, gravity, and sweet release. Could she sense the desperation on him? Some animals could smell fear. She gave him a weird look.

"No, of course not."

The two sat in silence for a series of hundreds of heavy seconds. Jason felt each one of them individually.

"We're going to stick it to them, Jessica," he finally said.

She smiled and the awkward silence rushed back in. Or was it just regular silence? Jesus, pull it together. Jason noticed that he was still holding the imitation artisan coffee. He threw it in the trash can in the corner.

The Prick

Thankfully, there was a knock on the door. "Come in," Jason said.

It was the potato. "They're here. Are you ready?"

"Sure, bring them in," Jason said. He noticed, with some satisfaction, that Rossi tensed and sat upright.

In they came. Trent and Nichols he recognized immediately. There was a third man he didn't know.

"Will Simmons," the third man said gruffly, shaking Jason's offered hand. The general counsel. All eyes in the room, however, quickly shifted to the Nichols/Rossi greeting. Nichols smiled at her and reached out his hand. "Hello, Jessica."

Rossi glared back at him icily and refused to shake hands, prompting Nichols to laugh and shake his head. "Alllllllll right," he said. He sat next to Trent with an ironic expression. Trent, per usual, was an emotionless cyborg.

Bass positioned himself at the head of the table and cleared his throat. "Okay, let's begin."

Bass gave his rote speech about the neutrality and confidentiality of the mediation. Rossi was listening politely and attentively. Nichols was looking at Rossi. Trent, typing on her BlackBerry, wasn't even pretending to pay attention. Simmons, who looked like he was in physical pain, nodded at the end of each of Bass's sentences, physical punctuation.

Jason had tuned out Bass's drone. He was cycling through his opening in warp speed, synapses super-powered by adrenaline and caffeine. The rehearsed lines roller-coastered through his head in random order. His hands were wet and he laid them on his knees under the table.

Then the drone stopped and everyone looked at him.

"Thank you, Jeff," Jason said. "And thank you to everyone for being here," he said across the table to all, but mostly Simmons, who was clearly the decision maker. "We are here today to attempt to resolve Jessica Rossi's claims against Levitt. It is our sincere desire that this happen. As everyone here knows, early resolution is far better for both parties than protracted litigation."

He took a deep breath. Now for the bad cop. "That said, if we are unable to resolve this matter today, Ms. Rossi and I are prepared to go all the way to trial." Simmons, gratifyingly, raised his eyebrows at that. Nichols may have rolled his eyes. Jason couldn't tell for sure.

"Ms. Rossi has a very strong case. As everyone in this room knows, she and David Nichols had an ongoing sexual relationship for months." He paused. "They had sex in the Levitt office. They had sex in Nichols's office. They had sex in the conference room." Now the big one. "They had sex while Nichols was on the phone with clients." Simmons was turning red. Nichols was staring at Jason like he was picturing his murder. Trent was periodically writing sparse and orderly notes on a legal pad. Jason wasn't watching Bass, but was sure he was smiling pleasantly.

"This all went on during and after regular business hours. When other employees were literally in the next room." Now for the part he wasn't sure was true, the part that had surfaced in his subsequent talks with Rossi, in which she seemed to increasingly understand that it was not beneficial for the sex to be entirely consensual. The narrative had shifted the more they'd discussed the case. The more Jason talked to her, the more she recalled that Nichols had taken advantage of the power dynamics in the work relationship and she began to remember that she had perhaps not been as consistently willing as she had initially indicated. Jason couldn't tell for sure if things were changing because Rossi was finally coming to terms with an abusive relationship and having related revelations, or whether her recollection was conveniently morphing to benefit her claims.

177

The Prick

"Ms. Rossi didn't feel right about this. It made her very uncomfortable. She asked Mr. Nichols if they could at least stop having sex in the office." Jason watched him. Fuck. Jason saw in Nichols the wide eyes of shock, and then the furious narrowing with comprehension of what was happening. It wasn't true.

"Truth is," Jason continued, "she wanted to stop altogether, for months. But she was worried about what would happen to her career if she broke it off. But she at least wanted not to risk having sex in the office."

"But Mr. Nichols insisted. Mr. Nichols insisted"—pause with partially feigned embarrassment followed by gritted teeth—"that she perform oral sex on him whenever certain clients called." Nichols's hands were balled fists on the table. "He made it part of her job. In fact, when he asked her to schedule calls with certain clients, she knew that she would be expected to perform oral sex that day. On her knees under his desk, his penis in her mouth, while he gave advice"

He let that hang in the air. Nichols's fists were still balled on the table and he was breathing heavily. Everyone else seemed to be holding their breath. There were no movements, no fidgets, everyone was stock still. Even Trent was temporarily frozen and staring at him.

"About a month or so before she was terminated, Ms. Rossi was told that she would no longer be assisting Mr. Nichols. At the time, nobody told her why. But the sexual demands didn't stop. If anything, they increased. Just a few weeks before she was fired, Nichols demanded that she meet him at the Ritz Hotel in the Levitt building during the middle of the day, as he had done numerous times before. She told him that she could not continue to have sex with him, that it wasn't right. He would not take no for an answer. She didn't think she had any choice. She met him in the room and, during the middle of a workday, he had his way with her."

A pause.

"He made her have anal sex for the first time."

Jessica started crying. Right on cue. Bass walked around the table and handed her a box of Kleenex. "It was ... horrible," she said between sobs. "It ... hurt so much ..."

Jason looked at the other side. Simmons was staring at Nichols, who was just shaking his head. He obviously wanted to say something, but he didn't break the unwritten rule of not interrupting the adversary during their opening statement. Trent had resumed typing on her BlackBerry.

"This abuse may have gone on indefinitely," Jason continued, glancing again at Simmons. "We don't know who in the firm knew this was going on. But we will find out in discovery if we file the lawsuit." All of this was mainly for Simmons's benefit. He wanted Simmons to hear what would be in the papers, what he would have to explain to the firm's management, and, maybe, what a jury would someday hear.

"But then Nichols's friend, Robert Spelkin, sexually assaulted another assistant, Margaret Moxley. And Mrs. Moxley filed a Charge of Discrimination with the EEOC, and then a lawsuit. Suddenly the Atlanta office of Levitt was under scrutiny. People were asking questions about sexual relationships in the office. The EEOC was going to investigate."

Jessica was still sniffling but had stopped crying. There were several balled tissues on the table in front of her.

"And somebody got nervous about what would happen if the wrong person found out about Jessica. What would happen if the EEOC investigated and she told them everything? So Levitt decided to get rid of her, and hope that she would just go away quietly."

The Prick

Jessica nodded. She was glaring openly now at Nichols. Jason hoped Simmons noticed it. Made her seem a bit more credible, maybe.

"So they terminated her. And they terminated Mrs. Moxley. And they called the whole thing a layoff."

Jason gathered himself. The hard part was over. "Ms. Rossi has claims for hostile work environment, assault, battery, invasion of privacy, intentional infliction of emotional distress, negligent retention and supervision, and wrongful termination," he said. "Again, it is our hope that we're able to resolve these claims today. But if not, we will file a Charge of Discrimination and a lawsuit immediately, and we will pursue the claims all the way through trial."

After all that, Bass still nodded serenely. "Thank you, Jason," he said. "Rebecca, do you wish to respond?"

Trent put down her BlackBerry. "Yes." She reached down, picked up her briefcase from beside her feet, and laid it flat on the table. From the briefcase, she pulled three manila folders, each about a half inch thick. Moving slowly but deliberately, she placed these on the table in a small stack. The room was quiet.

"I'm not big on these opening statements," Trent said. "I find that they're a waste of time, and normally just a lot of hot air."

Jason, who was experiencing a huge drop in adrenaline following his opening, smiled at Trent's snipe.

Trent turned and looked not at Jason, but at Jessica.

"You have no case," she said flatly. "I don't know what your lawyer here has told you, but consensual sex between two adults does not give rise to a lawsuit, regardless of whether it's at home, in a hotel, or under a desk. I think you know that. You worked at a law firm. As to this new invention that you felt forced to have sex with David, well, that's just a lie."

The Prick

Trent put her hand on top of the three folders and moved them to the center of the table. "I have three folders here. In the first one"—she picked it up—"are emails you sent to David in the last year. They are overtly sexual. You invite him to come over to your house, telling him that you want to perform various sex acts with him." Trent opened the folder. "Taking one at random, let's look at this message, from January 16th of this year.

Sexy, we should go to Miami for the weekend. Stay at the W. Last time, I couldn't walk for days after. Pack up your big cock and let's go.

Jessica, to her credit, merely looked at Trent stonily. Jason had seen that email before, but he wondered what else was in the folder.

"There are a lot of those," Trent said to Bass. "Does that sound like a woman being forced into sex?" She closed the folder and moved it to her right.

Trent turned back to Jessica. "In the second folder," she said, holding it up, "I have printouts of all of your text messages." Jessica maintained her poker face. Jason ground his teeth, waiting for it. "Let's take one at random." Trent opened the folder slowly and lifted out a one-page printout. "From February 23rd of this year, you wrote to David, quote, 'I want your balls in my mouth.'"

He had definitely *not* seen that particular text yet. It wouldn't exactly endear her to the jury. He wondered when Jessica had erased it. He'd had her whole phone imaged and it wasn't on there. Jason looked at Nichols, expecting perhaps a smirk, but Nichols just looked pissed. Trent put the paper back in the folder and closed it. She looked again at Bass. "There are many more," she said. "Does that sound like a woman being forced into sex?" Bass just blinked at her.

Trent turned to Jason. "You've made very serious allegations here today. You should be extremely careful about who you make those allegations to, if you don't have the evidence to back them up. Otherwise, as I'm sure you know, there are sanctions." Jason did not take the bait and stayed quiet. He hoped that his face was obeying his command to stay emotionless.

Trent put the second folder on top of the first. Jason braced for whatever was in the third.

"In the third folder," Trent said, staring at Jessica, "I have all the pictures you sent David." Trent opened it, slowly, tortuously, not breaking eye contact. "Let's take a picture at random." She took a page out. Jason could see through the back that it was a full-page color photo. Trent kept the picture facing her. Both Simmons and Bass were leaning forward in their chairs, heads extended forward, craning for a look.

"You sent this picture to David on March 4th. I'm sure you'll recognize it." She put it facedown on the table. Everyone was leaning in now, except Jessica, who had closed her eyes. Trent flipped the picture. "Look at it."

The picture was bad. Really bad. Jessica was bent over the end of a bed wearing nothing but a red thong, which she was grabbing with her right hand and pulling up about two inches above her ass so that it stretched and covered almost nothing. Her head was turned so that her profile was visible and recognizable. She was smiling seductively. Her right hand held a camera, which was obviously pointed at a mirror. On the bed next to her, standing upright and pointed toward the ceiling, was a red dildo. The whole setup looked like a porn shoot.

The Prick

Jason tore his eyes from the picture and looked at Jessica, who was quite obviously mortified and looking around the room at all the men looking at her in that pose. "Enough," Jason said. He reached out and turned the picture over, keeping his hand on it so that Trent couldn't flip it over again. Jessica looked at him gratefully, tears in her eyes.

"Did that look like a woman being forced into sex?" Trent didn't wait for an answer. "I'll take that." She pried the picture out from under Jason's hand and returned it to her third folder, closed the folder, and put it on top of the stack. She looked at Bass and raised her eyebrows.

Bass cleared this throat. "Okay. Thank you, Rebecca. Let's break into separate rooms." The defense team filed out, Trent leading the way.

"I'll spend some time with them first," Bass told Jason.

*****

As soon as the door closed behind Bass, Jason said, "I'm sorry you had to go through that; it wasn't called for." He wanted to yell at her for not telling him about the picture and not warning him there might be other texts that had been erased from her phone, but now wasn't the time. It was hard to yell at a crying woman who'd just been humiliated.

"Thank you," Jessica said shakily. "I can't believe she just did that. Can you ... can you please show me where the ladies' room is?"

Jason got up and walked her to the restroom. Luckily, the defense team had already been shepherded into another conference room. Jason opened the door for Jessica and stood as a sentry outside. He could hear her sobbing behind the door. Hopefully there was nobody else inside.

"Well, fuck," Jason said quietly. That had been brutal. Trent lived up to her reputation. The text and the picture were bad. They cut into his theme of the case a great deal.

The Prick

But they meant nothing in terms of the skin that Levitt had in the game. Even if Trent had thousands of pictures of Rossi in various voluntary sexual poses and a mountain of solicitous text messages, that didn't change the fact that Nichols told her to blow him while he was giving advice to clients, nor did it change the fact that they fired her to cover it up. He had to stay on theme. They had the emails, the texts, and the pictures. But they were here. They wanted out.

Jessica emerged from the bathroom. She had calmed herself down and reapplied her makeup. Still, she looked like she could fall apart at any moment. To Jason's surprise, she came over and hugged him, wrapping her arms around him and pressing her body against his.

"I'm sorry," she said.

Jason didn't move, not sure what to do. "It's okay," he said, looking around to make sure no bad guys were coming.

"Is the case ruined?" she asked, still holding on. Her breasts were pressed against him, he couldn't help but notice.

"No," Jason assured her. He very much wanted to disengage from her so that nobody caught them like this, but that wasn't really the etiquette with emotional women who might start crying at any point. "It's not over in the slightest. The text and the picture certainly don't help things, but they have problems on their side as well. And I'm pretty sure we've seen the worst of what they've got. Those selections were not at random."

"Okay," Jessica said, finally dropping the embrace. She backed up and looked him in the eye. "How much do you think we'll get?"

*****

"Five thousand dollars," Trent said. "That's our initial offer."

The Prick

Jeff Bass raised his eyebrows. "Is that really how you want to start?"

They were sitting in a conference room in the northwest corner of the office space. It was a nice, open room, with high ceilings and large windows taking up two sides. The High Museum was partially visible to the right, but I-85 dominated the view. Jeff was at the end of the table with his back to the door, and Trent, Nichols, and Simmons were spread out around the table.

"Their number is extremely high," Trent said. "They need to get real. This isn't a six-figure case."

"Are you sure?"

"Yes."

Jeff raised his eyebrows again, but wrote the number down. Time would tell if Levitt really believed that.

*****

"They're saying this isn't a six-figure case."

"Bullshit," Hunter said. Rossi looked concerned.

Jeff smiled. "It may be. Only time will tell. That said, I don't want you to be discouraged by their first number. It's meant to send a message. You started at 850,000, correct?"

"Yes," Hunter said.

"Their first number is 5,000."

"Ask them what time they want their interview with the *Daily Record* to be," Hunter said. "I'll file the Complaint this afternoon." His words had heat coming off them.

"I don't think that threat will be well received," Jeff said. He, like everyone else, had read the *Daily Record* article about Spelkin. A few times, actually. It was a reckless thing to do, but it had also been good to see a plaintiff's attorney take a stand. Too many were cowed.

"Well, tell them to stop wasting my time," Hunter said. "Our time."

The Prick

"The five thousand dollar mark isn't a good start," Jeff conceded. "Obviously. But it's a response to the initial demand, which they believe is way too high."

"It's not," Hunter said. Rossi nodded in agreement.

"Maybe, but at this point they aren't willing to pay it. With the emails, and the texts, and the pictures arguably supporting their position that the relationship was purely voluntary, I can see their point."

"They fired her."

"They say it was a layoff."

"Bullshit," said Rossi. Jeff found it a bit awkward to look at her after seeing her in that—ahem—position.

"The timing certainly doesn't look good for them," Jeff agreed.

"Normally," Hunter said, "I would talk this over with my client first, but I'm sure she'll agree to this. We will move to eight forty-seven, five hundred."

So that's how it was going to be.

*****

Jeff was exhausted. He'd been at it all day and the parties were still $425,000 apart. Rossi had descended, kicking and screaming, to $625,000. Levitt had clawed its way to $200,000 and was hanging onto the number with a death grip. Levitt had broken through the six-figure ceiling, with a great deal of cajoling from Jeff and several calls to Washington, around 2:30 p.m. Both sides were becoming irritable in the extreme.

Jeff sat at his desk and tapped his fingers together pensively. Levitt had just moved to the current number from $190,000, saying all the typical, tired things like "this is it" and "not a penny more." He didn't buy it. The members of the Levitt team were all still sitting in the room; nothing had been packed. Jeff had discussed with them ad nauseum the potential damage that Rossi's accusations could do to the firm. He wasn't telling them anything they didn't already know, but it sometimes helped the process to confirm the party's fears. Let this thing hit the press and it might be curtains for Nichols. And the Levitt firm couldn't afford another scandal. This thing would be on CNN. It was that salacious.

That said, Hunter and Rossi were being wildly unreasonable. Jeff didn't buy the whole involuntary sex thing one bit and neither would a jury. Not with that documentation. The pictures, good lord. Trent had showed him a few more in caucus, and while they weren't as scandalous as the first, they made an impression. Jeff wanted to get a good look at the whole file in private. He smiled, but briefly. He had a headache.

So what had happened to Rossi, really? Levitt wasn't even claiming anything was wrong with her performance. They kept pitching the line that she'd merely been caught up in a layoff. Jeff didn't believe a word of it. And, again, neither would a jury. Levitt just so happened to shed both Moxley and Rossi in the same layoff that only wiped out a tenth of the support staff in one office? No, there was something there. But people got fired unfairly every day. Most of them got nothing, let alone hundreds of thousands of dollars. Rossi had only been making just north of $50,000 a year, with overtime. So the real question was, how much would Levitt pay Rossi not to pull the trigger of the gun she had pressed against its big, corporate head?

It had to be more than $200,000. Maybe a lot more. But there was no telling how much. Trent, who Jeff secretly could not stand, had been deliberately feeding him false signals all day, hoping that he would pass them along to the other side, starting with the opening salvo that this wasn't a six-figure case. But it was 6:45 p.m. Jeff was halfway through the third season of *Breaking Bad*. He wanted very much to go home and continue it. He'd reached the point, as sometimes occurred in his mediations, when he was so sick of both sides that he no longer cared how much they were paying him. He was going to force the issue.

Jeff went back into the defense room. Trent looked up in surprise. "Let me guess," she said, "they moved another ten thousand."

"No. Before I go to them with your most recent move, I want to suggest something."

"Okay," Trent said, obviously annoyed at the deviation in play.

"We are now $425,000 apart," Jeff said. "That's a gigantic gulf. The mediator's handbook—to the extent you put stock in such things—says the parties won't settle today if they're apart by this magnitude."

Simmons and Nichols, who were both slumped in their chairs, sat up. Jeff kept himself from smiling.

"If we don't settle, then we don't settle," Trent said in her best steely tough-guy voice.

"Naturally," Jeff agreed. "Although since it's my job to try to resolve the case, and since we've all been trying to settle it for almost nine hours now, we might try something to break what's increasingly looking like a stalemate."

"What do you suggest?" asked Simmons.

Good. The decision maker was asking the right question.

"A mediator's number. I'll throw out a midpoint figure that I think the case can—not should—settle for. I'll present the number independently to both parties. If both say yes, then the case settles. If one or both parties say no, then neither party knows how the other responded. And we're in the same position we're in now."

"That sounds like a good idea," said Simmons. Nichols was nodding.

"Give us a minute," said Trent.

The Prick

Jeff lowered his head obsequiously and went to go pitch the idea to Jason and Jessica.

*****

"It's risky," Trent said once the door closed firmly behind Bass. "If they accept it and we reject it, it could blow up the whole mediation."

"Rebecca," Will said wearily—after hours of maneuvering, he was feeling his age—"chances are we're going to say yes to whatever number he chooses."

"Not necessarily."

This was Trent's downside. She became personally invested in every case and was obstinate as shit. Getting her to offer money was like trying to pry food out of her children's mouths. It was gratifying, at the beginning of the day, to see her fighting for every inch, but now it was just tiresome. The truth was that the actual value of settling far exceeded Hunter's current stratospheric offer of $625,000. If the case wound up in the *Daily Record* like the Spelkin disaster, the damage would be to Levitt, not to Trent.

Trent was probably worried about maintaining her reputation as a tough negotiator, Will mused. Sooner or later he was going to have to remind her who was really calling the shots here. He wasn't looking forward to that moment at all.

"Hunter is worse than my ex-wife," Nichols joked, perhaps trying to ease the tension. Trent glared at him.

They sat in silence.

"You know, she really doesn't have anything resembling a sexual harassment claim," Nichols said. Nobody responded. Everybody knew that. And everybody knew that wasn't the point.

There was a knock on the door. Bass had returned.

"They're interested in pursuing the mediator's number," he informed them. "Are you interested?"

The Prick

"Do you already have a number in mind?" Trent asked.

"Yes."

"We'll do it," interjected Will. "Anything that will get me back to my hotel room." He ignored the look from Trent.

Bass smiled and settled into a chair at the end of the table. He always smiled with his lips. Perhaps he thought showing teeth was too aggressive. He'd shed his jacket hours earlier and was sporting suspenders. Despite his girth, his pants were obviously too big for him. He looked like he was wearing one of those old wooden buckets.

"What I suggest is $325,000."

Trent threw her pen. It clanged off the huge window, shooting left in Nichols's direction. "Jesus Christ, Jeff. Why don't you just give the whole firm away? That's a hundred and twenty-five over our last number!"

Bass ignored her childish outburst and spoke directly to Will. "You all need this to go away quietly. There may not be much in the way of a substantive claim here, but Hunter is holding the doomsday device on David's career. I'm not sure he knows exactly what he has his hands on. If he did, he may not have come down to six twenty-five. Heck, he may have even started in the seven figures."

Will grimaced and nodded.

"I think," Bass continued, "that you all should give settlement your best shot today. If you don't, with all of the publicity this is going to get, $325,000 may seem like a real bargain in a couple years."

Trent slapped her hand on the table. "It is your job to make that child in the other room realize that he doesn't have any substantive claim. And to tell him that if he doesn't take the *extremely generous* 200,000, which is our *last offer*, he'll be in hard-fought litigation for years and wind up with nothing."

"Well—"

190

The Prick

"And that if he keeps pursuing this litigation," Trent said, "we'll seek attorneys' fees."

Bass cleared his throat and smiled weakly. "I don't think —"

She slapped the table again. "Or maybe we should call it off for the day and hire a decent mediator."

"That's your prerogative," Bass said icily. "I've spent my entire day on this, using tactics that I've found effective over a twenty-five-year career."

"Jeff," Will interjected. "Please give us a minute."

Bass nodded. "I'll go check with the other room."

*****

"Our answer is no," Jason said. Rossi, to his left, was nodding.

"Pardon me?" Bass said. "No?"

"No."

"You're serious?"

"Yes."

Bass exhaled loudly, his frustration wearing through. "What are you thinking?" he asked wearily.

"About what?" Rossi said.

"You have almost nothing resembling a case. You have consensual sex between two unmarried adults and a termination as part of a larger layoff."

"It was retaliation!" Rossi said.

Bass waved that aside with his hand. "There's no evidence of that besides timing, which is going to look very weak to a jury. In particular after they read all of those emails and texts, and see all those pictures."

Rossi looked down at the table.

"And that's in two years, assuming that you even make it to a jury. Trent is a pit bull. She's going to try to get the case dismissed at every available opportunity and, believe me, discovery's going to be hell."

191

The Prick

Jason nodded. "Our answer is still no."

"Then what's your plan? They threatened to walk out at 200,000. I have no idea whether they're going to accept the 325,000. Are you really going to litigate this case?" Bass scrunched his face up as if the mere thought made him physically ill.

"It's late." Jason smiled. "Our final number is $450,000. They can buy peace with that today. They don't and we walk."

Bass shook his head and wrote the number on his pad. "I hope you know what you're doing."

As soon as Bass exited the room, Jason let the veneer of confidence slip. "Jesus," he told Jessica, "this is incredibly risky."

Jessica frowned. She was getting testy. It had been a Herculean feat getting her down to $625,000 in eight hours. Moving her to $450,000 in one move wasn't without consequence. She was mad at him.

"We're giving away too much," she said. "We've got them by the balls. They'll pay whatever we want."

Seriously? How could she possibly say that?

"We have to be extremely careful not to blow this thing up," he said. "$200,000 is a hell of a lot of money that they already have on the table."

"Hmm," she said, and looked at her watch.

"And 325,000 now, if they'll do it, is a hell of a lot better than the risk of nothing two years from now." Jason tried not to sound like he was pleading. "And you don't have to go through discovery and have your deposition taken."

"I can handle it," she told him. "I'm going to go to the ladies room."

She walked out without another word and left him sitting there.

The Prick

"Goddammit," he said. Hundreds of thousands of dollars for what amounted to (pretty hot) consensual sex. And she was turning her nose up at it. He felt nauseous. They were going to walk. His firm was going to fold.

*****

Jeff stood outside the door to the conference room that held the Levitt trio. He took a deep breath and steeled himself for Trent's histrionics. In his hand was the notepad that had Rossi's "final number." He would be shocked if (a) Levitt took it, or (b) it really was final.

He wasn't paid enough for this. Why didn't he just retire?

He pushed in the door and found Simmons and Nichols, both looking at their iPhones.

"Rebecca in the restroom?"

Simmons cleared his throat. Jeff thought he caught a hint of a smile across the table from Nichols.

"Rebecca, um," Simmons said, "will not be with us for the rest of the mediation."

Jeff raised his eyebrows.

"She, ah, became rather irate when I decided—we decided—to accept your mediator's number." Simmons sighed. "She went back to her office."

Jeff suppressed a smile.

"So, against my better judgment, and over the ... strong objection of the firm's outside counsel, Levitt will accept 325,000." He leaned back in his chair, eyes half closed. "I imagine we have a deal?"

Jeff frowned and took a deep breath. "No," he said. "We don't."

"You're kidding," Nichols shouted. "What the hell are they thinking in there?"

"They're thinking they have a gun to our head," Simmons said, spitting the words out. Any pretense at a unified front had apparently left with Trent. "I may soon invite them to pull the trigger and let everyone face the consequences of their actions."

"I think you're right," Jeff said. "They're betting that you'll blink first. If this doesn't settle today, Hunter assures me the lawsuit will be filed tomorrow. And I'm sure the *Daily Record* coverage won't be far behind."

"Did they just reject your number outright, or did they send a counter?" Nichols asked.

Jeff nodded. "Their number, which they say is their final walk-away number, is 450,000."

Simmons shook his head. "Jesus Christ."

"That *is* down from $625,000 in one move," Jeff said. "It's progress."

Simmons nodded. "Please tell them we'll move to 275,000, and that's our final offer. If they won't take it, we'll walk, and won't talk settlement again after today."

Jeff's head was pounding. He was going to have to get some food soon or he would kill everyone in the office. "Why don't you at least offer them the 325,000 you were already willing to pay?"

"They blew their chance at that," Simmons said. "And I bet you a hundred they'll take the 275,000."

Nichols exhaled loudly. Jeff looked at his watch. It was 7:30. He would be equally happy if Rossi took the $275,000 or got up and stormed out. He stood to go deliver the message.

Just ten minutes later, Jeff burst back into the defense room, breathing heavily. "They're leaving," he reported. "They're walking to the elevators now."

Nichols sprung out of his chair. "Will, stop this." Simmons looked shocked. His mouth had literally dropped.

"Stop them," Nichols said to Jeff.

The Prick

"Are you willing to pay the 450,000?" Jeff said. "There's no reason to if not."

"I will pay the 325,000," Simmons said quietly.

"They've already rejected that," Nichols shouted. "You cannot let this happen! This will be the end of my career!"

"Will they take 350,000?" Simmons asked.

"I don't think so," Jeff said, still trying to catch his breath. He needed to get back to the gym. Finally make some appointments with that personal trainer who kept emailing him. "Hunter keeps saying $450,000 is their final number." There was the unmistakable sound of an elevator ding out in the hall. "And it sounds like he means it."

"Can we offer them the 350,000?" Simmons said.

"This is not a game!" Nichols yelled. He rushed around the table and pushed by Jeff through the door, roughly elbowing him to the side. He nearly sprinted down the hall and yanked open the door separating the hall from the elevator bank. "Stop!" Jeff heard Nichols order in the direction of the elevator bank.

Simmons shook his head and looked out the window.

Nichols stormed back into the room. "In or out?" he asked Jeff, who was still in the door frame. Jeff stepped into the room. Nichols slammed the door behind him.

"I've had it!" he shouted at Simmons. "Stop fucking around! I'll cover the extra hundred thousand, which, by the way, I will make back in a goddamn month. Stop toying with my life over this piddly little bullshit." He turned to Jeff. "450,000 is a deal. Go sit their asses back down in the goddamn conference room and put together an enforceable agreement. Jesus Christ."

"David ..." Simmons said.

"No! This is over." Nichols turned to Jeff. "Go get them."

*****

The Prick

Jason was still in a state of shock. It was 9:15 p.m. and the agreement was in front of him. Levitt agreed to pay a total of $450,000 to Rossi, 35 percent of which would go directly to his firm. The Law Offices of Jason Hunter had just made $157,500 in one day. This was where the one-person law firm paid off. By Jason's rough calculations $157,500 divided by 1 equaled $157,500. He had less than twenty hours in the case. That was just under $8,000 an hour. Not a bad rate if you could get it.

In the ninety minutes or so between the time that a disheveled and enraged-looking David Nichols had ordered him and his client to stop dead in their tracks as the elevator doors parted before them—an image that would surely be burned in his head as long as he walked the earth—and the time that the potato had dropped off the draft agreement, Rossi had said "I told you so" four separate times, in different variations.

As he powered through paragraph twelve of sixteen, she did it again. "I told you they would take whatever our last number was." She wasn't even reading her copy, he noted. She was checking her makeup in a pocket mirror rather than acting like someone who'd just received almost $300,000 for doing nothing. Well, not *nothing*.

As elated as he was, Jason was getting a little sick of that routine. "The gamble certainly paid off," he said. "It's going to be painful for Levitt to cut these checks."

She snorted. She had been snorting at things all day. If she weren't so hot, it would be a very unattractive trait. "They won't even notice it's gone. We should have held out for more."

Jason felt his blood rise at that. She was accusing him of not having the fortitude to take the big risk. Hadn't he been walking toward the elevator with her? He wondered if she sensed how desperate he was for the money.

The Prick

"I think we pushed them as far as they would go," he said. But he wasn't sure. The mad version of David Nichols that had pulled them back from the brink had been a man who looked like he'd pay quite a bit to keep them off that elevator.

"David would have gotten me more," she said.

Jason felt the sting acutely and immediately. He looked up from paragraph fifteen. She was still looking into the mirror, seemingly unaware of her shot's impact.

"Jessica," he said, "this is an incredibly good deal. I personally cannot believe they've offered to pay this much. That said, it's your decision whether to accept the terms of the agreement. You haven't signed anything yet. You can walk whenever you want."

"No, I'll sign it." She pursed her lips and ran a finger across both eyebrows, smoothing them down. "We agreed to the amount already."

She put the mirror down and plunged her hand down the front of her dress on the right, fixing her bra. She looked at him and he wrenched his gaze up to meet hers, feeling very much caught in a laid trap. She gave a half smile.

"But David would have gotten me more."

*****

Nichols drove north on Piedmont with the top down. Traffic wasn't bad, but nearly everyone on the road was taking Friday night seriously. A good deal of thumping bass and unnecessary swerving. He stopped at the light at the intersection of Cheshire Bridge, contemplating whether or not to blow off steam at a strip club. His phone rang and the caller's name came up on his dashboard. He hit the answer button.

"Are you serious?"

Jessica Rossi's throaty laugh answered him loudly over his car speakers. "What are you doing?"

The Prick

"Driving home," he said. "Trying to figure out how to get your knife out of my back, or maybe your cock out of my ass."

The laugh again. "You have plans the rest of the night?

The light turned green and Nichols hit the gas. "Shouldn't you be out celebrating with your infant attorney?"

"I was going to take him out and blow him if he got me over a half million, but he came up a little short."

Nichols laughed. "I would have gotten you more."

"That's what I told him."

"The last thing he wanted to hear, I'm sure. Seriously, Jess, why the hell are you calling me? You've already got my money, taken your shot at my career. What else do you want?"

"To fuck."

Nichols hit the brakes to avoid plowing into a Cadillac. "What?"

"You heard me."

"You must be kidding. After what happened today?"

"Especially after today. It was a dick move of you to use those pictures, but ... it made me real hot, all those guys looking at me."

"I had to use them, the position you put me in. You accused me of forcing you to have anal for the first time. So I ask again: are you fucking serious?"

"Uh-huh," she said. "Are you going home? I want you to fuck me on your balcony, like we used to ... so everyone can see."

"And wind up with another lawsuit tomorrow."

"Please," she said. "That's over. I'll sign a full release authorizing you to do what you want to me."

The Prick

He smiled as he pulled up to his building. "I'll get started on the paperwork," he said. "You get over here. And bring a video camera. You're going to say you want it on tape."

"My phone can record videos. Or did you forget?"

Fuck. Should have used the videos.

"You know where to find me."

"I do," she said. "You're hard to miss."

The Prick

Chapter 2

Saturday, June 8th
Park Tavern, Piedmont Park
Midtown Atlanta

It was a beautiful day in Piedmont Park. There wasn't a trace of a cloud in the sky, which was such a resplendent blue that it looked artificial. The scene looked like a goddamn postcard. People riding bikes, lying on blankets, kicking balls, walking dogs, flinging Frisbees, and even leading kites on strings, all frolicked on the expansive grass. They could be actors, hired by the park for a portrait. Georges Seuratian.

Jason watched the frolickers from a table in the shade at Park Tavern, a good microbrewery wedged at the corner of Tenth and Monroe overlooking the park's east end. He was suffering from a massive adrenaline hangover. The elation of the Rossi win and the salvation of his firm had started wearing off, and the comedown was steep. He had a pint in hand, which, against all instincts, he was only nursing. He had company.

Richard Weston specifically, who had suggested the meeting, and who was seated to his right. Weston was outfitted in old wrinkled khakis and a light blue polo that had a big yellow mustard stain on the left breast. Looked like a hot dog had gotten away from him. Also noteworthy was Weston's aggressive chest hair, which was exploding out of the collar of his shirt. It was hard to imagine that Weston—or at least Weston's wife—hadn't noticed it. Maybe he thought it was a sign of masculinity. And maybe it was. What it wasn't, however, was welcome around Jason's lunch.

"I had coffee with our client this morning," Weston said.

Jason was half listening, half checking out a couple of female joggers. "Oh, yeah?"

"Yes. Have you seen her recently?"

"Not for a few weeks, why?"

"She looks terrible," Weston said. "Putting on a lot of weight, it seems to me. She is not an attractive woman, Jason."

"I know," Jason said. Was this really why they were having a meeting?

"That gives me serious concerns about the viability of the case," Weston said. "No one's going to believe that somebody wanted to have sex with that woman."

Jason laughed. "That issue has actually occurred to me. But with alcohol, anything's possible."

"I'm not convinced. I mean, have you seen her recently? Looked at her stomach? It's disgusting." Weston made a face of disgust to show how disgusting it was.

"I don't think the judge is going to throw the case out because the plaintiff is getting too fat," Jason observed.

Weston snorted. Jason had been inundated lately by snorts. "It's not the judge I'm worried about. It's the jury, if we get that far. And it's Rebecca Trent in settlement negotiations if we let her get a look at our client. Has her deposition been scheduled?"

"No, we haven't even discussed it yet."

"Good," Weston said. "Do you think we can get her to start taking diet pills?"

"Maybe you can suggest that to her."

The Prick

"I'll have my assistant do some research," Weston said solemnly.

The Prick

Chapter 3

Sunday, June 9th
New Orleans

Robert was getting a hand job in the back room of a
Bourbon Street strip club. He'd stumbled by the club—one
of those neon affairs with narrow facades occupying just
about fifteen feet of street real estate—and a woman
wearing a G-string had grabbed his elbow and led him
inside, feeling for his wallet in his front right pocket. Now
his pants were around his ankles and he was sitting on some
disgusting plastic chair.

After more than a month of daily binge drinking,
interrupted only occasionally by twenty-four-to-forty-eight-
hour comatose sleep sessions, his brain had started to fold
in on itself. He lacked any aim, purpose, or direction other
than his need to not remember. Whereas in the beginning
he had set upon debauchery with an aggressive lust, as
though he'd unleashed an animal that had been strapped
down for decades, that had passed quickly, and now he
addressed the street and the ongoing nightlife with
disinterested listlessness. Lately he had just kind of thrown
himself on whatever current was moving. The only things to
which he applied any discipline were never letting anyone
near the money in his room and blocking out his thoughts.

Nevertheless, this was disconcerting, and brought his
mind back from the brink. Uncomfortably. It was a strange

turn of events that a woman without a full set of teeth would be giving him a hand job in what likely doubled as a broom closet in the back of this shotgun strip club. But every time he looked down, that's what was happening. Up and down. He supposed he should want—was probably expected to want—a blow job or sex or something. But he most certainly did not. He wasn't at all sure, in fact, that he wanted any of this to continue. She had been very assertive. Was she chewing gum? It seemed like maybe she was chewing gum.

"Is there anything to drink?" he asked.

She looked up at him quizzically. "What?"

She was chewing gum, he confirmed. A neon green gum. Robert estimated that she had about 75 percent of a normal human's allotment of teeth. She should switch to Trident, which might have the added benefit of improving the overall olfactory experience he was currently enduring.

"Is there anything to drink back here?" he repeated.

"No," she said. "You can buy me a drink after."

"Why would I buy you a drink? Is that part of it or something?"

"Part of what, honey?" Although she seemed puzzled by the sudden Q&A, she hadn't broken stroke. A real professional. Up and down.

"Is buying you a drink part of whatever hand job transaction I've entered into here?"

"No, it's just polite," she said.

He had no idea manners factored into this. Hand job etiquette.

"All right. Maybe I'll buy myself a drink for the road ... after, I guess. How long do you expect this will take?"

She looked at him again, confused. "Are you getting close?" She picked up her speed. A hundred strokes a minute, up from fifty, he estimated. She also cupped his balls with her other hand and did some kind of one-hand juggling thing. Odd.

"Not sure," he said. "I may just get going."

"Do you want me to put it in my mouth, for twenty more dollars?" she asked. She looked like she had no intention of letting him escape.

"Absolutely not."

"Well, what do you need me to do?"

He considered. "Can you turn your face the other way?"

She did it without further debate. He wondered if it was a routine request.

"I haven't had sex with my wife in five hundred days," Robert told her. It was five hundred days exactly. She didn't respond. She had probably heard stranger things, received stranger instructions.

Anyway, it didn't matter. He tried to concentrate so that he could pay the toll and get the hell out of there.

The Prick

Chapter 4

Sunday, June 9th
The Moxley House
Norcross, Georgia

"245," the scale reported. That just couldn't be right. There was nothing in her pockets. She stepped out of her slippers and tried again. Pete was still sleeping it off in the adjoining bedroom. She could hear him snoring through the door.

"244." Off came the sweatpants. And the underwear and bra. "244," the scale stubbornly asserted. It must be wrong, she thought. Had to be. Even at her worst she had never even broken into the 230s. But maybe *this* was her worst.

The scale was unfortunately positioned in front of the mirror. She hadn't seen herself naked in a while. Her whole body looked swollen, like the entire corpus was having an allergic reaction to something. At least her breasts looked big, too. She'd always had nice ones. Even Pete had to admit it. He was always grabbing at them.

She began to cry again. That did nothing good for the image in the mirror, which jiggled and folded on itself in places. Which of course just made everything worse. Her crying became louder and more severe, with wracking body convulsions. *Huh—huh—huh—huh.*

She got off the scale and sank to the floor in the middle of the bathroom. Her skin pressed against the cold tile, and

The Prick

she sat with her knees up and her head in her hands. She couldn't see the mirror from down on the ground. Her clothes lay in a pile next to her.

"What am I going to do?" she said.

The bathroom door opened. It was Pete, newly awakened and wearing nothing but boxers and socks, in which he had slept. His chest fur was grossly matted.

With glassy eyes, Pete looked down at her and the pile of clothes. She was still crying, but more softly now. Her gaze fixed on his as she waited for words of comfort.

"The fuck?" he queried. He pushed through the door and kicked her clothes to the side, out of his way. The beer stink wafted off him as he passed. He took five or six plodding and unsteady steps to the toilet, threw up the seat, and unleashed a stream. He looked over his shoulder at her as he pissed out last night's binge and cooed, "Some fuckin' reason you cryin' on the floor with your shit all over the fuckin' place?"

She stared at him. He turned his head and spat into the stream. It was like someone had tapped a keg.

He'd stumbled in the night before around 2:30 a.m., waking her up. He'd obviously driven home loaded. She had no idea where he'd been all night, but her best guess was Hank's Sports Bar with all of the guys from work. At least she hoped so. Occasionally there were late-night credit card charges to "Tropical, Inc.," and occasionally he came home with cheap perfume on him and a few scattered specks of glitter. Maggie hadn't checked his clothes or logged on to bankofamerica.com to check the statement, yet. She'd been too occupied with her ever-increasing body mass to even think about it. But now he had her attention.

"Where were you last night?"

He turned his head, looking surprised. She never outright asked him.

The Prick

"Out."

"Out where?"

He finished, finally, and shook a few times for good measure. He turned to look down at her on the floor, his face contorted in disdain. "Fuck you care?"

She had to crane her neck to meet his bloodshot eyes. She knew how she must look, all her fat on top of itself against the tile. She hated him for looking at her like that, hated him for seeing her like that.

"I know where you go," she said. "I know you go see the strippers."

"You don't know shit."

"I can smell it on you," she said, even though that wasn't presently true. "And I find your charges on the credit card statement."

He studied her. The accusation hung in the air.

"What do you 'spect," he said, nodding down at her body. "Look at the fat cow I have to come home to."

With that, he angled around her to plod back to the bedroom, but her foot shot out underneath him and he tripped. His alcohol-addled mind didn't communicate quickly enough to his arms that they needed to brace him and his face absorbed all of the impact as he hit the door frame. He collapsed down to the floor, holding his head in his hands, and landed with his back against the open door.

"What the fuck!" He tried to pick himself up. Blood was rushing freely from the side of his head, down through his matted chest hair and onto the floor. He tried to stand, then slumped down onto his back.

Maggie got up on her feet, grabbed a towel, and pressed it up against Pete's head. Streams of blood spread out across the floor in the spaces between the tiles.

"What did you do that for?" He spat blood. The towel she was holding covered his eyes. She lifted it for a second and

The Prick

blotted quickly. There was a huge gash on the left side of his forehead.

"Do what?"

"You fucking tripped me."

"Hush," she said. "You probably need stitches."

Chapter 5

Monday, June 10th
Atlanta Offices of Levitt, Bennett & Taylor, LLP

"It's the twenty-first century. People don't just disappear," Simmons growled over the phone. "This is just ridiculous. What Mickey Mouse investigator did we hire to find him?"

Rebecca was in no mood. After the pussy shit that Simmons had pulled in the mediation, she was in no mood at all. She and Maria Chan were sitting in Peters's office in front of his desk. Peters was behind the desk, staring into the middle distance.

"Listen, Will, it's not my goddamn fault that you can't keep track of your own goddamn partners. Nobody notified me that I was going to have to put a fucking GPS on Spelkin." She glared at Peters, really for no reason other than he was easy to glare at.

"Tell me exactly what we're doing to find him."

"The investigator is monitoring the use of his credit cards and cell phone, neither of which has been used in more than a month. We're also monitoring his email; same thing, no activity. The angry emails from people he hasn't responded to, by the way, are piling up. The firm will eventually have to step in and do something about it. We've been calling his wife every week to see if she's heard from him. Nothing."

The Prick

"Has she filed a missing person's report?" Burroughs asked in his gratingly nasal voice. He was in Washington with Simmons.

"No. I get the feeling that she'd be perfectly fine with him vanishing altogether."

"Should we file a missing person's report?" Burroughs asked.

"Sure," Rebecca said. "Great idea. Broadcast publicly that we can't find the only person who can contradict Moxley's story. Hunter won't be able to use that to his advantage at all. And I'm sure it would work wonders for your firm's image, which is just so sterling right now."

Rebecca caught the familiar Simmons sigh of resignation over the phone. The predator in her rose up at the sign of submission, and she felt a slight rush.

"So what do we do?" Simmons asked.

Yes. Ask for, and fucking follow, directions. "Attack."

"Attack how? We're the ones in deep trouble here. I thought about trying to book another mediation and making all of this just go away for good."

There was no way Rebecca was going to let that happen. She couldn't stand the thought of her client rolling over for that little dipshit Hunter again. And she had hours to bill.

"You do that and you'll end up writing a check for millions," Rebecca said. "The Moxley case is so much better than that horseshit Rossi case you just paid out on. We've got to have the balls to stand up for ourselves here, gentlemen. Hunter thinks he can have his way with us now."

"Fine. What do you have in mind?"

Questioning manhood worked every time. "We're going to attack on two fronts. We'll put Hunter on his heels and buy time to find whatever spider hole Spelkin's hiding in. We just filed an Answer in the Moxley case. We'll send Hunter a Rule 11 letter—calling the litigation frivolous and demanding that it be withdrawn or we'll seek sanctions—and file a motion to dismiss."

"On what grounds?" Burroughs asked.

"Not important. We'll find something. That should give us at least a few months, with briefing and waiting on the court's ruling. If he tries to take Spelkin's deposition during that time, we'll ask that discovery be stayed pending a ruling on the motion to dismiss."

"We don't have any basis to move to dismiss, or to call the litigation frivolous for that matter," Simmons said.

"Doesn't matter. We're just doing it to keep Hunter busy —keep him worried—and push out discovery until we can locate fucking Spelkin."

"And you're comfortable with that?" Simmons said. "Filing a motion that we'll lose?"

"Even if we lose, we win," Trent said. "A delay is a win. Who knows, Hunter may even lower his demand if we get him worried enough about this." Simmons would go for that, Trent thought. His primary motivation was clearly to just make this all go away.

"Okay. What's the other attack?"

Rebecca smiled. She liked this part. Especially after what happened at the mediation.

"Before Spelkin turned tail and ran, he puffed up big about suing Hunter for defamation for the *Daily Record* article. I'll go to Hunter and tell him the lawsuit is in the works. That I tried to prevent it from happening but couldn't talk Spelkin down."

"Isn't that just going to piss him off?"

Simmons had been powerful for too long. A federal magistrate judge and then a high-profile partner. He'd forgotten what it felt like to be vulnerable.

"Probably," Rebecca said. "But if he has a brain, it will also terrify him. He can't afford to even defend a lawsuit like that; forget what would happen if there was a judgment against his little firm. My bet is that Rossi gift you just gave him is 90 percent of his revenue." Rebecca was going to stick Simmons with the Rossi settlement whenever she could. Make him think twice about doing that to her ever again. "It may be the only thing funding the Moxley lawsuit."

"That was the right call, Rebecca." Simmons's voice was hard.

"Anyway, if it pisses him off, or scares him, or both, he'll be distracted. We'll keep him busy worrying about himself."

"Fine. That'll be the plan for now. Don't actually file any defamation lawsuit, of course."

"Not a chance. We just want to make a credible threat."

"Got it," Simmons said. "Jimmy, what are we doing on our end to get Spelkin back here?"

Peters's head shot up as if he'd been woken violently out of a dream. He shuffled papers on his desk. "We're monitoring his emails and ... we are on the lookout for any calls or, ah, messages from—"

"Rebecca mentioned all that," Simmons snapped. "Are you doing anything else?"

"I—"

"Talk to payroll and cut off his partnership draw," Simmons said. "That may bring him out of hiding."

"I don't believe he accesses his bank account," Peters said.

"Well, do something!" Simmons said. "Find him!" Then there was a dial tone.

"It's not my fault he's missing," Peters whined to Rebecca, who was already packing up and standing to leave.

Rebecca laughed. "Jimmy, that's true. All the same, it may be time to dust off the old résumé."

*****

The Prick

Jason was trying to get off the phone so he could get to his meeting in Dunwoody with Moxley's sister by 11:00 a.m.

"Listen, I hear what you're saying. You think they fired you because of your race. What I'm saying is that they have you on videotape slapping a coworker in the face."

"She hit me first."

"You told me five minutes ago that there wasn't even a fight."

"It wasn't a fight. It wasn't even nothing. She got in my face and then she slapped me."

"Amanda, I'm watching the tape right now. I can see you clearly in it. You hit her first. They told me in the beginning of the case that they fired you for hitting another coworker. You promised me that didn't happen. Now I've got a time-stamped video where it clearly did."

"They can change those videos, Mr. Hunter. You can't trust no videos."

"You hit her, didn't you?"

A moment of silence. "She got in my face. You can't let no bitch just get in your face, Mr. Hunter."

"Okay," Jason said. "Well, given this video, Amanda, there's no way we can go forward with the case. I've got to terminate—"

"How much they gon' pay?"

"Pay for what?"

"To not go forward with the case. How much I get?"

Jason arrived late at Moxley's sister's house, pulling in the driveway at 11:17. Kathryn Addison lived in a nice, family-friendly neighborhood in predominantly upper-middle class Dunwoody, a suburb of Atlanta that lay just outside of the I-285 perimeter that circled the city. The Addison residence was a stately colonial that looked manicured and well maintained, although Jason had to maneuver around a small bicycle and squirt gun in the driveway.

The woman who answered the door was prettier and slimmer than Maggie, but Jason could see the resemblance immediately. She had the generally disheveled look of a mother chasing children around and even sported a streak of what looked like green paint on her chin. She wore sweatpants and a T-shirt.

"Mrs. Addison?"

"Yes!" she said, smiling. "Call me Kate. You must be Jason. Please come in." She led him through the foyer and down the hall. The house was cheerful and brightly lit. Family pictures, professionally taken, lined the walls.

"Sorry I'm late," he said, trailing her.

"No problem at all. We're just painting." She ushered him into a living room with tall windows facing the backyard. In the center of the room was a trio of easels, two of them occupied by children who, from their respective works, seemed to be of the Jackson Pollack school. The boy looked to be about five, the girl three. Under the easels, newspaper was spread out all over the floor. Classical music played in the background. The whole environment was clearly meant to be a breeding ground for creative geniuses.

"Kids, say hello to Jason."

"Hello," they said in unison, not looking up.

"Jason, this is Charlie and Beth," Kate said, smiling and proud.

"Hi, Charlie! Hi, Beth!" Jason said dutifully, in his best sunshiny voice. "A couple of masterpieces there."

The children mercifully didn't prolong the conversation by responding.

"I thought we could talk here," Kate said, indicating the adjacent room.

The Prick

They sat down at the dining room table, he at the head, she on the side, in a chair facing her kids.

"I'm trying to make sure they confine the paint to the easels," she said. "It's important to encourage them to be creative, but not on my new walls!" Her delivery and tone indicated that she was hitting him with some humor. It was probably the kind of material that killed with the stay-at-home-parents crowd.

Jason managed to smile thinly. "Not the kind of interior decorating you had in mind, huh?"

She laughed at that like she was on nitrous oxide.

Jason took his notepad and pen out of his briefcase. She glanced, perhaps a bit nervously, at the pad. "I'll help you in any way that I can," she said, lowering her voice to a whisper, "but I really don't know anything. I mean, other than what she told me. What Maggie told me."

Jason forced the smile to remain on his face. "That's what I'm interested in. You may end up being an important witness in Maggie's case."

She swallowed heavily, and her lips tightened.

"It will be helpful," he pressed on, "to have someone verify and corroborate that she was claiming that her boss ... sexually assaulted her on the night in question." He matched her low volume when he said this, mindful of the young ears in the next room.

She nodded but looked very uncomfortable. Jason was starting to feel a bit uncomfortable himself. Something was wrong. This was supposed to be a cakewalk interview with a friendly witness. Maggie had said her sister was willing—even excited—to be a part of this.

"Is that okay?" he asked.

"Well, I suppose," she said. "I don't know if I'll have time to do much ... you know, with the kids."

The Prick

Jason felt the first physical manifestations of his own apprehension, consciously registering his pulse against his temples. "It won't take a lot of time. Just today, probably a deposition, and then a few hours of testimony at trial."

"Okay," Kate said, looking out the window. "I can only tell the truth, though, you know, about what Maggie told me. I don't really know that much. I mean, I wasn't there when it happened."

What the fuck did that mean?

"Right," he said, hopefully reassuringly. "All anyone will ever ask you is to tell the truth."

She blinked rapidly. Was she crying? Yes, she was crying a little bit, just welling, but still.

"So she can still win, even if I say it?"

Oh Jesus. "If you say what, Kate?"

"Paint only on the sheet!" Kate yelled into the other room. Jason, who had been leaning in to catch the whispers, reared back in the chair in surprise.

"Sorry," she said. Jason looked into the other room but didn't see any need for the interruption. Both painters were wholly focused on their canvasses. Not even the shout had distracted them.

"If you say what, Kate?"

"If I say what she told me that night, she can still win her case?"

"I'm hoping it'll *help* her win her case."

"Oh, okay," Kate said. She dropped all the way down to a whisper and Jason leaned in again, cautiously. "So you know what she said? Because when I talked to her a week or so ago, she said that if I, you know, gave a statement or deposition or something, I should say that she didn't do anything. But if I say the real thing, what she really told me, that's fine?"

The Prick

Jason felt like he was going to vomit. He put his pen down.

"I want you to tell me exactly what Maggie said to you that night."

"For the statement?"

"There is no statement," Jason said. Why did she keep talking about some "statement"? "Don't worry about that. You're just talking to me."

She shrugged. "Okay. You're the attorney."

"Yes. Just please tell me."

"Well," she said, whispering conspiratorially, "she texted me first and said she needed to talk. I said, what about. She told me her boss, you know, made her have sex with him."

"You mean *tried to* make her have sex with him?"

"Did I say the wrong thing? That's what I was worried about. Because after that night, a few times, she told me I should say that she didn't have sex with him."

Jason shook his head. This was very, very bad. "All I'm interested in," he said, "is what she actually texted you, and what she actually told you."

"I have the texts right here," Kate said, pulling out her iPhone. "Maggie told me to delete them, but I didn't, because I thought she might need them later. Maggie ... doesn't always think straight in stressful situations."

Jason stared at the iPhone in her hand. It was hard to believe that this housewife in Dunwoody who spent her days in sweatpants spreading out newspaper and keeping paint off the walls had been walking around with evidence that could destroy a seven-figure case.

"Can you pull them up?"

She hit a few buttons and handed him the phone. The screen read:

Mar 21, 9:21 PM

The Prick

I need to talk to you right away.

Mar 21, 9:21 PM
Can it wait until tomorrow? Just got the kids down and about to get into bed.

Mar 21, 9:22 PM
Now please.
My boss just made me suck his d***. Don't know what to do. Don't want to go home.

Mar 21, 9:22 PM
What?!?!

Mar 21, 9:22 PM
Don't tell Jim!
Don't tell anyone!

Mar 21, 9:23 PM
I will call in one minute.

Mar 29, 3:53 PM
I met with the lawyer today.

Mar 29, 3:54 PM
How did it go?

Mar 29, 3:54 PM
Good. He thinks I have a case. Pete thinks we're going to get a lot of money. ☺ Do me a favor and erase the texts from that night. I'm gonna do it too.

Mar 29, 3:55 PM
Ok ...

The Prick

Mar 29, 3:55 PM
Can you call me tonight?

Jason's heart beat rapidly and hard against his chest as he read through the messages and his already churning stomach registered seismic events. He tried to betray no emotion to Kate, who was studying his face closely. Jason scrolled down to the bottom of the text chain, moving forward in time until the day before, when the two sisters talked about Kate's then-upcoming interview, but there was nothing else of relevance, just a series of proposed dinner plans, recipes, and pictures of Kate's kids. He handed the phone back to Kate.

"Do *not* delete those messages," he said.

Kate's face brightened. "I knew it! She told me that I should delete them, but I thought they might be important."

Jason nodded grimly. Even though the texts made a liar out of his client and might destroy his firm's most valuable asset, he had an affirmative ethical obligation to take steps to preserve all relevant evidence, favorable or not.

"Did you end up talking to her that night? March 21st?"

"Oh, yes," she said, looking down at his pen, which was lying still on the table. He had no intention of writing any of this down until he figured out what the hell was going on.

"Please tell me what she told you," he said, eyes locked on hers.

Her voice dropped once again to a whisper. "When I called her she was still at the MARTA station trying to figure out what to do. She had missed her bus and she didn't know how to get home. She didn't want to call Pete to come pick her up ... and, you know, she didn't want to go back to the office."

The Prick

"Right," Jason said. "What did she say happened with Spelkin?"

Kate hunched over, elbows on her knees, and spoke so softly that Jason had to lean even farther in to make it out. "She was working at her desk after everyone else left. He made her stay late on some project. And then he came into her, you know, cubicle area or whatever. She heard him and turned around and he unzipped his pants and took his di— um, penis out of his pants."

She stopped, looking embarrassed. Stone-faced, Jason nodded for her to continue. This part at least was consistent.

"He told her that he wanted her to put it in her mouth. What did she say he said? ... Oh, yeah, that it was a 'project she had to work on.' She said 'no' and turned around to try to continue working and hoped that he would just go away. Then she felt it ...on her neck. She turned and it was ... right in her face. He told her to do it, to put it in her mouth, that nobody would know, and that she had to do it."

She paused.

"Go on."

"Well this is the part I'm confused about. I'm not sure what I'm supposed to say."

Motherfucker. Jason wanted to punch something. "Just tell me exactly what Maggie told you the night that it happened."

Kate nodded. "She told me she did it. That she gave him a bl—that she ... did oral sex with him or whatever, sitting down in her office chair with him standing over her. She said that she tried to get him to ... you know, have an orgasm for like five minutes. She said that he was squeezing her boob real hard. But then he stopped her from, you know, and told her to leave."

"He stopped her and told her to leave?"

221

"Yeah, he said he couldn't, uh, finish because she gave the worst head ever and that she should just get her things and go."

"He told her *what*?"

"She was so mad about that. He told her that he couldn't ... you know... because she 'gave the worst head ever' and that she should just leave. She said she was so humiliated that she ran away. She could hear him laughing."

Jason put his head in his hands. He couldn't maintain the poker face any longer. "Jesus Christ."

"She didn't tell you he said that?"

"No," Jason said from between his palms, "she did not. What about Pete? Did she tell Pete about all this?"

"Not the whole thing," Kate said. "She only told Pete that he tried to make her do it. She thought Pete would blame her and try to divorce her or something."

"Right."

"What did she tell you?"

"Not the whole thing."

"Oh. I hope I didn't do anything wrong."

"No," Jason said, rubbing his temples. "*You* didn't do anything wrong.

Kate's eyes narrowed. "I have to tell the truth, right? I'm going to be under oath."

"Yes."

"That's the only thing I can do."

"Yes."

"I mean, she wants me to say something different, but I can't do that, can I?"

"No."

"Right. That's what my husband thinks."

The Prick

Chapter 6

Thursday, June 14th
The Law Offices of Jason Hunter, Esq.

Maybe Jason was paranoid, but Trent calling to set up a meeting the hour after he returned from Kate Addison's house in a full panic hadn't seemed like a coincidence. Now here she was, sitting in the chair in front of his desk in his tiny, yellow, windowless office, looking at him like he was an insect. He had walked her back through the dingy hallway into his office, and she'd walked around the room, looking at the artwork on the walls like she was taking some kind of goddamn museum tour. He knew she was just trying to mess with his head, but he was very susceptible to head-messing at the moment, given recent revelations about how his entire case against Levitt was based on a big fat lie.

"How long have you had this space?" Trent said. She was wearing another ill-fitting pantsuit that was two sizes too big, this one scarlet. Yards and yards of scarlet cloth just for the legs alone.

"A little over a year."

"Just you?"

"Yes."

"No assistant?"

"No."

"I don't know if I could live like that."

"Hmm."

The Prick

"You ever think about going back to the defense side?"

"No," Jason said. "Lately the plaintiff's side has been very profitable."

Trent smiled. "Yes. Congratulations on the settlement. I was strongly opposed to it, as I think you know."

"Thank you."

"I wouldn't spend it yet if I were you."

"And why is that?"

"There are storm clouds on the horizon, kid. I wanted to come and warn you about it first in person."

Shit. Did she know? Had she known the whole time? On the way home from Moxley's sister's house he'd wondered if Trent hadn't confronted him because Spelkin didn't want to cop to any species of sexual interlude with Moxley. But maybe Spelkin had finally broken down and fessed up.

"What are you talking about?" Jason asked, heart in his throat.

She grinned. She was enjoying this. Whatever this was.

"Where to begin." Trent reached down to the right for her bag and lifted from it a manila folder. Jason looked it balefully. Nothing good ever came out of her manila folders.

"First," she continued, opening the folder, "I'm here to hand deliver to you a Rule 11 letter and a draft Rule 11 motion, which we will file unless you dismiss all claims except the individual battery claims against Spelkin."

Jason glared at her as he reached out to take the papers from her hand. "This is bullshit."

And it was. By handing him this, Trent was asserting that the Complaint he'd filed against Spelkin and Levitt was so frivolous that he should be sanctioned. A Rule 11 motion was exceedingly rare. It was a public shaming, and so intended.

"Not at all," Trent said. "You have claims in the Complaint against Spelkin for civil assault, civil battery, invasion of privacy, and intentional infliction of emotional distress, and a claim against Levitt for negligent retention and supervision."

"I know. I wrote it."

"The only claim that isn't legally frivolous is battery," Trent said. "As detailed in this motion to dismiss, which we're filing today"—she tossed another stack of documents on his desk—"the civil assault claim is nonsensical because, even if you believe the lies in the Complaint, Moxley claims that she had her back turned when Spelkin put his dick on her shoulder." Trent said the word "dick" with a level of comfort most women didn't possess, at least in Jason's experience. "She didn't see it coming, and therefore didn't have an apprehension of physical contact—and therefore has no assault claim." Trent reached out and tapped on the documents she'd just thrown his way. "Educate yourself. It's all in here. For the invasion of privacy and IIED claims, you simply don't have the requisite facts. Do you know how high the standard is for IIED in Georgia? Moxley may not even have a claim if he forced it in her mouth."

"We'll see about that," Jason said, trying to maintain the tough exterior.

"Finally," Trent said leaning back in her chair. "The negligent retention and supervision claim against Levitt is flawed because, even if the lies in the Complaint are to be believed, Levitt had no knowledge of any propensity of Spelkin to be a sexual predator ... alleged sexual predator. It cannot therefore be negligent."

Jason snorted. "The judge isn't just going to take your word for that. I get discovery on it. Discovery just opened."

"You have no evidence whatsoever," Trent said. "And so we are moving to dismiss."

"Again, I get to develop evidence in discovery. Surely you would agree with that."

The Prick

Trent rolled her eyes. "I guess you can make that argument if you want to, but I think Judge Barnes will see things our way."

"This is absurd," Jason protested, picking up the motion and thumbing through it. "You have no chance of winning this."

"We do. And if you don't dismiss the frivolous claims now, Levitt will insist that I move for sanctions. My hands will be tied."

"This some kind of good cop, bad cop routine? Levitt out to get me and you trying to help me?"

Trent leaned back further in her chair and put her feet up on his desk, crossing her hands behind her head like she was at the fucking beach. Her legs were so long that they stretched past Jason's monitor and right into his personal space. He looked down at the soles of her shoes in disbelief.

"I'm just telling you how it is, kid," Trent said. "Levitt is furious, at the highest levels. You've gone after their reputation, their livelihood. They're coming to get you. I can try to reason with them, say you made some rookie mistakes and didn't appreciate the gravity of your actions, but only if you dismiss now and walk away. Maybe I can even get Spelkin to pay your filing fees if you drop the battery claim."

"I'm sorry they're upset, but they have to take responsibility for *their* actions, and for the actions of Spelkin."

Trent shrugged. "It's your funeral. Don't say I didn't warn you."

The two looked at each other for a few long seconds.

"Is that it?" Jason asked.

She flashed the predator grin again. She looked so much like a shark when she did that he wondered if she practiced it in the mirror. Trent dropped her feet off his desk, reached down to her briefcase, slowly drew out yet another folder, and placed it flat on her lap.

Jason couldn't help staring at it. Trent caught his eyes.

"This one is going to become your biggest problem," she said, patting the folder.

"Okay ... what's in there?"

"A draft defamation lawsuit."

Life was becoming nothing more than a series of gut shots.

"You've got to be kidding me."

Trent shook her head. "Not at all. I can't hold off Spelkin any longer. Not after you got that article into the *Daily Record*. You went after his career, publicly humiliated the man. Now he wants your head—and certain other body parts."

"I didn't write the article," Jason protested. "I just provided them with the filed Complaint, which is a public document." His voice sounded whiny and weak, like a child complaining about being grounded. He forced himself to breathe.

"You may be right," Trent said. "But that's something the court is going to have to determine unless you can find some way to appease Spelkin. He's determined to file. He's probably going to get divorced because of you."

"What does he hope to gain from this?" Jason asked. "Look around. I don't exactly have deep pockets. Even if he manages to someday get a judgment against me, it'll be worthless."

A smile crept back across Trent's face. "You've got your portion of the Rossi settlement."

Jason gritted his teeth.

"You offer Spelkin the 160,000 you took from that bullshit case, and I'll do what I can to convince him not to file," Trent said. "I'm not sure he'll take it, but I may be able to tempt him by telling him that he's getting everything you have." Trent made a show of turning her head and looking around. "That really is everything you have, isn't it?"

"There's no way I'm paying him anywhere close to that," Jason said. "There's no way I'm paying him anything at all."

Trent put the file back in her briefcase. She hadn't shown it to him.

"Can I at least see it?"

"Not yet," said Trent, standing up to leave. "You'll see it soon enough, I assure you. In the meantime, I would set aside a sizeable chunk of the Rossi settlement for attorneys' fees."

"You file that horseshit lawsuit against me, I'll defend it myself," Jason blustered, standing up as well. "And I'm sure Richard Weston would defend it pro bono."

Trent laughed. "You'd be better off representing yourself, and as they say, the man who represents himself has a fool for a client. Weston's a dinosaur."

"He's still on some high-profile cases."

"With substantial oversight from his partners," Trent shot back. "It's widely known what goes on over there. His firm assigns another attorney to every case he's on to make sure he doesn't make any colossal mistakes. They've done that for years now, ever since your new nemesis, Robert Spelkin, destroyed him."

Jason blinked. Trent's jaw dropped. "Did you really not know that?"

Jason didn't respond.

"You didn't know why the legendary Richard Weston agreed to be on this case with you?"

"Because ... it's a strong case," Jason said softly.

"Wow," Trent said. "I guess maybe you were still in law school or even college when it happened. It was all over the city, let's see, about fifteen years ago now."

228

The Prick

Jason looked at her blankly and sunk back down into his chair.

"Let me give you a history lesson here, Jason. Robert Spelkin is the reason that Weston's firm no longer represents Rinks Industries. Spelkin was representing a class of retailers suing Blue Atlantic for fraud. Blue Atlantic is a subsidiary of Rinks. Weston and his firm were the lead counsel for Blue Atlantic. This was back when Weston was still in his heyday, when people took him seriously. Turned out, however, that Weston didn't know shit about saving electronically stored information, and, under his watch, Blue Atlantic automatically deleted millions of relevant emails, just through their standard deletion protocol. We're talking millions of emails directly relevant to the case. Weston just whiffed on it—he had no ESI litigation hold issued whatsoever, and didn't suspend the company's biannual permanent deletion of emails. Spelkin got a hold of that and took a huge bite out of Blue Atlantic. Moved for sanctions, got the company's Answer struck as a discovery violation, and got a boatload of attorneys' fees on top of it all. Blue Atlantic was forced to settle, I forget for how much, but it was a huge payout. Weston, of course, was completely discredited as a bet-the-company high-stakes litigator. His firm lost all Rinks business. We're talking millions in fees annually."

Jason couldn't think of anything to say.

"That's why he took on this bullshit case," Trent said. "He wants revenge against Spelkin. Look it up. I shouldn't know more about your co-counsel than you do, for Chrissake." With that, she turned and walked out of the little space that he occupied in the universe.

*****

Donald Jeffries had a lot of time on his hands lately. Time to think. He spent most of his days sitting in his underwear on the white fabric couch in his mother's basement, watching the TV on mute, and thinking. He'd collected all of the facts and sorted through them in his head until he had them lined up the right way. Finally, that morning, they all made sense, had slotted themselves correctly into place like the correct sequence of characters in a password. He had been fired because of Robert Spelkin. The Moxley lawsuit, her firing, his firing, the timing.

His career was over because of Robert Spelkin. He'd been arrested and made his mother cry because of Robert Spelkin. He wanted to kill himself because of Robert Spelkin.

He was driving around and around the Levitt building in his old light blue Ford Taurus. Left onto Peachtree Street, left onto Ellis, left on to Peachtree Center, left onto Andrew Young, left onto Peachtree Street, left onto Ellis, and around and around he went, in a circle that was actually a square, looking. Surely Spelkin would have to emerge at some point, on foot or in his fancy car. Donald wouldn't go in the building. Couldn't. They had his picture up in there. He didn't have the radio on, nor did he have the AC on, and nothing rattled in his car, which he kept immaculately clean. The Taurus was suffocatingly hot and deathly silent in its orbit around the building, except for the intermittent click-click of the blinker every half minute, signaling another left-hand turn. He stared into the crowds and into the cars that passed, searching.

Donald's mother's Glock 19 was under the passenger seat. She was careful about locking it up with the others, especially after The Incident, but he knew where she kept the key to the chest she stored them in, so locking them up didn't do much of anything. He had snuck in and spirited away the Glock that morning, when she was at work, after he'd figured out that Spelkin had ruined his life.

The Prick

Donald had never actually fired a gun—as he had also told that damn judge when he was arrested and his mom cried in the courtroom pews and he had to wear the orange jumpsuit and everyone talked to him like he was a criminal —but how hard could it be? Point and shoot.

The Prick

Chapter 7

Friday, June 15th
Weston, Brenson & Alps, LLP
Midtown Atlanta

This was the meeting before the meeting. Jason was in
Weston's spacious but cluttered corner office on Peachtree
Street in Midtown Atlanta. The door was closed. There was
no shortage of things to look at on Weston's walls, which
were covered floor to ceiling with photos—mostly of Weston
with former Atlanta dignitaries, including several mayors
and congressmen—nestled amongst a lifetime supply of
golf-themed artwork. Weston's undergraduate diploma
from Harvard and law diploma from Yale were prominently
featured directly behind Weston's chair so that when you
looked at the man he was buttressed by his pedigree.

There were stacks of papers and files all around on the
floor. It looked like a miniature cityscape of all-rectangular
white and brown buildings. Weston's desk was likewise a
patchwork of binders, legal pads, Post-it notes, and loose
sheets of paper intermixed with legal knickknacks,
including a gavel, brass scales of justice, and a granite block
that sat upright and advised, "Talk is cheap, unless you're
talking to a lawyer!" Jason also saw pieces of a fancy gold
male grooming kit scattered haphazardly through the mess,
including a small comb, tweezers, and a nail-clipper.

The Prick

Neither of them had said a word for ten minutes. Reclined in his aging leather swivel chair, Weston was reading through the Rule 11 letter, Rule 11 motion, and motion to dismiss that Trent had dumped on Jason the day before. Jason had forwarded all three to Weston yesterday afternoon in advance of the meeting but Weston hadn't bothered to read them until Jason arrived. Some message there about how much Weston valued Jason's time, perhaps? Jason himself had read and reread the documents about seventeen times between his meeting with Trent and this one. Compulsively. Every time he forced himself to put them down and do something else, he found them back in his hands within a few minutes.

All other waking minutes had been devoted to worrying about the defamation lawsuit and cycling back through everything Trent had said and trying to decipher when the lawsuit would be filed from what he could recall of their conversation. He had slept fitfully, only logging about an hour or so at a clip, and waking up each time in a sweat. Trent had really done a number on him, which had been the point. He hated himself for knowing that and still being spineless enough to succumb to it.

"Goddamn invertebrate," he said under his breath.

"What?" Weston asked, looking up from the papers.

"Nothing," Jason said. "You make it through everything?"

"Not yet," Weston said gruffly. "You should've faxed these over. It's easier than printing them out as an email attachment."

What year was this? A mayor on the wall smiled at him from the 1980s. "Yeah, okay."

Jason looked down at his iPhone. 4:15 p.m. Moxley was scheduled to be there in fifteen minutes and he wanted to have a real discussion with Weston before she got there.

233

The Prick

Roughly one eternity later, Weston sat up in his chair and swiveled in Jason's direction. "They've got nothing," he declared, tossing the papers carelessly across the desk. "This is just Trent churning the file."

"I agree completely," Jason said, and physically felt himself trying to convince his panicking brain that maybe he did. "They're just drowning us in paperwork, and trying to get us to back off."

"Admittedly," Weston continued, "the Complaint could have been more precisely drafted, could have better spelled out the claims. But there aren't grounds for a motion to dismiss. And there certainly aren't grounds for a Rule 11 letter."

Jason ignored the slight to his drafting. "What about the threatened defamation lawsuit?"

Weston looked at him like he was an idiot. A dumb idiot wasting his time with dumb idiot questions. "There's nothing to it!" he exclaimed, throwing his hands in the air. "You don't need me to tell you that. They're just trying to scare you. Spelkin's an asshole but he's not stupid. I'd wager that they never even file it."

"There's some case law out there stating that an attorney can be sued for defamation based on an article that reports what's in a Complaint, if he supplied the Complaint to the media." Jason had spent roughly seven hours researching said case law in manic spurts.

"It's just a tactic! You have to recognize that!" Again Weston gesticulated wildly. Maybe it was some kind of goddamn workout. Condescendrobics.

"Got it," said Jason, wondering if Weston would be so cavalier if Spelkin had threatened *him* with a defamation suit. Annoyed, he decided to prod at him a bit. "Trent told me that you and Spelkin have a history."

The Prick

Weston glared at him from beneath a furrowed and furry brow. The male grooming kit littering his desk didn't seem to get much playing time. "What of it?"

"Nothing. I just didn't realize."

"I've been doing this for over forty years!" Weston snapped. "There aren't too many high-profile litigators in this city that I haven't had a case with or against."

"Trent made it sound like you might have some kind of, I don't know, grudge against Spelkin. Something involving Blue Atlantic."

"She doesn't know what the hell she's talking about," Weston all but shouted at him. "Spelkin sandbagged me regarding electronic discovery after we'd reached a previous agreement about what should be saved and the client misunderstood my direction—express direction—about what to preserve. You can read through the file if you want." Weston gestured vaguely toward the stacks of documents to his left. Were any of those really decades-old files?

"It's all public record!" Weston continued, highly agitated.

"I don't need to do that, I just…"

"Focus on what matters! They're trying to bully you off the case. To distract you with nonsense! Are you going to let them?"

"Well, no, I—"

"Then don't!" Weston said, looking wild and exasperated. His golden mane had become increasingly disarrayed during his little temper tantrum. Jason glanced down quickly at the small comb on Weston's desk.

"Let's talk about what matters, then. Principally that our case is founded upon a lie."

Weston seemed to calm a bit. "We'll give her an opportunity to explain it. That's the point of today's meeting."

The Prick

Jason knew the point of the meeting. He had called the goddamn meeting. He took a deep breath. "I can't think of any explanation that would fix the problem. She told me that she refused to blow Spelkin. Accordingly, that's how I drafted the EEOC Charge, which she signed under penalty of perjury. That's also the way I drafted the Complaint, which *I* signed and filed. *Now* it turns out that Spelkin may be able to argue that it was consensual at worst, and can show—quite convincingly, I might add—that she's a liar. A jury could easily believe, if she's willing to lie about, oh, I don't know, whether she put his dick in her mouth, that she might be lying about some other things, like, for example, whether the whole thing happened at all."

"Try to calm down," Weston said. It was an odd thing to hear from a man who'd been shouting about a decades-old case not thirty seconds prior.

"She's playing with my reputation here," Jason said. The reputation card would strike the right chord with old Weston, who seemed to value public perception highly.

"Maybe the sister got it wrong," Weston said, patting down his golden hair with both palms. So he was at least that self-aware. He didn't want to appear crazed.

"I saw the text messages. One in particular said that Spelkin made her suck his dick, or rather suck his 'd, asterisk, asterisk, asterisk.'"

"Shit."

"Yes, shit. Unless her sister is a pathological liar who's so determined to undermine Maggie's case that she's creating fake text messages, Maggie lied and committed perjury."

"Spelkin still forced her into a sexual encounter that she didn't want, and did it by exploiting his power as her boss," Weston countered.

"Very true," Jason said. "*Says* she didn't want. And if she had presented it that way from the beginning, the case would still be in fine shape. Maybe even better shape, given what Spelkin apparently did and said to her during and after. But now I think we may be fucked."

"I'm not sure about that," Weston said. "We'll figure out how to handle it. And, in any event, there's still the retaliation claim."

Jason had been mulling that over himself. It didn't matter if the Charge wasn't 100 percent true if they retaliated against her. Incredibly, in the end, that might be the best claim standing. The compensatory and punitive damages on that claim, however, were capped at $300,000.

"But we still may be sunk by the original lie. How are the judge and/or jury supposed to take our word on anything when they find out?"

"The reason is understandable. Have you ever been married?"

"No, but—"

"It sometimes requires a bit of cover-up."

"That doesn't extend to lying under oath," Jason said. "Now I've got this defamation issue to worry about and it turns out that some of the statements in the damn Complaint may actually be false!"

Weston's eyes widened a bit, and he gave Jason a searching look. Then he sighed, like he was disappointed in a pupil. "You can't let your concern for yourself compromise the pursuit of the case," he said. "You have an obligation to Maggie to zealously pursue her claims."

"Bullshit. I have no obligation to pursue a case based on material misrepresentations. She lied to me about the most important thing in the case."

"It still doesn't excuse what Spelkin did."

"Of course not, but—"

"And you're assuming they're going to find out."

Jason stared at him. "How are they not?"

The Prick

Weston opened his mouth to answer just as someone knocked on the door.

"Come in," Weston growled. Weston's tiny secretary opened the door just enough to squeeze through and tiptoed in. The woman constantly looked like she was afraid of being hit by something. Like she had been rescued from the pound. She stood there, perhaps awaiting permission to come aboard.

"Well?" Weston asked.

"Yes, sorry, Mr. Weston. Um, Mrs. Moxley is here."

"Show her in, then!" Weston bellowed. "We've been sitting here waiting for her."

Clearly accustomed to this manner of communication, the secretary scurried out to fetch the woman who was threatening to become the bane of Jason's existence.

In came Moxley in all of her glory. Perhaps taking office-entrance cues from Weston's secretary, she entered the office trepidatiously, stepping in slowly like she was testing the water.

Weston was right, Jason thought as they stood to greet her. Moxley really had gained a hell of a lot of weight. The door had to swing open fully to admit her. On top of everything else, his damn liar of a sexual harassment plaintiff was flirting with morbid obesity.

"Hi, Maggie." Jason quickly extended his hand to prevent an awkward hug. He felt a sudden urge to choke her. The fucking position she had put him in. And what the hell did Weston mean, "*assuming* they're going to find out she lied"? Of course they fucking were.

Maggie's hand was cold and clammy, per usual. The woman had cornered the market on unpleasant traits. He wiped his hand on his pants leg and sat back down.

The Prick

Weston remained behind his desk. Jason noted that he didn't offer his hand. Veteran move. "Please have a seat, Maggie," he said. "Do you need anything—water, coffee?"

"No, I'm fine."

"Laura!" Weston yelled.

The secretary reappeared so quickly, she must have been hovering in the hallway.

"Yes?"

"Go make me some tea, please, and close the door behind you. Thanks." She scampered away. Weston sat.

"The chairs you're sitting in," Weston said, addressing both Moxley and Jason, "come all the way from California. They were a gift from my cousins on my mother's side, members of Pebble Beach. Played there many times."

Great. They were embarking upon yet another involuntary Weston biographical voyage. This had happened so often recently that Jason wondered whether Weston thought he'd been tasked with ghostwriting his memoirs. For every minute he spent actually discussing the case, he spent three on the life and times of Richard Weston.

"Hmm," he responded.

"In fact, they used to be in the players' lounge before it was refurbished. So, you never know who sat in them— could be Arnold Palmer, or Bobby Jones!"

"Wow," Jason said, thinking about his IKEA chairs, model 804A-2. Moxley didn't seem to have anything to contribute. Maybe she wasn't into chairs.

"Jones was actually from Atlanta, you know," Weston prattled on. "Played at the same golf club as my father, East Lake, although it later fell into disrepair. It's been revitalized recently as the neighborhood has improved. I've always been a member of the Oak Club."

239

The Prick

"No need to go to California for a Bobby Jones chair, then, really," Jason said.

"Well he was just one of the great golfers that played at Pebble Beach over the years," Weston said, ignoring the insouciance. "It's been one of the sites of the Open Championship numerous times. Have you been?" he asked Jason. Weston did not seem to consider it likely that Moxley had been to Pebble Beach.

"No, haven't had the chance. You know how work can be."

"If you make it out there," Weston said, "let me know. I can get you a tee time without a problem."

"Super."

There was a knock on the door.

"What?" Weston shouted.

"Your tea."

"Yes, come in."

The small woman pushed the door in and arranged the tea neatly on his desk, doing everything with a rush that bordered on panic.

"Close the door behind you, thanks."

Jason seized on the interruption in Weston story time to try to get things back on track. He pivoted his chair to face Moxley, who looked at him anxiously and squirmed in her Bobby Jones chair like a trapped animal.

"Maggie, the reason we asked you to come in today—"

"I know, I know!" she cried out, looking back and forth between Jason and Weston. "Kate called me. I'm sorry, she just told you the wrong thing. That's not what I told her to say."

Mouth open, Jason stared at her, fighting for composure. "What do you mean, what you 'told her to say' about what happened?"

The Prick

"I told her to say that he put his thing on my neck and I wouldn't do it and I ran away to the bathroom and he tried to grab me," she said with a catch in her throat. The obligatory waterworks were warming up.

Jason looked at Weston, who seemed more concerned with how hot his tea was, blowing on it carefully.

Jason picked up his chair and moved it a foot closer to Moxley. He sat down and leaned forward, putting his elbows on his knees. "Maggie, I want you to tell us right now what actually happened that night. I want the God's honest truth about everything that happened between you and Robert Spelkin. And I want it right now."

"Just what I told you! Just what I said."

"Maggie," Jason said. "The truth. Now."

Free-flowing tears. Of course. The crying was so ubiquitous with Moxley that it no longer had any impact on him. Weston conjured up a box of tissues from behind the desk and handed it to her. "Thank you," she said, dabbing and wiping.

"Maggie," Jason repeated.

"But won't—won't it hurt our case, my case?"

"That's not what's important. What's important is what actually happened."

She was quiet for a good solid minute. She stared at the floor. The only sound in the room was Weston slurping his tea and the clink of cup on saucer. Finally, she took a deep breath.

"He came into my cubicle. I could hear him coming all the way down the hall. He was stumbling bad from the booze. He knocked into the wall a couple of times. You could hear the banging."

"Okay."

"Okay," Maggie echoed. "So he came into my cubicle, and just like I said, he took it out and said that it was a project that I had to work on before I left, you know. He said I had to, that I couldn't leave until I ... finished it."

"Right."

"Right," Maggie agreed. "I didn't know what to do. He was between me and the cubicle exit. I couldn't get out. So I turned around and tried to keep working on corrections he had given to me. I was hoping he'd just zip up and leave me alone. He had never done anything like this before. But I know how men are when they've been drinking. They can't control theirselves."

"Then?"

"Then I felt it. Against my neck. He'd come up behind me and put it right on my neck."

Nobody said anything for a few long seconds. This was it.

"I turned," she said, "and it was right in my face. He backed up just a little but it was, the head was, like, an inch from my mouth."

"Then?"

"Then I told him, 'No, I can't.' He said that, yes I could, and that nobody would know, and that I had to, before I could leave." She stopped again and looked down.

"What did you do?" Jason prompted.

She didn't pick her head up. Just stared at the floor. No eye contact. "I did it," she said, softly. "I put his thing in my mouth. And I, you know, sucked it. I don't know. He made me."

"Okay," Jason said. "It's okay, Maggie." Even though none of it was remotely okay from any angle.

She nodded, her eyes still locked on the floor. "I did it for a few minutes," she said. "I don't really know how long. He was mostly, um, hard, erect, I mean, but not a lot seemed to be happening. Except then he started grabbing my breast, real hard, and squeezing it. I even had bruises for a couple days. I had to hide them from Pete."

"How did it end?" asked Jason, knowing the answer.

She tensed up. "He's such an asshole."

"That's been well established," Weston said, weighing in. "What happened, Maggie?"

"After a few minutes or whatever he told me to stop. He said he wasn't going to be able to ... finish ... because I gave, according to him, 'the worst head ever.' He said to just get my things and leave."

There was another long silence.

"I was so humiliated," she said. "I got up and ran away down the hall to the bathroom. Behind me I could hear him. He was laughing."

Hell hath no fury. That's what the defense theme would be, once it all came to light. She had a bad sexual episode with Spelkin, he rejected her or spurned her or whatever word you wanted to use, so she lied about it being nonconsensual. Once she admitted to doing it, her allegation that it was forced would ring hollow. Because she lied about it in the beginning. The defense would accuse her of just being angry—wrathful—about Spelkin finding her performance deficient and claim that she fabricated how it was initiated. And people would buy it. It was buyable. He was having more than a few doubts of his own about this new version of the story.

Either way, a jury would hate her. Women would think she was a homewrecker. Men would think she was a vengeful and jilted lover, a rejected and unattractive woman lashing out. Jason would have to push to settle this quickly, for whatever they would pay. In a way, that was a relief. There'd be no reason for them to press the defamation case if the main action settled. Spelkin would just want to be done with the whole thing.

The Prick

To get there, to achieve settlement, he would have to convince Moxley to accept a low number. Much, much lower than his original demand. And to get her there, he was going to have to break her down.

"Maggie," he started, "I understand why you didn't tell us this in the beginning. Why you wanted to keep it from Pete. I get that."

She looked at him and nodded gratefully, mashing the balled-up tissue against her eyes. "Thank you."

Jason looked at her arms, which had the girth of an offensive lineman's. She had been big before, but she was huge now.

"All the same," he continued, "we're in a lot of trouble now. The case is in a lot of trouble now."

"But—"

"You signed a statement, under penalty of perjury, that wasn't true, Maggie. Even worse, we filed a Complaint in court that alleged that you didn't do it. When the defense finds out that you actually did, your credibility will be completely shot."

She was really crying now. Blubbering. He didn't care. He had to beat a low-number authorization out of her. Plus, he was goddamn pissed off and it felt good to let her have it.

"The case might have been worth what we demanded in the beginning if you had told me the truth. Hell, it might have been worth even more. But now that you've lied about it, how are we going to get anybody to believe you? The lie ruins it."

"Assuming that they find out," Weston said.

Jason glared at him. Why did he keep saying that?

"They're going to find out, Richard. Of course they are."

"Not for a certainty," Weston said, with a small smile. "Consider why Trent hasn't pushed this story at all. Spelkin is lying to them about the entire encounter, denying everything. He's not in a position to admit that *any* of this happened. Which means he will never testify, and they will never argue, that this was a consensual sexual encounter, or that Maggie lied specifically about certain parts. It's either Maggie's story or a complete denial. There is no middle ground."

"That's not the point. The point is that Maggie is going to have to change her story when she testifies about what happened, under oath."

"Well, that depends," said Weston.

"Why should I have to tell the truth if he's telling a lie?" Moxley asked.

Un-fucking-believable. Jason glared at them both, the prospective suborner and the prospective perjurer. "I can't sit there and permit you to lie under oath if I know it's a lie. At this point, knowing what I know, I may even need to amend the damn Complaint."

"I wouldn't do anything too hasty," Weston said. "She may not even be deposed. Discovery is just getting underway. The case may settle well before any witnesses are sworn in."

"Couldn't I just say in the deposition or whatever what I told you in the beginning?" Maggie said.

"No," Jason said. "Even if I *could* sit by and knowingly let you commit perjury, which I absolutely cannot, they'll have the text messages you sent to Kate. We have to tell them about them and Kate will have to produce them. They very clearly state that you—"

"Oh don't worry about those," Maggie said.

"What? Why?"

"Kate called me after you left her house and told me how upset you were. I drove over there, made her give me her phone, and deleted them, which is what she should have done from the beginning. The texts are gone."

The Prick

Sitting in Atlanta's perpetual traffic on the way back to his office, Jason regretted the rage-fueled tirade he'd unleashed at Moxley, and then at Weston, who'd attempted to interfere. But in the face of that sobbing mess so nonchalantly hand-delivering an ethical torpedo that threatened his livelihood, Jason had simply exploded, using quite a few words he shouldn't have.

"Fuck!" Jason slammed his hand against the leather steering wheel. That was one of them, "Fuck," and had probably been the most prevalent among the various and sundry vituperations he'd issued to Moxley. "Goddamn it!"

A woman in the lane next to him was staring. He stared back at her until she averted her eyes.

Jason took a deep breath as his car inched forward on Juniper and tried to settle down. He'd already alarmed a number of people who worked in Weston's firm, including two worried senior-partner-looking persons who thought the authorities might need to be summoned. No reason to frighten additional villagers.

The needle on the BMW's fuel gauge was closing in on E. He would at least be able to fill up with regular when he was forced to sell the BMW and buy an aging Honda or maybe a gently used Ford Pinto. He stared at the GPS on the dash; the triangle that marked the car was in stasis. He was going to miss watching the little triangle maneuver around the city.

The dash switched screens to notify him of an incoming call. Jessica Rossi. She was probably calling to bitch about the "low" settlement or the taxes she had to pay on all her free money.

"Hi, Jessica."

"Well, if it isn't my favorite young attorney."

The Prick

Jason smiled. He much preferred flirting Jessica Rossi to bitter and bitching Jessica Rossi. Maybe she'd come around and realized what an incredible windfall she'd received for having consensual sex and losing a $50,000 a year job.

"To what do I owe the pleasure?"

"I thought I'd call to give you the update."

"On what?"

"Well ... I'm sleeping with David again ..."

"What? Since when?"

She laughed. "We actually started back up the night of the mediation."

"You can't be serious."

"Sure am. He invited me over. And I guess I wanted to, so I went. We've been at it every day since, sometimes multiple times a day."

"Jesus."

More laughter. "Yeah, I thought you would find that interesting."

"Yeah, I mean, I can't believe it. Do you want to? I mean, obviously you do. But are you going to keep doing it?"

"Doing it?"

"You know what I mean," Jason said, feeling a bit of adrenaline course through him. The slow-moving traffic was suddenly a bit less tedious. "Are you going to keep seeing him—Nichols?"

"I might not, you know, if another attorney would ever get around to asking me out ..."

How many ethical dilemmas could he be presented with in one day? "You mean Jimmy Peters?"

"Gross! Don't make me sick."

"I'm going to tell him you said that."

"No. You know who I mean."

"I, ah, guess I do."

The Prick

"Let me ask you something," Jessica purred. It really was a purr. "Do you ever look at those pictures of me, you know, like not for work?"

"Uh ..."

"David thinks you do. I think he's jealous. I told him I wasn't sure. But there are some hot ones in there, don't you think?"

It was hardly an ethical violation to state a fact in response to a direct question. "Yes," Jason said, "very hot."

"I guess David was right to be jealous." Another throaty laugh. "I may send you another one, you know, for your file or whatever. Any objection, counselor?"

"I mean, I guess not. One that you forgot to send before?"

"No, a new one. It's sent. Check your inbox."

Jason hurriedly complied.

"That's me in my new Porsche convertible," Jessica informed him. "With the top down."

"Good lord. I can see that. You didn't waste any time cashing that settlement check."

"I took it just for you. You can think about that when you're getting ready to take me to dinner tomorrow night to celebrate the settlement."

"Tomorrow?"

"Yes, counselor."

"All right," he said. It was customary to take clients out to celebrate settlements. The state bar could hardly fault him for that. "Anywhere you want."

"I like the sound of that. We can celebrate our settlement, my new car, and from what I hear, the pile of money you're going to get on the Moxley case."

Jason couldn't tear his eyes off the picture. He hoped Nichols hadn't been the photographer. The guy behind him honked at him to tell him it was his turn to move up ten feet. Jason waved his apology.

"Celebrating that case may be premature."

"Really?" she asked. "I'd think they'd stroke her a big check. How are they going to defend the case when the guy's MIA?"

Jason forgot about the picture. "What?"

"Spelkin," she said, sounding surprised. "David told me he's been missing for weeks. You didn't know?"

"Son of a bitch."

Chapter 8

Saturday, June 16th
Tulane Medical Center

"What's your opinion, Dr. Reynolds?"

"Herpes, I guess?"

"Differential diagnosis?"

"Ah ... I mean, it's herpes, isn't it?"

"What the fuck?" Robert shouted.

A crowd of white-coated persons loomed over him in a semicircle. He was completely naked from the waist down, prone on an absurdly uncomfortable twin bed. Blinding florescent white light blasted down at him. It was apparently Judgment Day. Robert grabbed a sheet and pulled it over himself.

"You people better have a goddamn good lawyer," he barked out at the white mass. "Just what in the hell do you think you're doing?"

"Dr. Reynolds, our patient seems to have rejoined the living. Judging from the state and smell of things, I would expect that he was on a bit of a bender last night, would you concur?"

"Definitely."

"He may need some orientation as to his current environs and predicament."

"Yes, Doctor."

"Provide it to him."

The Prick

One of the whitecoats stepped out of the pack. Robert's eyes felt swollen and he was having a great deal of trouble getting them to focus. He remembered once reading about visual distortion brought on by severe migraines.

"Sir," the person said, "my name is Dr. Reynolds. Do you know where you are?"

"Some level of hell inhabited by perverts."

That brought laughter from the semicircle in the background. Robert tried to glare at them all at once.

Approacher tried to work a different angle. "What is your name, sir?"

"First name A. Last name, Walking Lawsuit."

No semicircular laughter at that one. That one wasn't funny. Robert smiled. His vision was kaleidoscopic. He thought he saw the kid doctor glance back in the direction of the group, perhaps unsure of how to proceed in the face of such patient-doctor aggression. There was no response. Sink or swim.

The kid doctor elected to reroute back to the initial subject matter, geographic location. "Sir, you are in the hospital."

Robert did not respond. He had to concede, however, that this seemed correct.

"Do you know why you're here?"

"No, I don't. I assure you, however, that it's involuntary. Are you familiar with the laws regarding informed consent with respect to patient care?"

"That's enough, Dr. Reynolds. I'll take it from here," the original authoritative voice said. Robert couldn't make out which whitecoat it was but it was obviously the pack leader. The shape identified as Dr. Reynolds slunk back toward the white mass. A new one didn't emerge, and Robert was confronted with a commanding faceless voice from the void.

The Prick

"Sir, you seem rather learned for a person discovered in his own vomit and urine on Bourbon Street at four in the morning." Laughter from the group.

"You seem rather brazen for a person about to wind up on the wrong end of litigation," Robert retorted. "Kindly direct me to my clothes and the exit."

"I will chalk these threats up to your alcohol-addled mind. Your clothes, which I understand are covered in your own vomit, urine, and blood, are in a sealed bag under your bed. It is not presently advisable either that you put them on or leave the premises. You're still extremely intoxicated and dehydrated, you have two black eyes, you almost certainly have a concussion, and frankly, sir, you have an unusually aggressive case of genital herpes. At a minimum, you should sober up and allow the IV fluids to do their work. You should also remain under observation for the concussion. That is, if you value your brain."

Robert wished his attacker would separate from the school of doctors so that he could try to make him out. It was all a blur of white coats and featureless skin tones.

"Write me a prescription for whatever is curable and I'll be on my way," Robert said.

"You'll have to give us your name for that, sir. You have no ID on you."

"Ask Dr. Reynolds what my name is."

"All right, group, let's move along," the voice said. The white group edged out of focus and Robert was alone. He felt the flesh on his face and it, combined with his pounding headache, corroborated the suggestion that he had two black eyes. He felt a strong impulse to pass out again, in hopes that he would awaken upon a better reality. But he fought it. This was no place for a nameless man. He had to get out of here.

The Prick

He pushed himself up onto his elbows and pulled the sheet back. Herpes? He didn't see anything to indicate that but allowed that he couldn't really make out much of anything at all. No real reason for the gaggle of doctors to lie to him, unless that was just another part of the sadistic torture they inflicted in morning rounds on severely hungover and disoriented persons who washed up in the ER. He sighed. Which one of the godforsaken venomous whores had given him herpes? Probably most of them. The identity of the culprit was immaterial, regardless. No redressability. The back alley strip joints probably didn't have much in the way of a complaint department.

The most important thing, at present, was to extricate himself from this hellhole posthaste. He tried to puzzle out his surroundings. His eyes continued to present him with a confused map of color. He was in a white room, which, as best he could decipher, was separated by a gray curtain. Did he have a roommate?

"Hello?" Robert ventured, "Anybody there?"

No response. Robert felt for and detached the IV. He pushed himself onto his feet unsteadily, clinging to the bed's metal rails. The hospital gown tied around his neck dropped helpfully to his knees, covering up his allegedly infected business. He tied the gown around himself and threw the curtain back in an unsteady lunge, one hand still secure on the bedrail. The curtain swung to the right with a clang. Through his distorted vision, Robert made out another hospital bed with an occupant.

"Hello!" Robert shouted at that person.

No response. Robert tried to balance himself, took two careful steps across the divide, and grabbed onto the rails of his neighbor's bed.

The Prick

It was a man. White hair. Robert lowered his head within a few feet of the man's face to get a better look. Lots of wrinkles. Sallow skin. Guy didn't look good.

"You alive?" Robert inquired. No discernible reaction. He smelled terrible, the man. And that was from a person recently derided by a group of alleged medical professionals for his own odor. The guy smelled like decay and sewage. A dead man? Did they room him with a cadaver?

Robert reached out and lightly slapped a wrinkled cheek. "Anybody living in there?"

The man's eyes flitted open. They were pale, watered down, blue. They focused on Robert's face and, although everything was still blurry and confused, Robert saw the man's eyes register fear.

"No cause for alarm," Robert said.

"Who ... who are you?"

"Your roommate, apparently."

"Why are you here?"

"Involuntarily receiving medical treatment, I suppose. You?"

"Why are you in my room?"

"I could ask you the same question."

"I don't understand."

"You don't have to tell me that. That's obvious. I thought you might be dead."

"Dead?" The man's eyes widened, or at least it looked like they did.

Robert sniffed at him. "Are they not making the bedpan rounds regularly?"

"What? Who are you and why are you here?"

"This conversation is becoming a bit redundant. Listen, friend, do you know the hospital layout outside of this room? I can barely see and I need some help. What's down the hall? Where are the elevators? Maybe I can find a nurse to come clean you up."

The last bit apparently struck a chord with the man. "Nurse!" he shouted, right in Robert's face. "Nurse!" The man had surprising lung capacity for somebody plausibly mistaken for dead.

"No need for that," Robert said, backing away. The last thing he wanted was more hospital attention. "Was just trying to check on you. To make sure you were all right."

"Nurse! Nurse!"

"Just calm down," said Robert in a soft but urgent voice, retreating fully to his side of the room.

"Nurse!"

"Goddammit, shut up!"

The last "Nurse!" had apparently done the trick. Two female nurses bustled into the room. Unfortunately for Robert, they'd arrived in time to hear him shouting. One of the nurses, built like a linebacker, put a hand heavily on Robert's chest and pushed him back into the rails. "The hell you think you doing to Mr. Peterson?" The other nurse, who was strikingly diminutive by comparison to her colleague, rushed over to coo at Mr. Peterson. The bed rails dug into Robert's back. He had drawn the wrong nurse of the duo. She must be swiping steroids from the medical closet.

"Get your fucking hands off me," Robert ordered.

"You need to be quiet and get back in bed right now," the nurse said, keeping her hand firmly on his chest.

"He's in my room!" Mr. Peterson yelled.

"The man's a delusional idiot."

"He said I was dead!" Mr. Peterson cried out.

"Did you threaten him?" The bodybuilding nurse asked Robert threateningly.

"Far from it. I was just checking on him. I said he looked dead. Look at him!"

The Prick

"That's enough!" yelled the other nurse who had been cooing at Mr. Peterson. "You're being abusive."

"I'm the one being abused," Robert retorted. "Tell your large colleague here to get her paws off me."

In response, the musclebound nurse gave Robert a rough shove. Robert lost his balance and fell backwards across the bed, slamming his head against the rail on the bed's opposite side as his legs flailed up in the air. A jolt of pain shot through Robert's body and his vision became completely white.

"You bitch!" he yelled out, and kicked out as hard as he could with his right foot, which made solid contact with something that felt like a face. He could see nothing and was fighting for consciousness. The last thing he heard was "Oh, God! Security! Security!"

The Prick

Chapter 9

Saturday, June 16th
Weston, Brenson & Alps, LLP

"I told you," Weston said. "You may want to call Maggie to apologize."

Jason was back in Weston's office, seated in what might have been Bobby Jones's chair or whatever the hell. Weston worked most Saturdays until about 2:30 p.m., which Weston had told him approximately six times. Jason had tried to call Weston with the Spelkin news the night before, but Weston's timid assistant had timidly told him that Weston had left for the night. And the man was impossible to reach by cell phone.

Jason had just downloaded the news to Weston, naming Rossi as the informant but leaving out the part about his potential—client?—dinner that night with her. And nothing, of course, about the convertible picture. Weston was smiling at him smugly, like he had known all along that Spelkin was missing.

"This has nothing to do with what Maggie did," Jason said. "She still willfully destroyed damning evidence."

"You don't seem to care as much now that you know the defamation lawsuit is a complete bluff. Which, as I recall, is exactly what I told you."

Jason nodded at that. "Trent lied to my face."

The Prick

"Well, what a surprise!" Weston said, throwing his hands in the air. "Maybe we don't need to rush to tell her *our* bad facts when she's going out of her way to misrepresent hers. And trying to intimidate you with horseshit motions."

There was something to that, Jason had to admit. Why should he play by the rules when nobody else was? If everyone is cheating but you, chances are you're going to lose.

"You should call Maggie to apologize," Weston said again. "She was very upset."

"I'll go see her."

"Today," Weston demanded. "We don't want her running off to retain some other lawyer."

"Yeah, you're right. I've had similar problems with her in the past."

*****

Jason pulled into the Moxleys' driveway. He parked behind an aged blue Dodge pickup truck that he could only assume belonged to the resident behemoth.

This was going to be a surprise visit, unfortunately. Maggie wasn't picking up her phone. Jason had called about fifteen times, like a jilted high school girl. After call number fifteen went unanswered, he decided to just look up her address and drive out to her house.

Jason was dressed to impress because he had his Rossi dinner later that evening in Buckhead. After some deliberation, he'd selected one of his newest gray suits, which his tailor had assured him was very stylish. As it turned out, it was hard to decide what to wear to a dinner with a former/current client who might or might not be trying to sleep with you and whom you definitely wanted to sleep with but knew you shouldn't for various reasons, including certain ethical rules. So, the suit, sans tie.

The Prick

Probably not particularly suitable attire for *this* visit, however. Jason got out of the car and squeezed between the pickup truck and the small patch of unkempt lawn, which had clearly not been mowed in months. Jason had to contort his body uncomfortably to avoid brushing up against Pete's unwashed truck.

He knocked on the metal screen door. He could hear the TV blaring inside. There was definitely somebody home. He pushed the doorbell but didn't hear it sound.

"Hello!" he called out and pounded on the metal door with his fist.

"In a goddamn minute!" a male voice sounded from inside.

In roughly three to four minutes, the interior door opened, and Pete loomed in the doorway with a scowl, Keystone Light in hand. He had a ragged, uncovered cut on his forehead.

Pete snorted when he recognized Jason. "The teenage lawyer. What are you doing here? She owe you money?"

Jason didn't have it in him to try to explain a contingency fee agreement again to Pete, who seemed well on his way to intoxication. "Nothing like that. Just need to talk to Maggie. Is she here?"

Pete laughed and pushed open the screen door to let him in. "She's here, all right. But good luck talking to her. Hasn't left the bathroom for almost a day. Got the door locked and won't come out. I've had to piss in the goddamn kitchen sink," he said, gesturing to a sink half full of dishes. Jason tried to keep his expression free of loathing and disgust.

"Can I go try to talk to her?"

"Uh-huh. Be my guest," Pete pivoted his prodigious bulk to let Jason pass and took a swig of Keystone. "Better you than me, buddy. You lose her case or something?"

"No."

The Prick

"Must be on her period or some shit, then. You know how they are."

"Hmm."

"Well the bathroom is just down the hall there," Pete said, pointing. "You need me, I'll be in the living room."

"She's been in there since last night?"

Pete nodded, walking back to the living room and the TV, his voice trailing off. "All night and all goddamn day. Not a fuckin' word except 'Go away.' Real nice, right?" He settled back into his chair with the remote, mumbling to himself something along the lines of "Can't believe I have to put up with this shit."

Jason walked down the dimly lit hallway and saw on the left a small and messy bedroom with clothes strewn all over the floor. Adjacent to the bedroom, at the end of the hallway, was a closed door.

He knocked gently. "Maggie," he said softly, "Are you in there?"

No response.

"Maggie, it's Jason. We need to talk."

Jason heard some movement in the bathroom, shuffling sounds, but there was no verbal response.

"Listen, I know you're there. I'm ... sorry about yesterday. I shouldn't have lost my temper like that."

There were some muted feminine sounds. Knowing his client, Jason was sure they were crying or crying-related.

"I was just upset," Jason started hesitantly, "because of the texts ..." More whimpering sounds with increasing volume. Wrong direction. "*But,* I have some good news. Some potentially really good news...so you should come out of there so that we can talk."

"I thought I had ruined the case, and gotten everyone in trouble," Maggie finally said in a small pathetic voice. "You said that."

The Prick

That wasn't *exactly* what he had said, but it was in the ballpark. "Things may have changed."

"What?"

"Come out of there and I'll tell you."

There was a sigh. And then silence.

Jason waited about thirty seconds. "Maggie?"

"I took some pills," Maggie said. "Some of the pills that Pete gets from Doug at work."

"What? Jesus Christ, what?"

"I think I'm going to take some more. Pete won't care."

"Do *not* do that, Maggie." Jason turned and yelled down the hall, "Pete, get down here!"

"What?" Pete yelled over the TV.

"Get the fuck down here!"

"Give the money to Kate, okay?" Maggie said from behind the door. "Whatever money comes from the lawsuit."

"It doesn't work like that," Jason said. "Pete!"

"In a goddamn minute!" Pete shouted back.

"Maggie, what pills did you take?" Jason asked, trying to sound calm. "Please tell me what you took and please don't take any more, okay?"

"Oxy something. Pete takes them a lot."

"Please unlock the door."

"Just give the money to Kate and her kids. Don't let Pete get it all."

"That's not my decision to—there is no case without you, Maggie. You need to please open the door."

"I'm sorry," she said, "for all of it."

"It's all going to work out."

No response.

"Maggie? Maggie! Open the door! Pete!"

"The fuck do you want?" Pete yelled from down the hall. "Come in and shout at me in my own house, why don'tcha."

The Prick

"What pills do you have in the bathroom?"

"Lots of them," Pete yelled back. There was some network sitcom blasting from the TV.

Jason knocked on the door again. "Maggie. Maggie, please open the door. Maggie."

There was no response. Jason made a quick decision. He took a few steps back and flung himself into the door, leading with his left shoulder. There were a few cracks. He did it again. A few more cracks, but the door was still in the frame.

"The fuck is going on down there?" Pete shouted.

"Get down here and help me!" Jason yelled, ramming his shoulder back into the door. The top of the door cracked satisfyingly and separated a little from the frame. Jason stepped back and kicked it with his right foot as hard as he could. It smashed open and he rushed through. Maggie was on the floor in nothing but her underwear, with her back against the bathtub. She was looking at him wide-eyed. She shrieked and covered her breasts with her hands.

"Did you take them?" Jason demanded.

She stared at him.

"Where are they?"

"In ... in the cabinet."

There was only one cabinet, and it was above the sink far out of Maggie's reach. Jason looked at it for a moment, and then back down to Maggie cupping her mammoth breasts on the floor.

"How many did you take? We need to get you to a hospital."

"I, um, only took one."

"*One*? Jesus Christ, Maggie. I just broke the door down."

Maggie started to well up.

"Don't you dare start crying."

The Prick

"I'm sorry," Maggie said, "I just wanted to make you go away. So that I could be alone."

"You thought pretending you were about to commit suicide was going to make me leave?"

Maggie shrugged. Jason grabbed a towel off the rack and tossed it to her. She wrapped it around herself and sat up a little straighter.

"I'm so embarrassed."

"About which part?" Jason asked. There were a lot to choose from. Maggie's face got red. But she adjusted the towel, deliberately opening and shutting it to give him another quick topless shot. They were just huge. Maggie looked at Jason and Jason tried to look at the ceiling. Then he heard the flow of liquid behind him and turned to see Pete urinating into the toilet.

Pete made eye contact with him and shook his head reprovingly. "You know you're paying for this fucking door, right? Come into my house, yell at me, break down my goddamn door, and then perv out at my naked wife. You got some balls, kid," he said, spitting into the sink. "Some fucking balls."

"You can take it out of what you owe me in fees," Jason said. Pete snorted and spit in the sink again. The urination continued unabated.

Jason turned back to Maggie, who was staring at him with sort of—almost—a Mona Lisa smile.

"Spelkin's missing," he told her.

*****

Robert woke up on a cement floor. He stared at the ceiling and noticed that his vision was no longer beehive-ish. His headache, however, was blinding, and the rest of his body felt like it had been hit by a truck. With great effort he lifted his head off the cement and saw that his hospital gown

263

had been replaced by an orange jumpsuit. His situation hadn't improved since his last bout with consciousness.

He pushed himself to a sitting position. He was in a cell with no windows and a steel door. There was a shiny metal bench attached to the wall and a shiny metal toilet. By the grace of God, he was the only occupant of the room. Something in the cell smelled terrible and Robert suspected he was not without blame in that department.

He pulled his knees in to try to stand up.

"Oh fuck," Robert said.

His fingertips were black. They had ink on them. The bastards had taken his fingerprints. He had to get out of here before they figured out who he was. Before they found him. Fingerprinting was a requirement of bar admission. His fingers were on the grid.

Robert slowly and gingerly pushed himself to his feet. He swayed, thinking he might either faint, throw up, or both simultaneously. But he soldiered on to the door. He leaned against the concrete wall and slapped his palm on the metal door. It made a horrible clanging sound, but he kept at it.

"Shut the fuck up!" came from down the hall.

"Medical emergency!" Robert called out.

"Sergeant, the inmate in cell 204B is up," a different voice said.

"Go check on him."

"I'm saying, I've got a medical emergency, too," said the first voice.

Robert heard footsteps coming toward him. A slat opened in the door at eye level and Robert was partially face-to-face with an angry-looking deputy built like a pit bull.

"Back away from the door, inmate."

Robert complied.

The Prick

The door opened. The deputy entered, looking extremely large. He was black, as wide as a lineman with pads on, and intentionally bald. He wore a Taser around his belt. Not that he likely ever needed it.

"Sit on the bench, inmate."

Robert complied, finding his new title deeply troubling.

"What's the medical emergency?" the deputy asked. He had a clipboard.

"Extreme dehydration."

The deputy raised his eyebrows. "You thirsty? That's the emergency?"

"It's a serious medical condition."

The deputy took a pen out of his pocket. "Okay, I'll put down 'thirsty' on the form, inmate." He wrote something which may or may not have been "thirsty." That accomplished, he raised his eyes to Robert again. "State your name."

Robert looked at him for a few seconds. "I may pass out," he said. "I need some water, please."

The deputy glared. "Name,"

"Water, please,"

The deputy put the pen back in his pocket. "You don't got a name, you ain't nobody. You ain't nobody, you don't need no water."

"I could die," Robert said.

The deputy nodded. "My cousin at the hospital said you wouldn't give a name. She said you broke her friend's nose. What I think—I think you got a record, I think you got outstanding warrants. But don't worry, we gonna figure all that out."

"I need to call a lawyer," Robert said.

The deputy smiled and walked out of the room. "How you gonna call a lawyer without a name?" The steel door slammed shut with a terrible bang.

The Prick

*****

Jason had made a reservation at Bones, a first-rate steakhouse on Piedmont Road in Buckhead. It was the kind of place you could take a client, or a date, and thus fit the bill perfectly. Given that Rossi had already put her hand on his thigh under the table three times—noticeably closer to his business each time—and the appetizers hadn't even arrived, Jason judged that she perhaps didn't consider this a strictly professional gathering. He was still a bit shaken up from his first encounter with a faux suicide, or what do they call it, a "cry for help," however, and had other things on his mind.

Jason took a sip of his whiskey. He had ordered Knob Creek, neat, as that seemed like a manly thing to do in a steakhouse with a hot blonde who occasionally put her hand on your thigh, just over an hour after you'd broken down a bathroom door to prevent a suicide that wasn't actually happening. He was drinking it too quickly, though. Present circumstances were conspiring to require the exercise of considerable discretion and willpower.

"Did you know Maggie well when you two worked together?" he asked Rossi. She was on her second, quite expensive, glass of champagne.

She looked bored by the question. "Not really. She kept to herself. Was quiet."

"Did you think her behavior was ... strange? Or did other people around the office say that?"

Rossi drained her glass and Jason fought back a wince. $18 a glass, down the hatch. "Let's not talk about your other clients," she said. "It makes me jealous." There was that hand again. It was definitely closer. By a few solid inches. "Tonight is about us," she said, leaning in.

The Prick

"All right," Jason said. He was glad the tablecloth was covering her advances. "Are you still seeing David?"

"Seeing him?"

Jason laughed. "Not this game again. We're in public. You know what I mean."

She shrugged. "On and off. It's not as much fun now that, you know, we're allowed to."

"Does he know that I know?"

"Yeah. He said he didn't care. He said not even you could make up a bullshit claim about a consensual sexual relationship between two people who don't even work together." She smiled. "David's funny."

"Yeah, hilarious."

"Boy is he mad at you."

Jason grimaced. The waiter arrived.

"Oooh, the oysters are here!" Rossi said. She had ordered a dozen. "I'll have another glass," she told the waiter.

"The same, miss?" the waiter asked.

"We'll just take the bottle," Jason interjected. Might as well save the $20.

The waiter smiled at him. "Very good, sir."

"We're celebrating," Rossi informed him. The waiter nodded and left, and Rossi turned her attention to the oysters.

"Here," she said, putting one on his plate. "They're Blue Point, my favorite." She sucked one down. "And you know what they're good for."

"What's that?" Jason asked with a smile.

"Let me see if they're working," she replied. This time her hand made no stops and ran all the way down his leg right to his crotch. Jason just sat there, not sure exactly how to handle it. He looked at the other tables around him but nobody seemed to notice. The tablecloth hid everything.

The Prick

"Hmm," Rossi said. "Seems like they're working just fine." She gave a squeeze and got up suddenly. "I need to use the restroom. Too much champagne and excitement. Don't let them pop the bottle without me." She swayed away. Jason watched her and watched all the men in the restaurant watch her.

He went straight back to his iPhone and read the rule again,

> Rule 1.8(j) A lawyer shall not have sexual relations with a client unless a consensual sexual relationship existed between them when the client-lawyer relationship commenced.

He had read the rule five times that day with growing discomfort. There wasn't a lot of give to this particular rule. The key would be establishing that she was no longer a client.

Yeah, that's it, convince your inebriated client/date that she is no longer your client so you're free to fuck her in compliance with the rules. That should go over nicely with the panel of impotent elderly lawyers who'll be conducting the inevitable disciplinary hearing. But his representation of her really was over—although she kept referring to him as her lawyer and referring to herself as a client. It was almost as if she was making a point of doing that, in fact.

Jason was Googling the application of Rule 1.8(j) to former clients when Rossi returned. "I'm back," she announced. Jason quickly pocketed his phone.

"So, what's next for you?" Jason said.

"I think I might eat some more oysters." The waiter came and popped the champagne, and Rossi held her glass out for the refill.

"Are you going to go back to work?"

The Prick

Rossi downed half her glass and grabbed another oyster. "Well, we certainly didn't get enough money for me to retire. But I'm going to take a few months off until I look for work again."

"That sounds good," Jason said, ignoring the not-so-subtle complaint about the settlement amount. "Are you going to go back to legal work?"

She smiled. "Are you offering me a position?"

"Ah ..."

"You must have liked what you heard about my skillset under David."

"I mean ..."

Her hand was back on his leg, but in a much more PG location. "I don't think we should work together, counsel," she purred at him. "I think we should fuck and then see what happens next."

"That's ... quite direct," Jason sputtered.

"And grabbing your junk a few minutes ago wasn't?"

"Decent point."

"You ever hook up with one of your clients before?" Rossi asked with a mischievous smile. "Certainly not poor Maggie."

"Um, no. About the client part of that, Jessica, technically I would say that we—our—relationship is no longer attorney/client, just because, unless you need further representation, you know, the case you retained me on is now over." Ouch. Very articulate, idiot.

Rossi drained her third glass and poured herself a fourth. "You don't want to be my attorney anymore?"

"Well, just because—"

Rossi laughed. "You're so nervous, counsel. Relax. I know about Rule 1.8. You're fine."

"What? You do?"

The Prick

"Of course," Rossi said, running her hand up and down his thigh and sipping champagne. "David sent me the rule and an article about it when he heard we were going to dinner."

Jason took a big sip of whiskey. "I see," he said. Somehow, that was not comforting.

"He's sooo jealous," Rossi said. "He thinks we're going to fuck." She took her hand off his leg to take the last oyster.

"He does?"

"Ummm-hmmm." She downed the oyster in one swallow and dispensed with the last of her fourth glass with the same dispatch.

"Why?"

"I told him that I thought you were going to try to fuck me," Rossi said. Her hand ran back down his leg and settled in on his crotch again. "Are you?"

Jason drank the last of his whiskey. "That certainly seems to be the question."

The Prick

Chapter 10

Monday, June 18th
New Orleans Superior Court

"Your Honor, the next case is the State versus Robert Spelkin."

Robert was seated in the pews behind the public defenders' table. The courtroom deputy motioned for him to stand. Just an hour earlier, the gigantic, khakied clipboard-wielding harbinger who'd so kindly responded to Robert's medical emergency, had gleefully explained to Robert that they had indeed figured out Robert's identity. The jailhouse deputy's exact phrasing was, "Oh, yeah, we got yo' ass." Robert tried to appear stoic but his insides felt like a plummeting elevator. It was only a matter of time before Atlanta knew where he was. The key was to try to extricate himself from Louisiana's atavistic criminal system and flee before they sent someone to collect him. Posthaste.

Not that he would have to go back, necessarily, if they found him. But it would be easier to fly further into the nothingness if he wasn't forced to confront anyone who knew his former self.

So here he was, back in a courtroom. Robert stood up and shuffled the few steps up to the table. He was wearing the same orange jumpsuit, his eyes were purple and puffy, and he hadn't showered in days. He looked, he was confident, the part of a typical Bourbon Street arrestee.

271

The Prick

The man who'd announced his name, a middle-aged, balding prosecutor, stood behind the bench on the other side of the courtroom. He was the kind of middling non-achiever that Robert had always looked down upon. Pushing papers in a government job until he racked up sufficient years for a pension. This man, this unimportant mite voicing his name, was singularly demonstrative of how far down the societal rungs Robert had fallen. The system had gotten him in its teeth and mid-level government stooges wearing off-the-rack suits felt empowered to summon him to answer for his sins.

The courtroom was packed, though, thankfully, not because of Robert. This was a preliminary hearing, and various and sundry charges were being levied against various and sundry lost souls, easily identified in like orange jumpsuits, and their families were there to cry about it, or shake their heads at the injustice, or look on passively because they were used to it. The prosecutor had already rattled off about twenty names in steady monotone. The charges were read and the potential consequences discussed, some pleas were taken, and some bails were set. Most of the pleas were guilty, worked out with the prosecution beforehand. The judge, a portly black man with glasses, was slumped back in his chair, looking bored. Just another day on the job and so forth.

Robert sidled up next to the public defender, who was a diminutive young black man bursting with energy and overcome with righteous indignation that any charges had ever been brought against anyone ever. Robert guessed he had been on the job for less than a year. Eventually, the system would beat his energy out of him. But, for now, every time a defendant he represented pled not guilty, the young man launched into theatrics about the injustice of the charge, the lack of probable cause, the defendant's status in the community and strength of character, and how bail should be set low, if at all. He invoked the United States Constitution with regularity and familiarity. The judge was obviously annoyed with him, and obviously had been annoyed with him on previous occasions.

The public defender had tried to consult with Robert before this hearing. Robert had told him precisely where he could stick his advice. The public defender had looked disappointed in him but left without much of a fight, shaking his head.

"Case Number 024042," the prosecutor continued, "charge of aggravated battery."

The judge cast a disinterested look at the public defender. "Has the defendant been duly apprised of the nature of the offense and the potential consequences of conviction?"

The tiny public defender was standing bolt upright, getting every inch out of his frame. "No, Your Honor. Mr. Spelkin has declined representation from the public defender's office."

The judge sighed deeply. "Do you have other representation, Mr. Spelkin? In other words, have you hired an attorney?"

"I will be representing myself against this baseless charge, Your Honor. And then I will be suing the state for wrongful and malicious prosecution."

The judge sat up a bit in his chair and raised his eyebrows at the prosecutor.

"Are you aware of the elements of the charge of aggravated battery, Mr. Spelkin?"

"My previous understanding was that it consisted of an offensive or wrongful touching resulting in grievous bodily damage of such an egregious nature that criminal liability is appropriate."

The Prick

"Hmm," said the judge.

"But now, apparently," Robert continued, "it's charged when a man is acting in self-defense after being assaulted by an individual outweighing him by about a hundred pounds."

The judge looked back at the prosecutor, who was staring at Robert.

"Mr. Faugno? What are the background facts in this case?"

The prosecutor looked down at his file. "Apparently, Your Honor, Mr. Spelkin here broke the nose of a *nurse* in the emergency room by ... kicking her in the face. A *female nurse*." He had obviously been happy to find the words "nurse" and "female" in the file description and leaned on them heavily.

"I see," the judge said.

"That *nurse* may have been *female*, Your Honor, but she was built like a truck." There was laughter behind Robert in the pews. "I was merely defending myself any way I could after she shoved me over my own hospital bed with considerable force, her full weight behind her. And I doubt very much that her jaw is broken, even if that's what Mr. Faugno is able to make out from his clearly extensive investigation."

"Self-defense?" The judge said, clearly amused. "Did the nurse give you those two shiners?"

"She charged me like a bull, Your Honor," Robert said. More laughter. "I think the black eyes were a preexisting condition but she didn't help the matter any. Incredibly, she assaulted me after I was admitted in the hospital following a vicious attack on Bourbon Street. Mr. Faugno should check his file to see if there is anything in there about same. I will certainly be investigating whether that *nurse*, whose name I did not happen to catch, has had prior rage-induced physical altercations with the people for whom she is supposed to be providing care."

"Mr. Spelkin," the judge said, "I get the sense that you might have a legal background."

"It says here, Your Honor," Faugno interjected, "that Mr. Spelkin is a lawyer practicing in Atlanta. He refused to give his name, but we discovered it in running his prints."

The judge looked back to Robert. "Is this true?"

"Yes, Your Honor." No point now in trying to hide from it.

"At what firm?"

"Levitt, Bennett and Taylor."

Everyone in the courtroom was one Google away from figuring that out. The judge raised his eyebrows at the name. The firm had an office in New Orleans. "Position?"

"Partner."

Now all the lawyers were staring at him. The spritely young public defender's jaw had dropped slightly. This had the makings of a scandal.

"Hmm. May I assume, Mr. Spelkin, that you will have representation going forward in this matter?"

"Well, Your Honor, I would think that Mr. Faugno will soon drop the charge after he's bothered to do some investigation. But if he insists on pursuing this, I certainly will retain competent counsel and would appreciate any recommendations in that regard." What he was going to do —with great alacrity—was retain a competent car and drive it the fuck to Mexico.

"I cannot recommend defense counsel from the bench," the judge said. "But I'm sure you'll have no problem finding a criminal defense attorney here in New Orleans." He turned back to the prosecutor, "Any priors?"

"No, Your Honor, not that we found...ah..."

"Suggested bail?" the judge interrupted.

The Prick

"Twenty-five thousand dollars."

"Bail is set at five thousand dollars," the judge ordered. "Get yourself an attorney, Mr. Spelkin. Plea hearing is set for two weeks."

"Thank you, Your Honor," Spelkin said. He turned to make his way back to the holding cell and hopefully a quick call to a bail bondsman. Out of the corner of his eye, he saw someone who looked vaguely familiar looming in the back corner of the crowded courtroom. Shit. Don't look. Just keep walking, head down.

He looked. It was Rebecca Trent. She smiled at him.

*****

Robert was not surprised when, within an hour of returning to the cell, the massive deputy came around to tell him that he had made bail. Robert had been so sure that Trent was going to stroke a check for his bail the minute he was escorted from the courtroom that he hadn't even called a bondsman. The deputy had a sour expression, not pleased at being the bearer of what he thought was good news. The game was over and it had been a lot less fun than anticipated. But he did seem to take some pleasure in discovering that the news of bail didn't brighten Robert's day.

"You ain't happy to be gettin' out?"

"It's worse out there than it is in here."

The deputy grunted and gestured toward the hallway. Robert walked in front of him and stopped in front of the locked door leading to the building's entrance. The deputy inched close to him and looked him in eye, issuing him an intimidation stare that he had doubtless administered to many jumpsuited persons over the years.

"Don't you be hitting any females," the deputy said in a low baritone.

"I'll leave them alone as long as they leave me alone," Robert said. "Feel like opening the door?"

"You cocky motherfucker, you're going to get yours." The deputy pushed open the door. Rebecca Trent was standing on the other side, smiling. There was a very large man next to her. Robert didn't recognize him, but he looked dumb and dangerous. He was dressed in black, like he was trying to mimic Johnny Cash, he wore a diamond earring, and his blond hair was pulled back in a ponytail. He looked at Robert with scorn.

"Looks like you're right," Robert said to the deputy.

"Hi, Robert," Trent said, "how's it going?"

Trent had an Escalade waiting outside, and they drove to her hotel. The large man with the ponytail sat with them in the back. Other than Trent directing the driver to take them to the hotel, nobody said a word. The SUV pulled into the hotel driveway.

"Let's go," Trent said.

Robert complied without a word, trailing her. The large man walked behind him and seemed intent on keeping him within arm's distance. Robert didn't care for the way the man looked at him. It was a look of ownership. People in the lobby stopped and stared at Robert, still in his orange jumpsuit. There had been no clothes for him to change into as the outfit he sported into the misadventure had been consigned to a hospital HazMat bin. Trent briskly walked him to the front desk. There was a room reserved in his name. The clerk, wide-eyed and pimply, quickly issued the keycards, and Robert got to the elevator as fast as he could. The doors closed on a room full of stares.

Trent led the way off the elevator and stopped at the door to his room. "There are fresh clothes for you inside," she said. "Go in, shower, put yourself together, and lose the jumpsuit. Jesse here is going to wait outside the door for you."

It was the first time the man had been identified. Robert nodded and looked at his new jailer. "Is that necessary?" Robert had in mind his hotel room at the Crowne Plaza, the bag of cash in the safe, and an expeditious exit.

Trent smiled. "Very much so. Jesse here works for the bail bondsman. I explained that you're a flight risk, and the firm has paid a premium for him to make sure you don't run off somewhere, you know, in the middle of the night without telling anyone where you're going."

Robert sighed.

"Now go inside and get cleaned up," Trent said. "I'll be back in an hour."

"Don't try anything stupid," Jesse said.

"This isn't necessary," Robert said to Trent.

She handed him a key card. "Forty-five minutes. Don't make me send Jesse in there after you."

Robert sighed again and pushed into his room. He had come to New Orleans for complete freedom and now he was the ward of a ponytailed imbecile named Jesse.

The door closed behind him. He was immediately grateful to be alone, and in a somewhat civilized place. This beat jail, even if it wasn't the hotel room he wanted.

He walked into the bedroom portion of the room and saw a pile of clothes on the bed. On top of the pile was a manila folder. He opened it.

"That fucking manipulative bitch."

Inside the folder were pictures of his children. They were recent. His daughter at her ballet recital. His son at bat in a baseball game. The two of them eating dinner, not looking at the camera, a candid shot. Who the hell had taken this? Not his frigid wife, surely, if she'd known it was for him. Unless she thought maybe it would hurt him.

The Prick

He held each picture a few seconds, dropped it, picked it back up, and stared at it again. He was crying now, which he hated because it meant he was weak, and because he knew that was exactly what Trent had wanted when she'd left this emotional landmine perched innocently on top of the clothes. The droplets hit the pictures and rolled onto the sleeves of the goddamn jumpsuit.

"Jesus Christ," he said, looking, really for the first time, at the thing he was wearing. The highlighter orange shame outfit. Holding a picture of a little girl he had named spinning in a ballerina outfit, just bursting with innocence, while he was in a jumpsuit made for murderers and rapists. He took it off and hurled it at the wall. He was naked now.

There was a note in the folder. He picked it up, crying harder and shaking. It was written in pink and red crayon.

I miss Daddy when he goes away. I want him to come home soon. I love my Daddy.

Underneath was a stick figure with a briefcase, standing next to a smaller stick figure in a skirt.

It was too much.

He shoved the letter and the pictures away from him. Still sobbing, he walked into the bathroom. He turned the faucet on so the cretin outside wouldn't hear him breaking down and threw water at his face. "Pull your fucking self together," he said. But he couldn't. He saw his reflection in the mirror. Beat up and ragged and without any self-worth or self-control. Not a free Dionysian man living without inhibition but a cowardly, rejected wretch.

Then he thought about it. Made himself think about it. The Destroyer. The thing that he had been running from more than anything. The blackness in the back of his skull. What had happened that night? He didn't know. He had no memory. He didn't think himself capable of the accusations, but something about them seemed eerily resonant, like they were receiving a signal of acknowledgment deep within the nastier, baser, primitive parts of him. His raw animal desire for power and dominance. Maybe, unchecked, he would demand to be blown by some small, nothing person with an insistence approaching sexual assault. But, no. He couldn't have done that. He tried to force his brain to remember not doing it or, failing that, to deny the possibility. But there was resistance. His brain refused to not believe he could do such a thing. And when he tried to recall an actual memory of what happened after the bar, there was nothing. Only a void.

He glared at his image in the mirror. And then he threw his face down into the pool of water. "Fuck you!" he screamed, face fully immersed in the water. "*Fuck you!*" It bubbled up.

He faintly heard pounding on the door.

Robert pulled his head out of the water and stared at himself in the mirror again. His face was red and purple, swollen. Monstrous.

"I'm fine!" he shouted at the pounding. It stopped.

Robert looked at himself again. And he decided. He wasn't going to Mexico. He wasn't going to be weak anymore. He was going back home. He was going to fight. He was going to get the people who'd done this to him.

The Prick

Chapter 11

Monday, June 18th
The Law Offices of Jason Hunter, Esq.

Jason was simultaneously exhausted and elated. Too
elated to let anything bother him. He didn't even mind that
Pete Moxley, who seemed to have taken the day off work to
berate him to his face, had insinuated that he was a pussy,
kept mentioning how Jason should pay for his bathroom
door, and spit chewing tobacco into one of the two potted
plants that Jason had bought from Home Depot in an effort
to spruce the place up before Richard Weston deigned to set
foot in it. Minor, temporary annoyances.

Thanks to Moxley and the missing Spelkin, he was going
to make a killing. He was going to get the fuck out of this
office. He would leave the potted plants. The next down-on-
his-luck jackass could have them. He'd move to a chic office
in a Midtown building. Hire an assistant and maybe a junior
lawyer and start a firm that would still bear his name when
his grandchildren had grandchildren.

On the wave of that optimism and supremely positive
worldview he had spent the weekend gloating and having
copious amounts of sex with his former—probably,
hopefully former—client Jessica Rossi. They had ordered in,
watched movies, talked some about the future, and, mostly,
explored different ways of fucking each other. Fucking was a
vulgar term for it, of course, but there was no other accurate

The Prick

way of describing what went on. If Jason had violated Rule 1.8, he had done so in a variety of ways, some of them quite creative. And he had done so with a smile on his face.

Despite the fact that several of the main characters in the Moxley drama were in his cramped office, Jason found his mind frequently drifting to some of the weekend highlights. He forced himself to tune back into the redneck, who appeared to be wrapping up his closing remarks.

"All I'm sayin' is, you gotta let these people know you mean business. You can't be worried about this and that, who sent what text or whatever, you've gotta just stay in their fuckin' face, you know? Let them see you ain't goin' nowhere."

"I understand what you're saying," Jason responded. "These things take some time."

Jason took some pleasure out of Weston's expression of obvious disbelief that he, Richard Weston, was sharing the same oxygen as this man, who was surely the son of a pig farmer. Weston hadn't said a word since Pete had started his little opus. He had just stared at him as if encountering a different species for the first time. Redneck Galapagos.

"Uh-huh," Pete said, "seems to me like y'all could've gotten us some money by now if you had just put your shoulder into it. I know you know how to fucking do that," he said, glaring at Jason. Jason took this to be another subtle reference to the broken bathroom door.

Weston decided to try his hand. "Look, ah, Mr. Moxley, it—"

"Call me Pete."

"Very well, Pete," Weston said, adopting a professorial tone. "The litigation process can be very complex and lengthy. There are many procedural niceties that need to be addressed before any real substantive progress is made. The typical life cycle of a particular litigation, depending on the facts, the parties, the complexity of the issues, and the litigiousness of the parties, can take many years. While I know it seems like this is taking some time, we are actually very close to the beginning of a—"

"We gotta show them we mean business!" Pete slammed his hand on Jason's desk. "Enough is enough! We need to see some movement!"

Weston visibly recoiled. He clearly wasn't accustomed to being interrupted or yelled at, and certainly not both at the same time. He turned his shocked expression to Jason. Jason smiled back. *You wanted to take on this case, esteemed Richard Weston.*

"That's what we're doing, Pete," Jason said. "That's why we're all sitting here today. We're going to discuss our plan for showing them we mean business."

"Awright. That's what we need to do."

"Good. So here's the plan. We've been holding off on pushing depositions in this case, both because we were unsure of how to handle the text-message issue and because we wanted to get some document requests out. Now, given that Spelkin is missing and apparently on the run, we'll ask to depose Spelkin immediately. They won't be able to produce him and we'll file a motion to compel his deposition. Trent, the opposing counsel, will have to explain to the judge why she can't make Spelkin available. This will force them to admit to the court and to us that he can't be found. That should drive settlement quickly. We have the only witness. They can't contradict Maggie's testimony."

"How you know he's missing, again?" asked Pete.

Jason cleared his throat. "Another client. It's not important. What's important is that they can't produce him, they have no one to tell their story, and that should definitely drive settlement."

"How much?" Pete said.

"At this point, I wouldn't recommend settling for anything under seven figures," Jason said. For the first time since he had met him, Jason saw Pete smile.

"Well, awright, then," Pete said.

"So at least a million dollars?" Maggie asked. She was smiling too.

"I don't know if they'll pay that," Jason said, glancing at Weston, "but I wouldn't recommend settling for anything less than that, given what we currently know, unless Spelkin reappears. Which is why, if he's on the lam, we want to push things forward quickly."

"Will I have to give a deposition?" Maggie asked, nervously.

"Maybe. If we ask for Spelkin's deposition, my bet is that they'll want to take yours."

"Oh."

"Nothing to worry about," Jason said. "You'll just have to tell the truth." At least 75 percent of the people in the room knew The Truth was actually something to worry about. But Jason was going to cross that bridge when he came to it. For now, it was time to ramp up the pressure on Trent, her smug face, and her Jason-bane manila folders. Jason wondered how much of the actual truth Maggie had disclosed to Pete after the big blowup in Weston's office. She had obviously told him that texts to her sister had been deleted. Whether she'd told him what those texts had actually said was another story. Jason's money was on nondisclosure.

"Just answer a few questions, say what happened, and get out of there, right?" Pete said.

"That's about the long and short of it," Jason said. He was done with this meeting. Recently arrived was an email from Jessica Rossi with no subject line and an attachment. Time to get everyone on their way and have a look. He could only handle the Moxleys and his royal highness for limited quantities of time under the best of circumstances anyway.

"So," he said, "that's the plan. We'll move forward and let you know as soon as we hear anything. You have anything else, Richard?" Weston shook his head, likely still stewing with indignation over Pete's lack of respect.

"Okay, then," Jason said, "let's get you all on your way."

Pete stood up. "Good work," he said. Jason smiled at the compliment. He could see the dollar signs in Pete's eyes. Jason had finally said something that made Pete feel good.

"Thank you," Maggie said. She hadn't mentioned the faux-suicide night the entire time she'd been in the office, not even to apologize or to attempt an explanation. Jason could still picture her on the floor in the bathroom. As a courtesy to her, he hadn't mentioned it, either. He was no longer angry. After the weekend he'd had, he wasn't angry with anyone or anything. And prior to the meeting, Weston had lectured him about being more gentle with her. He didn't buy that Moxley was as fragile as she was making out. Not at all. But it was coming through loud and clear that she was mentally ill. Nuts. And she was a million-dollar asset. So, from here on out, he would handle with care.

Pete and Maggie exited. They were such an unattractive couple, Jason observed, despite himself. Weston stayed seated and waited until the door audibly closed. Jason looked at him, annoyed. He wanted to check out the Jessica attachment.

"The man's a Neanderthal," Weston complained.

"He is," Jason said. "Maggie has a knack for surrounding herself with abusive men." A little pop psych and maybe Weston would also exit.

"She really needs to lose some weight," Weston said, shaking his head. He gave no indication that he intended to leave.

The Prick

The door chime sounded, signaling that someone had come back in. It was Maggie, sans Neanderthal.

"Hi, Jason, hi, Richard," she started, breathlessly, "I just forgot to ask you one question. In my deposition. Do I tell the truth about what happened with me refusing to, you know, do it, or do I tell the truth with me ... giving in and the whole thing?"

The Prick

Chapter 12

Thursday June 21st
The Law Offices of Jason Hunter, Esq.

Rebecca Trent had finally called him back. Jason had tried to reach her right after the Monday Moxley meeting and again the next day. Her assistant had said she was out of the office for a few days but wouldn't say where, or when she would be back.

Jessica had come to his office to go get lunch. They were about to leave when the call came in. When Jason recognized the number, he told her he had to take it quickly. Jessica frowned, sat down in one of his guest chairs, and took out her iPhone, pointedly looking bored.

"Rebecca, nice to finally hear back from you."

At the sound of Rebecca's name, Jessica's eyes popped up from the screen. "Trent?" she mouthed to Jason.

Jason nodded. Jessica put her phone on the desk and got up.

"I've been out of town," Trent replied coldly.

"So your assistant said. Vacation?" Jason leaned back in his chair and looked at Jessica, who was walking around his desk with a mischievous look on her face. He covered the phone. "This will just take a minute."

"Work," Trent said.

"Okay, well, the reason I was calling is that ..." Jason stopped midway through the sentence as Jessica had dropped to her knees in front of him and started massaging his piece.

"Is what?" Trent asked. Jason shook his head at Jessica. "No," he whispered.

"Is that I wanted to get Spelkin scheduled for deposition. Soon." Jessica undid his belt and unzipped his fly. Jason stared at her.

"Already?" Trent asked. "Discovery just opened. The Title VII claims aren't even in the case yet."

"I'll get the Right to Sue, amend shortly." That would take the EEOC out of the case and surely disappoint his good friend Ryan but the time to apply pressure was now.

"Fine. But we haven't even exchanged documents yet."

"This case is not, ah ..." Jessica had taken it out and put it in her mouth. It was somewhat distracting.

"It's not ... going to be very document intensive. I say we get moving on the depos."

"Fine," Trent repeated. "When?"

Jason was confused. He tried to stop Jessica with his hand, but she brushed him away and kept bobbing. Jesus, she was a skilled practitioner. Was Trent bluffing? Good God, Jessica had this thing where she would run the tip of her tongue around just the—

"Jason?"

"Sometime in the next few weeks," Jason said.

"Fine," Trent said. "My schedule gets very busy next month, so let's schedule Moxley's deposition and Robert's deposition on back-to-back business days. How do July 13th and 16th work for you? July 13th for her and July 16th for him."

What the fuck? Jason had expected tremendous pushback. Had they found Spelkin? If so, this plan could backfire quickly. Jessica stopped a few seconds to take her top off. This was the first time since he'd moved in that Jason was happy his office had no windows.

"Jason? The 13th and the 16th?"

"I'm ... checking my calendar." Jessica, now topless, had put it back her mouth, and he was physically incapable of checking his calendar. He closed his eyes. "Yes, that should be fine."

"Okay, it's booked." Trent said. "Let's do it at my office. Yours doesn't have enough space."

Jason ignored the insult. He couldn't give a shit about the insult at the moment. "I'll send over a depo notice."

"Likewise," Trent said. "See you in a few weeks." She hung up.

"What the fuck?" Jason said aloud.

Jessica stopped. "What? You want me to stop?"

"Not that," Jason said. He very much did not want her to stop. "I thought Spelkin was missing. Why is she scheduling him for a depo?"

"He's missing." Jessica assured him from his lap, talking in between fellatios. "David would have told me if he was back."

He wasn't a huge fan of hearing David's name while she was giving him the business. "So what the fuck?"

"She's just bluffing. Again. Don't get rattled."

That might be right. She'd certainly bluffed before.

"How did you like getting blown while you were on the phone?" Jessica asked, looking up at him.

"It was ... distracting. First time for me on a work call."

"You weren't a baller before. You're a baller now. Ballers get blow jobs."

Jason liked his new status. He watched as Jessica stood up, dropped her shorts, and bent over his desk. "They also get this," she said.

The Prick

Chapter 13

Friday, July 13th
Midtown Atlanta

Jason was back in the square chair in the lobby of Trent's building, drinking coffee, waiting for a client in a sexual harassment case. He was just as nervous as the last time, but better outfitted. His suit had cost just over 2,000 dollars. He looked down at the fine fabric on his right knee, which was bouncing with anxious energy. Trent hadn't called off Moxley's depo and hadn't said a word about postponing Spelkin's, either. Jessica, whom he'd showered with that morning after another sleepover, assured him that Spelkin was still MIA. To Jason's great annoyance, she was still in touch with Nichols and had asked him about it just yesterday. Jason didn't want to think about whether she was still sleeping with Nichols. He sure as hell hoped not. Part of the reason he didn't ask, he was honest enough with himself to admit, was that he didn't want to risk cutting off the flow of information from the enemy camp.

If it was true that Spelkin was still missing, Trent might try to eviscerate Maggie today, then try to settle immediately after, or suggest that they stay discovery to pursue settlement. Or maybe she would just say they needed to move the Spelkin depo. There was no telling. The only thing out of Trent since the blow job scheduling call had been silence. That silence kept Jason up at night. Trent was never without a plan. And he couldn't figure out what it was for the life of him. He was having nightmarish visions of her manila folders.

Jason watched the lobby's revolving door and, behind it, the walkway from the parking lot. The depo was scheduled to start at 9:30 a.m., and he had told Maggie to meet him at 9:00. If she didn't show, Jason wasn't entirely sure he'd be able to avoid murdering her.

Weston had a court hearing in the morning but was supposed to attend the afternoon portion of the depo. It was going to go all day.

Most of the morning was likely to be preliminary background bullshit. Trent was going to take her time, tire Maggie out, wear her down. She was going to put Maggie through the goddamn ringer, was what she was going to do. Jason wasn't at all confident that Maggie would survive intact. But in a Spelkin-less world, hers was the only story.

To prepare, Jason had put in four marathon prep sessions with Maggie. In the second, third, and fourth sessions Weston had cross-examined her. He'd seemed to enjoy it and, Jason had to admit, was pretty damn good at it. The first time, Weston had destroyed Maggie and her story. She'd collapsed under the pressure, and after the first hour started agreeing with whatever he said. Jason went through yet another box of Kleenex. In the next cross she had done better. And in the last one, two days prior, Maggie had actually approximated a decent and believable witness. She made eye contact. She focused on the question. She stood up for herself, as much as could be expected, and didn't fall apart when the tone of the questioner suggested disbelief. And she was able to articulate what happened.

What happened. That, of course, was the real trick. In the first prep session, when the subject came up of what happened, Maggie had again looked to him for guidance.

The Prick

"Just tell the truth," Jason said. Clearly unsure, Maggie tried out the version of the "truth" in which she rejected Spelkin's advances outright. The picture of purity and moral rectitude. Jason hadn't corrected her; instead, he'd asked specific, detailed questions about this version of the "truth." They concluded the topic and moved on. Neither of them said a word about how The Truth was not the truth.

When the topic came up in second prep session, with Weston crossing her, Maggie again trotted out this truth, unsteady and unsure, like a newborn colt. She said the words and looked at Jason and Weston questioningly. Weston didn't bat an eye. Jason didn't say anything. Weston continued his attack on her story, but never broke character.

By the third session when Maggie told the purity version, she did so confidently. She told Spelkin "no." She ran away. By the fourth session her recitation was even stronger, approaching vehement. Self-righteous anger, with some helpful embellishments, insights into her shock, outrage, embarrassment, humiliation, and, most importantly, fear. Jason had stressed her fear to her. She was a victim. Following the fourth session, Maggie was as ready as she could be. To lie under oath.

Jason and Weston hadn't talked about it, the perjury. They'd both instructed her to tell the truth, repeatedly, and the tacit unspoken agreement was that if this was Maggie's truth, who were they to say otherwise. Jason felt shitty about it, of course. There was no way not to. But he rationalized it through the lens that Weston had initially supplied—if they were completely honest and forthright, they would be the only party doing so. And that would mean they'd almost certainly lose.

Jason looked at his phone. It was 9:23 a.m. Where the hell was she? Probably crying in her car. Or sending incriminating texts to her sister. He called her. Straight to voicemail. Goddamn it. She was going to blow the whole goddamn thing.

No, there she was. Coming through the revolving doors. Jason was struck by the differences between her entrance and Jessica's months earlier. No men in the lobby stopped what they were doing to stare at Maggie, that was for sure. Jason thought for the millionth time that she didn't look like a sexual harassment plaintiff. He'd been trying to eject the image of her topless from his brain.

She had chosen for the occasion a white sweater top thing and a huge flowery skirt. Jesus, she was enormous. She scanned the lobby, saw him, and made a beeline in his direction.

He rose to greet her. He noted his noticeable lack of any kind of pride in meeting a woman like this in public, again only because his last such encounter in this exact place had been with Jessica. That was completely unfair to Maggie, and a petty and stupid thing to be thinking about at the moment. Still, though.

"How are you?" he asked, knowing the answer. She was terrified.

"I'm okay," Maggie said, breathlessly. "So sorry I'm late."

"Not a problem at all. You're ready," Jason said, leading her to the elevator bank. "Let's get up there and get settled in. Now remember, listen to the question asked, and answer only that question. No need to volunteer information. Do not change your answer if you're asked the same question multiple times. She's only doing that because she didn't get the answer she wanted the first time. The first two hours will probably be fluff. Just vanilla questions about your background, employment history, where you went to school, et cetera."

"Right," Maggie said. She had heard all of this at least ten times by now.

The Prick

The elevator doors opened. Jason continued to issue rapid-fire instructions to fill the nervous space. "If you don't understand the question, ask her to rephrase it. If you don't know the answer to a question, 'I don't know,' is the correct answer. Don't guess or speculate. Remember, even if Trent is nice to you, she is the enemy. Her job is to kill your case." Though Jason doubted highly that Trent would try the nice-guy routine.

"Right," Maggie responded. She was grasping her purse tightly.

They arrived at the floor. "And remember, no matter what, tell the truth," Jason said. She looked at him.

That probably hadn't been necessary, but Jason wanted to be sure that he said it right before the deposition. Just in case, God forbid, there was ever a question as to whether he had suborned perjury, Maggie would have to admit that he had told her to tell the truth. Unless she lied then, too.

They went through the doors and to reception, where they were directed to the conference room. The court reporter was already set up at the end of the table. There was also, as Jason had expected and prepared Maggie for, a videographer, set up on one side behind a gigantic camera. Small microphones rested in front of the seats for the witness and attorneys on the table, cords running back to the camera. There was a circular blue screen set up behind Maggie's chair. This was going to be the backdrop for her debut performance.

"That's your seat," Jason said, and sat immediately to her right. He passed his business cards to the court reporter and videographer and watched Maggie settle uncomfortably into her chair, putting her purse on her lap. He took the microphone in front of him and clipped it to his tie.

"Where do you want her mike?" he asked the court reporter, a bearded bear of a man.

The Prick

"Anywhere on her sweater around the bottom of her neck is fine," the videographer said. Maggie picked up the little microphone and looked at it like it was an alien life form.

"Just clip it to your sweater, Maggie."

She tried. Her hands were shaking. Jason took his mike off and leaned over to whisper in her ear. "Take some deep breaths. Remember, the first couple hours are likely just to be introductory questions. Just like you're having a conversation. Nothing you can't handle."

She nodded but didn't make eye contact. She was staring at her trembling hands, which were still fumbling around with the microphone clip. Jason looked up and saw that everyone in the room was watching them, too. Maggie closed her eyes and deeply inhaled and exhaled. After her third deep breath, she was finally able to operate the clip. The court reporter, a miniscule woman who wore glasses and looked like a librarian, asked Maggie the spelling of her name in a quiet and overly nice voice, the voice you would use to comfort a scared child, and Maggie managed to answer without too much trouble. The court reporter looked at Jason. She knew what he knew. This was going to be a bloodbath.

They waited. Jason looked at his phone. It was 9:45. He attempted to make some small talk with Maggie, but all he got back were mumbled, one-word answers, so he decided to leave her alone. He looked at espn.com. 9:50. He read a few *Times* articles, glanced at the weather for the weekend, checked his email, looked at his bank accounts. As nervous as he was, the accounts still brought a half-smile to his lips. That Rossi settlement had really saved him. 10:00. What the hell was going on?

"Have you seen Rebecca Trent this morning?" he asked. The court reporter and videographer shook their heads.

The Prick

"I'm going to see what's going on. This was supposed to start at 9:30."

Maggie nodded. She was looking at the table in front of her, still holding onto her purse like she was gripping the safety bar on a rollercoaster.

Jason walked over to the receptionist, a squat young woman with unkempt blonde hair who had let her makeup get away from her. "Any idea where Ms. Trent is?"

She smiled at him. "I'll call around and—oh."

Jason turned. There Trent was in all her lanky, oversized-pantsuit glory, striding toward him with purpose. She was flanked by a young Asian woman carrying a redweld full of manila folders, gigantic Jimmy Peters, and, Jesus fucking Christ, was that Robert fucking Spelkin? The supposed-to-be-MIA Robert Spelkin? The case-depending-on-his-absence Robert Spelkin? Jason stared at him as his insides did somersaults. He felt a powerful surge of panic.

Trent smiled her carnivorous smile at him. "You ready?"

Jason didn't answer. He was mesmerized by Spelkin, or whatever Spelkin had become. The man looked awful. He had put on maybe twenty pounds and his skin was pale, pallid, except for the area around both eyes, which were a muted shade of purple. He looked like he'd been in a fistfight. And he just emanated grotesque unhealthiness. He looked like what he was really—a fucking bloated corpse, back from the dead.

Spelkin wasn't returning Jason's gaze. His purple-rimmed eyes were fixed on the back of Moxley's head in the conference room, and they glowed with pure malevolence. You could almost feel the air tingle with his hatred.

"Something wrong?" Trent asked.

Jason swallowed. "Just surprised at the turnout," he said. Had she played him? Had Jessica played him? Why would she? Had Nichols played Jessica?

The Prick

Trent laughed. A caustic laugh. "I bet," she said. "Let's get started, shall we?"

Jason, feeling numb, followed her into the conference room, continuing to stare at Spelkin. He felt like a sucker. Of course they wouldn't have let this go forward unless they had him where they wanted him. Of course Trent wouldn't put herself in that position. He had been blinded by the money he thought awaited him in his future. Goddamn fool. Goddamn child. Goddamn blow-job-distracted imbecile.

He watched Maggie. He had told her Spelkin wouldn't be there, wouldn't be anywhere near there, that he had run for the hills. She just stared at the table, didn't raise her gaze to the people filing into the room.

Trent sat down in the seat opposite Maggie, and Spelkin, or Spelkin's animated corpse, sat in the adjacent chair. The Asian woman and Peters filled out the rest of the side of the table, Peters at the far end.

"Mrs. Moxley," Trent said, "I don't think we've been formally introduced."

Maggie looked up at her like a timid rabbit. A pasty, fatty, timid rabbit. Then she glanced to Trent's right. She saw him. The look on her face was sheer terror.

"You remember Mr. Spelkin," Trent said, her cadence quick and sharp. "He's here to witness you tell the truth."

"Yes," Spelkin said. His voice was much weaker than Jason remembered but his eyes burned potent hatred at Maggie. "The truth. To my face."

"That's what you'll get, Robert," Jason interjected. His protective instinct broke the spell and Spelkin finally looked away from Maggie to glare at Jason.

"You'll find out soon what you're getting," Spelkin said.

Whatever the hell that meant, it couldn't be good, and it was downright unsettling to be threatened by the undead. Jason elected not to respond.

The Prick

"Enough prelude," Jason said to Trent. "Ask your questions, Rebecca."

"Let's get the video rolling," Trent said. "And let's get her sworn in."

The videographer started the camera, announced the date, time, and case caption. The court reporter read the oath to Maggie and managed to coax her to raise her right hand and swear to tell the truth. Trent reached for the redweld full of manila folders. Jason eyed them warily.

"All right, Mrs. Moxley, are you currently employed?" Trent asked her first question.

"No."

"Where did you go to high school?"

Jason relaxed and leaned back in his chair, preparing himself for the typical one to two hours of introductory fluff. He saw Maggie relax a bit as well. She was prepared for this. Jason pulled out his iPhone and started emailing both Weston and Rossi. To Weston, "Big problem. Spelkin is back and in the depo." To Rossi, "Spelkin is here! What the fuck?!!!"

"Dacula High School," Maggie answered.

"In Dacula, Georgia?"

Maggie nodded.

"You have to give a verbal response, Mrs. Moxley," Trent instructed.

"Sorry, yes."

"Are you married?"

"Yes."

"What is your husband's name?"

"Peter. Pete."

"You call him Pete?"

"Yes."

"How long have you and Pete been married?"

"About nine years."

The Prick

Trent pulled out one of her manila folders and put it in front of Maggie without opening it.

"And how many times have you cheated on Pete?"

"What? Objection!" Jason said.

"What's the matter, Jason, too vague?" Trent said. "Okay, fine. Mrs. Moxley, how many times in the last nine years have you had sex with a man other than Pete Moxley?"

"Objection," Jason said. "This is just pure harassment and you know it."

"You have got to be kidding me," Trent shot back. "I'd be happy to call Judge Barnes right now and let you explain to her, and to all of us, how Mrs. Moxley's sexual fidelity is not relevant to this case."

"You have no basis whatsoever to ask these kinds of accusatory questions."

Trent smiled at him. Spelkin smiled, too. He looked down the table. Even goddamn Jimmy Peters was grinning at him. He was fucked.

Trent opened the folder in front of her. "I'll withdraw the question for the time being and ask another one." She handed one of the stapled documents inside to the court reporter and handed Jason his courtesy copy. "I'm going to mark this as exhibit one."

Jason looked down at the paper and then up at Moxley. It was a Tinder profile. With Maggie's fucking picture on it and her fucking name on it. Maggie M. Wearing a low-cut top. The picture had obviously been taken in her bathroom.

Trent pushed the exhibit in front of Maggie. "Recognize this?"

Maggie didn't answer. She began to cry.

"Recognize your Tinder profile page, Mrs. Moxley?"

Maggie shook her head but whispered, "Yes."

"How many times, Mrs. Moxley? How many times have you committed adultery?" Trent asked, her voice raised.

The Prick

"I ... I don't know," Maggie stammered.

"You don't know how many times you've had sex with a man other than your husband?"

"I—I don't ... I'm—"

"If we asked the good people at Tinder for their records on your communications with other men, what would we find?"

"I—I'm sorry ..."

"What are you sorry for, Mrs. Moxley?"

"For ... for everything. For all of this."

"You made it all up, didn't you? It's all a lie, isn't it?"

Maggie sprang up out of her chair and ran out of the room, sobbing. Her microphone was still attached, and the cord sprung up and knocked a glass of water all over the table.

"Goddamn it!" Trent said, trying unsuccessfully to push her documents out of harm's way. Her hands full of sopping wet paper, she swung over to Jason, furious, and pointed at him. "You go get your client," she demanded, sounding like the wrath of God. "She is going to answer my questions. She is going to sit in that chair and she is going to tell the truth." She shouted down the table, "Somebody clean this up and get me some new exhibits." She turned around, directing all of her force in the videographer's direction. "You got her running out of the room, right?" The big man recoiled, but nodded. He had gotten it.

*****

Around and around. Left, left, left, left. He would have to show his face eventually. Eventually he'd have to come out of there.

"That's when I will get him," Donald said. "When he comes out, I will get him." He counted the turns around the building. "One, two, three, four. That's when I will get him. When he comes out, I will get him. One, two, three, four."

The Prick

He spent every weekday this way now. Doing the same thing. Saying the same thing. It was soothing. But this morning was different. There was a kink in the hose. His mother. She'd grown suspicious of how he was spending his time. He had told her and told her and told her that he was out looking for another job, but she wouldn't believe him. She thought that he might be getting in trouble, that he might be out doing bad things. So, this morning, she had made him an appointment with a therapist who worked out of an office on Peachtree Street in Buckhead. She was making him go, and told him she'd be calling the therapist to confirm that he'd gone. So, this morning, a new phrase kept breaking into his mantra.

"One, two, three, four. That's when I will get him. She is making me go. I don't need to go but she is making me go. When he comes out, I will get him. One, two, three. She is making me go. I don't need to go but she is making me go. Four. That's when I will get him."

Donald looked at the digital clock on the Taurus console. It was 10:25. The session was at 11:00. He was going to have to leave his sentry soon. He looked again. 10:26. He screamed and punched the clock. "She is making me go! I don't need to go but she is making me go!"

*****

Jimmy Peters was positively giddy. Hunter couldn't even get his client out of the women's room. After Moxley had fled the deposition in the face of her whorishness, she'd locked herself in one of the stalls in the bathroom outside of Trent's firm. Crying and crying. Wailing, really, so that you could hear it in the hallway. After about five minutes of that, Hunter had gone in after her, announcing his intentions honorably, of course—"There's a man coming in," et cetera —the little sanctimonious shit. The wailing subsided but Jimmy, who'd positioned himself next to the men's room taking a fake phone call, could still make out softer crying and Hunter's muted attempts to console his client and coax her out.

This had gone on for about thirty minutes, with Jimmy stationed in the hall, phone pressed to his ear, soaking up the sounds of suffering. He grinned from ear to ear.

Trent's lackey, what was her name—Chen? Chang?—collected Jimmy from the hallway and led him outside the building to where Trent and Spelkin were waiting. Neither seemed to share Jimmy's joy. Spelkin was on the phone, describing to someone in a hoarse voice what had happened. Jimmy hadn't known they'd even found Spelkin, or that he was coming back, until that morning. So much for keeping him in the loop. But he had been so glad to see him, one of his problems fixed, that he didn't care at all. He'd tried to ask Spelkin a few questions, you know, like where the fuck he had been and what the fuck had happened to him, and whether someone had punched his lights out and for what, but Spelkin had just straight up ignored him. Whatever. Maybe things were going to work out for Jimmy Peters after all.

Trent was sitting on one of the stone benches immediately outside the doors, tapping away on her phone at typical breakneck speed. She didn't look happy. She looked furious, actually. She had the prey within her claws, grievously wounded, and it had managed to wriggle free before she could make the kill. But surely they had to be happy about how things had gone?

"That footage is going to be gold," he said in the general direction of Trent.

She glared up at him. "That fat bitch is going to answer my questions. I will get a court order compelling her to sit there and answer my questions. And if she pulls that shit again, I'll have her thrown in motherfucking jail."

The Prick

"Right ... okay," Jimmy said. "But the video is great, don't you think?"

"It will definitely have its uses," Trent said, looking back down at her phone. "But she didn't answer my fucking question." Her fingers started flying again.

Jimmy looked at Chan, that was her name, Maria Chan, to try to get some support for his position that everything was going great. She quickly looked away. She wanted no part of his that-went-really-well platform.

Jimmy stood there, tapping his leg. Trent typed, Spelkin talked on the phone, and Maria Chan looked at her notepad. It was a beautiful day out, but heating up.

"Anybody up for some Starbucks while we wait this thing out?" Jimmy said.

Spelkin glared at him, but nodded, still on the phone. He looked like he should be in the hospital.

"Fine," Trent said.

Jimmy led the way to the corner of the four-way intersection of Fourteenth and Peachtree and the crosswalk. The street wasn't busy. The lunch rush hadn't yet begun. The sun beat down on them as they waited for the white walking man to illuminate. Atlanta in the summer was no place to wear a suit.

The white walking man appeared and they began to cross, Jimmy still leading the way. Out of nowhere, a light blue car ran the light and came to a screeching halt in front of them. Hadn't it just been stopped?

"Pay attention!" Trent yelled at the driver.

The car wasn't moving, front end in the crosswalk, back end hanging into the intersection. The sun shone on the windshield and Jimmy couldn't make out the driver. He hoped it wasn't some gang member Trent was yelling at.

The door opened. Trent moved aggressively toward the driver. "You've gotta watch where the fuck you're going!"

The Prick

A tall, bald man stepped out of the car. He looked oddly familiar. Trent continued to walk in the man's direction, but the man wasn't looking at Trent. He was staring at something to Jimmy's left. At Spelkin, who'd walked back to the corner of the street and was watching the scene with amusement.

"Are you even listening—" And then she screamed. The man raised a gun. Holy shit, it was Don Jeffries! Crazy Don Jeffries with a gun! Jimmy turned to run and behind him he heard *pop pop pop pop.*

He felt a searing pain in his upper leg and fell to the black pavement. Looking up, he saw Spelkin lying on the corner, half on the sidewalk, half on the street. Blood was running out of his white shirt. And then Jeffries was standing over him.

"You made me!" Jeffries screamed. Spelkin put a hand up. Jeffries fired three more shots into Spelkin, point-blank.

"No!" Jimmy heard himself cry out.

Jeffries turned to him, looked Jimmy dead in the eye, put the gun to his own temple, and pulled the trigger.

The Prick

Chapter 14

Monday, December 10th
United States District Courthouse
Northern District of Georgia, Atlanta Division

The wind whipped through the space between the large, blocky federal courthouse and the abandoned building across the parking lot. Jason got out of his car and stiffened as the frigid currents pummeled his face. He picked up the exhibit boxes from the backseat with a grunt, kicked the door shut, and made his way across the uneven parking lot to the courthouse. It was the first day of the Moxley trial.

Everything was warped now. Inverted. That poor pale lunatic Jimmy Peters fired had crashed into everyone's life like a mad asteroid and shifted the world on its axis.

Spelkin was dead. He had died before they put him in the ambulance. The madman was dead, too. Maggie had cried through it all, but Jason had heard the sirens from the bathroom.

The Peachtree shooting was a front-page story and led the local news for over a week. It had even received some national coverage. CNN had come to Jason's shitty office to interview him about it. Everyone had done interviews for a while. Trent even got herself a few minutes with Anderson Cooper. Nichols was a talking head on two shows, touching on tort reform and how we as a society handle the mentally ill, respectively. Even Jimmy Peters had done an interview

305

with the local news from the hospital. He'd been shot in the ass.

And Spelkin's wife, for whom Jason had never before spared more than a passing thought, now The Widow, was everywhere. Goddamn everywhere. Local news, national news, newspapers. Pictures of the whole family. Spelkin, The Widow, the kids. They flooded the airwaves, images punctuated by sound bites. Loving father. Caring husband. Well-respected lawyer. Pillar of the community. Most importantly, victim. Victim of a madman with a gun. Victim of a meritless lawsuit brought by a disgruntled former employee and an unethical lawyer. The Widow expressed to countless news outlets that she hoped this tragedy would *at least* shame the plaintiff into dropping her blatant money grab. The Widow took out a full-page ad in the *Atlanta Journal-Constitution* to post her own version of Spelkin's obituary, with a picture of his children immediately beneath it.

There was a good reason for The Widow's sudden defense of her dearly departed husband. Because of the armed lunatic, Jason found himself no longer suing Spelkin, but Spelkin's estate—the money that would otherwise go to his wife and kids. An extremely sympathetic estate. Two adorable grieving children. What fucking luck.

The Levitt law firm was still a codefendant, of course. The retaliation claim against the firm was turning into his best and easiest claim. But the claims asserted against Spelkin were getting the headlines. Jason saw one interview in which The Widow appealed to him directly to drop the lawsuit. She looked right into the camera and said, "I ask Maggie Moxley's attorney to drop the frivolous claims against my deceased husband. He is no longer here to defend himself. You are hurting his memory. You are hurting his family. You are trying to take money that will be used to care for his children." Then the news station flashed a picture of Spelkin with the kids.

"Powerful words," the reporter said, before throwing it over to the weather.

It got worse. Jason's conscience was acting up of its own accord, *sua sponte*, even without the guilt-tripping interviews and pictures of children whose dead father he was maligning and whose college funds he was attempting to appropriate. After Spelkin's death, Jason found himself wondering on a daily and sometimes hourly basis what, if anything, Spelkin had done to Maggie that night. He didn't trust either version of Maggie's Truth. The woman was near pathological. And now Spelkin would never be put under oath about what happened. Tinder. She had actually signed up for Fucking Tinder during the lawsuit.

Before, when he knew that Maggie was lying about what happened, he had successfully rationalized the lie, and his facilitation of the lie, because Spelkin was also lying, and Trent was facilitating his lie. When the Gander was a mendacious prick, it was appropriate for the Goose to deny actually giving the blow job. And maybe it was even okay that Maggie had willfully destroyed evidence. But now there was no counterpart. The Gander had been shot dead. The trial was no longer Maggie Moxley v Robert Spelkin et al. It was Maggie Moxley v The Truth. And what if the whole thing, everything, was made up? What if both Truths were lies?

Richard Weston didn't seem to enjoy the new dynamic, either. He'd been doing everything he could to distance himself, starting right around the time the media had begun excoriating the bloodthirsty lawyers. Whenever Jason met with Weston to discuss the case Weston looked like he had a bad taste in his mouth. "Do you think she's telling the truth?" Weston had asked him out of the blue, a few months after the shooting. Like the cagey old bastard wasn't fully aware that Moxley was lying.

Jason wasn't buying the feigned senility or naiveté or whatever the hell it was that Weston was attempting to convey so that he might be permitted to disembark the sinking vessel. But he understood where it was coming from. This wasn't how things were supposed to have gone. Weston was supposed to have slain his old nemesis in open combat on a white horse, not rob his grave.

Jason wasn't shocked when, about a month before the trial, Weston told Jason he thought maybe it would be best if Jason handled it himself.

"Fine," Jason said. It wasn't fine, of course, but he was too proud to admit that.

"I'll stay on in an advisory capacity," Weston assured him.

He hadn't heard from him since. Jason was on his own. And now it was D-day.

He reached the unceremonial entrance to the courthouse from the parking lot. A marshal held the reinforced metal door open for him. Jason nodded thanks and stepped in out of the cold.

Inside was a line for security with a metal detector. To the right of the line was a separate security line for parties bringing in exhibits with the same X-ray machine they had for bags at the airport. A bored-looking marshal manned the machine. Jason nodded to him and put his boxes on the conveyer belt. The parking lot door opened again and Rebecca Trent came in. With her were Will Simmons, Ned Burroughs, David Nichols, Trent's associate Maria Chan, Jimmy Peters, who was still sporting a slight limp, and *four* paralegals. Each of the paralegals carried two boxes. Immediately following them came Joseph ("Joe") Clifford

III, his associate whose name Jason could never remember, and a fifth paralegal carrying two boxes.

Clifford was a high-profile trial lawyer whom The Widow had hired to represent the estate individually. He was a former federal prosecutor, completely bald and built like a fire hydrant. Hiring him was smart. Create separation between the estate and the moneyed law firm in the eyes of the jury and give the defendants two shots at the opening statement, cross-examination, and closing argument. Not to mention the guy was close to a living legend in Atlanta.

Jason was more than grossly outnumbered. He had a sinking feeling that he was also horribly outmatched. A public humiliation seemed to be gathering like a storm on the horizon.

Trent noticed him standing at the conveyor belt and nodded curtly. Nichols smiled darkly and winked. The rest of the defense lawyer group made no gesture of greeting. Clifford looked at him like he was an insect to be squashed. The five paralegals broke off with their exhibit boxes to stand behind Jason in the conveyer belt while the lawyer battalion marched ahead. Jason said hi to the paralegals, who murmured awkward semi-audible responses, not wanting to consort with the enemy.

The marshal gave Jason the all clear and Jason collected his meager boxes. "Here we go," he said under his breath.

Jason lugged his boxes up to the third floor and pushed through the wooden doors into Judge Barnes's courtroom. Like most district court judges' courtrooms in the federal building, hers was impressive. It was spacious with high ceilings, wood paneling, and a large gold seal above the judge's bench. An eagle with arrows in its claws. The bench itself was about fifteen feet from the lawyers' tables and at least five feet above floor level so that the judge and all of her invested power could visibly lord over the applicants for justice. The jury box was to the left.

Each juror seat was equipped with a monitor so that when the attorneys wanted to highlight a document in evidence, or a deposition transcript, they could pull it up on a computer and the jury would be able to view that very page. The witness stand was to the left of the courtroom as well, directly in front of the jury. In front of the judge's bench, on floor level, desks were set up behind a wooden wall for her law clerk, her calendar clerk, and the court reporter. These were presently empty, as was the bench. The only people in the room were two uniformed deputies and a couple of people who looked like reporters in the pews. Of course, Maggie had not yet arrived, despite promising him that she would be in the courtroom by 8:15. He would have to check the bathroom, follow the sound of weeping.

There were two sets of lawyers' tables, each with two rows and three chairs per row. One on the right, one on the left. Jason walked over to the one on the left, the plaintiff's side, nearest the jury box. Only he and his client would be occupying that side of the courtroom. The right side, the defense side, would undoubtedly be packed.

Jason took out his juror sheet. Juror selection, probably the most important part of the trial, was going to happen first thing that morning. They were going to pick twelve people from a group of forty to fifty citizens who were there against their will. The juror sheets that Jason always used were grids that looked like modified bingo cards. Each juror was given a number, and the idea was to get them all on the sheet and write down pertinent information and/or pluses and minuses when they responded to questions from both the judge and the lawyers. In all of Jason's previous trials on the defense side, he'd had with him at least one other lawyer and a paralegal to help keep track of everyone and provide

The Prick

input. Jason found himself wishing that Weston were there, or somebody. Some backup. He looked across the courtroom at the army assembling in the rows. They would have no shortage of input.

One of the many paralegals looked up at Jason, and Jason averted his eyes, looking back toward the doors. Still no sign of Moxley. But the reporters were filing in. This case, and Jason's likely demise, would be well covered in the media. Jason took a deep breath and tried to calm himself. He could feel his heart beating wildly.

Then Clifford walked over to him. He was wearing suspenders. A real statesman.

"Good morning, Jason," Clifford said, casually and coolly, like it was any other day. Maybe for Clifford it was. He had practically lived in this building for a decade as a federal prosecutor.

"Morning, Joe," Jason said.

In the weeks prior to the trial, Clifford had been sounding off whenever a microphone was put in front of his face about how frivolous the case was, what a liar Moxley was, and how dishonorable it was of Jason to smear Spelkin's name after his untimely and violent demise. Jason had grown to hate the man. But it was customary to be civil, and civil he would try to remain.

"Your client going to make it today?" Clifford asked.

"I think so," Jason said. "She's pretty critical to my case."

Clifford laughed at that. "I would agree, son. I would agree. She's not going to run out of the courtroom crying if I ask her a tough question, is she?"

"I wouldn't rule it out."

"Mmmhmm." Clifford glanced back at the reporters, some of whom were obviously watching the exchange. "This your first trial?"

Fuck you. "No," Jason said. "Yours?"

The Prick

Clifford frowned. "Juries don't like cockiness, Jason. Believe me. You may use it as a defense mechanism, but don't let them see it."

"Got it."

Clifford put a hand on his shoulder, lowered his voice, and looked him in the eye. "Listen, son, you're out of your depth here. You know it and I know it. If you have questions about how things are going to go, you can ask me. I won't make a big deal about it. I'm not here to make you look bad. Not here to embarrass you. I'm here to get the truth out."

Jason glared at him and moved slightly so that Clifford's arm dropped from Jason's shoulder. He was about to say something extremely inadvisable when the door opened and his client walked in. All eyes went to her.

"I'll leave you to it." Clifford walked back across the aisle to confer with Trent, who was sizing up Moxley.

There was so much to size up. So much more than when Maggie and her husband had first darkened Jason's door. Maggie's reaction to all the news coverage and attack pieces had been to binge eat. Jason estimated that, all told, she had gained a hundred pounds since Spelkin's untimely demise. It was almost impressive. He'd had no idea that a person could put on that much weight in so short a time—in between the tens of trial prep sessions at Jason's office, which were routinely interrupted by Maggie's need to go to the bathroom and cry, or go outside and cry, or go to her car and cry, or call her sister and cry. Pete Moxley, who'd insisted on attending most sessions, had bitched to Jason about the fact that Maggie had needed to buy all new clothes. "Fucking maternity wear, you ask me," Pete said.

In any event, she had crossed the line. She'd always been overweight, but now she was so morbidly obese and just ... *gross* ... that Jason bet eleven out of twelve people wouldn't even believe that she was capable of prompting a male of her species to want to do anything with her. The jurors would never say that, as it would be un-PC and offensive, but they'd all be thinking it. Everyone in the courtroom was thinking it as she waddled in Jason's direction. The only benefit to the disastrous Tinder profile, which he had failed to keep out of evidence on a motion *in limine*, was that it might show the jurors that she'd been more attractive just months ago.

That would of course be the only advantage. Married women were going to hate her. She was an adulterer, attempted at least. The intent was all that mattered. Failing at adultery doesn't make you any less morally culpable than a successful adulterer. Right?

Jason had wanted to suggest to her that she wear something slimming but didn't want to deal with the associated tears, and also didn't know what the hell that would even be. Besides, it wasn't going to matter. They were going to get slaughtered regardless of Maggie's outfit.

Maggie was flushed and out of breath by the time she got to Jason. She knew, Jason thought. She knew what everyone was thinking.

"Sit right here, Maggie," he said, trying to sound kind. "Next to me." He watched with trepidation as Maggie sat down, hoping she'd fit into the standard-sized chair, which she did after some difficulty. Good. The last thing he wanted to do was ask the deputy if they had any larger chairs.

He caught Clifford watching Maggie lower herself into the chair. Clifford saw Jason looking at him. And smirked. Jason wondered if Clifford's suspenders were long enough to stretch around his neck.

In came The Widow. Perfect timing for maximum compare and contrast with Moxley. The Widow was a slender, graceful, poised, statuesque blonde. Beautiful but not sensuous. Cold beauty. Hard beauty. She had the two children with her, both of whom also looked the part. The son was about ten or so and wore a sports coat, the daughter, about five, a muted dress. The Widow, of course, was all in black. You couldn't look at her without remembering what she was.

They were trailed by a carbon copy of The Widow, whom Jason took to be her sister. The Widow kissed her children and left them with her carbon copy to sit in the pews. She walked around to talk to Clifford, who pulled out a chair for her to sit next to him in the front row. The Widow sat down and turned to look at Maggie. She stared, boldly, purposefully. Jason got the sense that The Widow intended this to be a Moment. Maggie, sensing it, looked up and caught her eye, blushed horribly, and looked back down at the table in front of her. The Widow nodded and turned to whisper to Clifford. Jason heard it. It was meant to be heard. "She can't even look at me." Jason watched the reporters watching this. They were riveted.

And so the table was set.

Jason sat and waited. He felt like he was going to throw up.

"All rise!" the courtroom deputy sounded. "The Honorable Judge Barnes presiding."

Jason shot up out of his chair and helped Maggie get up, lifting her right arm. It was like grabbing a pillow. He glanced around behind him. The only people on his side of the courtroom were reporters. The other side, behind the defense benches, was packed.

In came Judge Barnes, trailed by her law clerks. The judge sat down in the massive elevated chair and her two clerks took their seats in front of the computer screens in the lower, still elevated portion of the courtroom just below her. As Jason had come to expect in federal court, the clerks were nerdy and young, fresh out of law school. They stared at Moxley, looked at each other, and smiled. Not a good sign.

Judge Barnes was a black Republican who had been nominated in the late '90s by President Clinton. She, like most judges in the Northern District of Georgia, was no friend to the plaintiff, but she was a better draw then some of the more conservative Reagan and Bush appointees. It could have been worse, which was something Jason couldn't say for other aspects of the case.

"Be seated," Judge Barnes said. "We have somewhat of a full house today, and I see some familiar faces." She nodded to the press corps in the back. "I will remind you of the rule, which I see you are currently abiding by, that there will be no cameras whatsoever in the courtroom. I know there has been considerable press in this case. This is a court of law. It will not be biased. It will not be influenced by outside forces. The media will be permitted in the courtroom to observe and report. Period." Judge Barnes glared at the audience to emphasize the period.

"Furthermore, and more importantly, there shall be no contact whatsoever with the jurors during the length of the trial. If anyone in this room, or anyone with the same organization of anyone in this room attempts to contact a juror while this trial is going on, I will not be happy and I'll make sure that they will not be happy. If that is not understood, or there are any questions or issues, I will hear them now."

The courtroom was silent.

"All right. Before we bring in our potential jurors, are there any issues we need to address?"

Jason stood. "Not from plaintiff's side, Your Honor."

The judge nodded and looked at the defense side. Trent and Clifford, seated on either side of The Widow, both stood.

The Prick

"No, Your Honor," Trent said.

"Good morning, Your Honor," Clifford said. "We don't presently have any issues to address and we're looking forward to meeting our jury."

The judge smiled at Clifford, which made Jason wince on the inside. "Very well, let's bring in our candidates." She motioned to one of the courtroom deputies, who exited a side door to the jury room, returning a few seconds later trailed by the ragtag group of malcontents that Jason had come to expect. People who had received a letter in the mail, cursed when they realized it was for jury service, unsuccessfully tried to get out of it, and resigned themselves to their respective fates. The people whose attention Jason was going to have to command. The people Jason was going to have to convince to be sympathetic for the corpulent homewrecker instead of the grieving widow and two children who had lost their father. He smiled at the jurors, but they weren't looking at him. They were either looking at the judge or eyeballing Maggie, not in a malicious way (yet), but curiously, like, damn, that is a fat lady standing at that table.

Jason glanced over at The Widow. She was returning the jury's gaze, trying to make eye contact. He looked at Maggie. Her eyes were on the table in front of her. She looked ... guilty? Hopefully not. Hopefully just shy, or embarrassed, or nervous. Hopefully not guilty.

Jason wrote down rough descriptions of the jurors in his boxes as the judge issued the typical preliminary spiel (honor to be a juror, appreciate your service, vital role in the justice system, and so forth). He looked up when the judge mentioned that the case had been in the media and asked whether any of them had read or seen anything about it. A few of them raised their hands and were immediately excused. One of the excused jurors nodded to The Widow on the way out. She returned the nod, ever so graciously.

When the excused jurors left, the judge explained to the remaining candidates that the media coverage was likely to continue and that they should avoid any exposure to the coverage if they were selected. The judge then asked if anyone knew the parties or their attorneys. Nobody raised their hand.

It was time.

"Now the lawyers for the parties get to ask you some questions to help us select our jury. Please listen to the questions and answer honestly," Judge Barnes said, and nodded to Jason. "Counsel, you may begin."

"Thank you, Your Honor," Jason said, standing. He squeezed Maggie's shoulder and whispered, "Look up, make eye contact." He attempted a casual and comfortable walk over to the podium, juror chart and pen in hand. He was going to have to take notes on the fly. He reached the podium and scanned the jury pool. There were twenty-four of them, fourteen women and ten men. They were mostly white, with three black women, one black man, and one Asian man. Jason had wrestled with the type of pool he wanted, and whether gender or race was going to be a factor. After many hours of deliberation and running through it with Brunnell, he decided it wouldn't. What was going to matter was socioeconomic status, and, more precisely, whether the jurors felt empowered in society or vulnerable. If the jurors believed Maggie's story, which was a big if, those who felt that they were constantly oppressed, taken advantage of, or bowled over by more powerful forces would be the ones who wanted to punish Levitt.

"Good morning," Jason began. "I want to first echo the judge's comments and thank you for your service here today. My name is Jason Hunter and I represent Margaret

Moxley, who goes by Maggie." He gestured in her direction. Sometimes it was a good idea to ask the client to stand up, but Jason decided against it.

"My first question is whether anyone here has been the defendant in a civil lawsuit—that is, a lawsuit that isn't a criminal allegation." No takers.

"Thank you," Jason said. "Next, has anyone here ever owned their own business?" One woman who looked like the grandmother in illustrations of Little Red Riding Hood timidly raised her hand. A middle-aged white guy in a blue blazer at the end of the row raised his.

"You, sir. Can I please have your name and juror number please?"

"Mark Price," the man said, "juror number 17, I believe."

"Thank you, Mr. Price. Do you currently own your own business?"

"Yes, I do."

"In what industry?"

"Finance."

"Do you have employees?"

"Yes."

Jason put an X in his box.

"And you, ma'am?" he asked the little elderly woman.

"Well, my sister and I had our own tailoring business for years in Macon," she said. "But I retired a few years back. I live in Dunwoody now. With my son and his wife."

"Very good," Jason said. "Now does anyone here believe they were ever treated unfairly at work?" Several hands went up. Some luck at last. Jason remained pleasantly expressionless and put pluses by the names on this chart. "Okay, let's talk about that." Even if these jurors eventually got stricken (and the defense would surely try to strike them), it was good to start a conversation regarding employer maltreatment. He noticed a few jurors were

318

looking at Maggie, so he glanced over. She had started crying, softly.

*****

Lunch at the federal courthouse was a bleak cafeteria-style affair and Jason had no appetite whatsoever. Neither, he saw, did Maggie. There was good reason for that. In just about an hour, she would be testifying. They sat at one of the circular tables with largely untouched food on plastic trays. Jason was looking over his notes for his opening statement; Maggie was texting, hopefully to her sister or Pete and not some fetishist she'd met on Tinder.

It had taken them almost three hours to pick a jury. Trent had wisely let Clifford do the honors for the defense side. Clifford had turned on his Southern charm and seemed genuinely interested in each and every juror and their thoughts and feelings. His command of the courtroom and its space was complete. He moved easily and smoothly, and his voice filled the room without being oppressive. He just sort of *fit* in the courtroom as if there were some sort of symbiotic relationship that allowed each to enhance the other. Even Jason, who hated Joseph Clifford III, found himself almost liking Joseph Clifford III, which, of course, made him hate Joseph Clifford III even more. He also hated fate for arranging his first performance in a courtroom filled with media such that he was opposite a trial legend with thirty-plus years' experience, setting up the perfect juxtaposition to make Jason look like an amateur. He also found the energy to hate Maggie, Spelkin, the armed lunatic, Trent, and The Widow.

He was okay with the jury that had been picked, however. There were eight women (seven white, one black) and four men (three white, one Asian). The grandmother had made it, as had one of the women who'd raised her hand when he'd asked whether anybody had been treated unfairly at work. The unfair treatment had to do with not getting a promotion she thought she'd deserved, not a termination, but it was still The Man keeping her down. Jason had struck the blazer guy with his first peremptory strike, and Clifford et al. had struck a black woman who felt she'd been discriminated against. They proceeded down the list, eliminating jurors based on largely indescribable criteria, mostly guesswork. Jason found himself wanting to strike the skinnier jurors, which was more amusing than anything. Because the more overweight jurors would believe that Maggie could be sexually desirable? It was possible. The highly trained trial attorney at the top of his game, he thought, biased against thin people.

But there was no one else there to help him decide, or to weigh in, so to speak, so he just went with his instincts.

And then there were twelve.

The court broke for lunch with opening statements to be made immediately following the recess. Jason was up.

He fought back jitters as Maggie continued to peck at her phone. At the other end of the room, the defense team had three tables pushed together and were huddled around them like a nerdy football team.

Jason looked at Maggie. She was very pale.

"How are you feeling?" he asked her. "You doing okay?"

Maggie threw up a little on her salad.

*****

"Mr. Hunter, you may proceed," said the judge.

Jason stood. All eyes were on him. He walked slowly around his bench to stand in front of the jury. He took no notes with him. Nothing between him and the jurors. It was time to connect. And it was time to play the only card he had that might throw off Trent, Clifford, and the rest of their battalion.

The Prick

"Levitt, Bennett and Taylor is a large international law firm. Maggie Moxley worked there for years as a legal secretary. Then, one night, when Maggie was working late, one of the most powerful and profitable partners in the Atlanta office, Robert Spelkin, drunkenly sexually assaulted her." Jason let that big pronouncement fill the room and hang there, and he saw all of the jurors take it in, register shock/disgust/delight, look at him, and look at Maggie.

"Maggie reported it. She had the *courage* to report it to the Equal Employment Opportunity Commission. Then, after she told the EEOC what happened, Levitt *fired* her," Jason thundered, pointing over to the defense table. "Unlike Maggie, however, Levitt was cowardly. They called the firing a layoff." Jason smiled and put "layoff" in quotes. Several of the jurors smirked at this. They knew what big corporations were like.

"Levitt tried to disguise its retaliation against Maggie by also 'laying off' several other employees, at the same time, so it could claim that Maggie was just caught up in this layoff wave. This cover-up attempt would have tragic consequences for Robert Spelkin, and for his family. This is the story of what happened."

Jason took a few steps back and looked over at The Widow, sympathetically. "This case involves Robert Spelkin, and his unfortunate actions that night started the chain of events that brought us here today. But this case is *not about him*. It is about Levitt and its wanton retaliation against a powerless employee who had the temerity, the strength, to stand up for herself."

"Now," Jason said, "I notice that Mr. Spelkin's wife and his children are in the courtroom. This next part is very adult and I think it might be best if the children left the courtroom for it." Jason turned around and looked toward the defense table. The Widow stared back at him, an ice queen.

The jury stared at him and The Widow with delicious rapt attention. It was the first test of her character.

Trent stood. "Your Honor," she said, "this is highly improper. Please direct Mr. Hunter to continue on with his statement or be done with it and sit down."

"That's enough, Ms. Trent," the judge said. Judge Barnes didn't like Rebecca Trent, Jason noted. That was interesting. "I think it's all right to give Mrs. Spelkin the option to make the choice regarding what she wants her children to hear."

The Widow looked wide-eyed at the judge, seemingly surprised that she'd shot Trent down and not Jason, and whispered something to Clifford, who got up, grabbed an associate, and escorted the kids out of the room.

Jason turned back to the jury. Several of the women were nodding at him approvingly. They were on the edges of their seats. He was no longer nervous in the slightest. He was rolling.

"On March 21st, Robert Spelkin told Maggie to stay late to finish a project. Maggie was his secretary. She had to do what he said." Clifford reentered the room and grabbed a notepad from a paralegal. "She had to do what he said, so she stayed late, working on a filing that Robert Spelkin said had to go out. But for a while Maggie was alone in the office. That was because Mr. Spelkin was upstairs at the Peachtree Club, celebrating. He and some of the other attorneys ran up nearly a two thousand dollar bar tab at the Peachtree Club, toasting each other on settling a big case. Nobody disputes that Mr. Spelkin had a lot to drink that night. *Nobody* disputes that."

Jason stepped forward toward the jury again, trying to keep their attention with movement. People were accustomed to constant stimuli from their entertainment. The reporter on the screen and the picture in picture of the scene of events and the news stream at the bottom on the page. "Now, I'm not here to judge Mr. Spelkin or to tell you that he was evil. I'm just here to tell you what he did to Maggie after running up that bar tab. And then I'm going to tell you what happened after Maggie was brave enough to complain about it."

Jason nodded to himself as if agreeing that what he said was right, and paused to let those two distinct events set in: (1) the sexual assault; (2) the retaliation. Hopefully the jury was getting that there were two issues, separate and distinct. He couldn't take anything for granted, though. He would have to keep drilling it home over and over. The message: Even if you feel bad for The Widow, and even if you think Maggie is a slut, the large and powerful law firm still maliciously retaliated against a woman who complained that her boss sexually assaulted her. Punish it.

"Maggie was sitting at her desk. It was late and dark in the office. She was the only one left. Everyone else either had gone home or was up drinking at the bar. She heard Robert Spelkin coming down the hall before she saw him. He was making a lot of noise. She turned and saw him walking toward her unsteadily. She thought he was coming to check on her progress, so she turned back to her computer to keep making the changes to the brief he'd directed, as quickly as possible. Then he came into her cubicle area, behind her. She could smell the booze wafting off of him. She turned around. Mr. Spelkin smiled at her. And then he unzipped his pants and pulled out his erect penis."

The courtroom was deathly silent, except for the soft scratches of pen on paper from the reporters in the back pews.

The Prick

"He told Maggie, who was obviously shocked, that it was the quote-unquote *project* she had to complete before she went home. He told her that she had to do it or she was fired."

"Picture this. A woman trapped in her cubicle with her drunken boss barring the exit, his erect penis thrust at her, and she is told that she has to gratify him, or that she'll lose her job."

Jason shook his head at the image. "Maggie didn't know what to do. She was trapped. So she turned around to her computer screen, hoping that he would just go away."

Jason paused and scanned eye contact through the back row of jurors. "But he didn't. Instead, the next thing Maggie knew, Mr. Spelkin was right behind her. And he was pushing his erect penis against her neck. That's how she felt it. *Right against her neck.* And then he demanded that she put it in her mouth."

The jurors looked shocked. Every single one of them. And they looked very, very interested. Every single one of them.

"But Maggie has strength in her. You'll see that in this trial. She isn't perfect. But she is strong. She told her boss no. She told him that she couldn't. His response?" Jason took a breath. "Of course you can," he said in a powerful, booming voice to simulate the power Spelkin wielded. "Nobody will know. I know that you want to. Do it!"

Jason dropped his voice now, to assume the voice of the powerless yet chastely defiant victim. "But Maggie refused. She pushed him away and got past him. He tried to grab her, but he was drunk and so she was able to dodge him. She escaped the cubicle and ran down the hall. Do you know what she heard behind her?"

Jason stopped and made eye contact with one of the female jurors in the front row, a schoolteacher. "He was laughing. Maggie heard him laughing." The schoolteacher shook her head in disgust. Jason nodded at her and shifted to her neighbor, the one African American on the jury, who held a customer-relations job at Delta.

"But that's only *half* of the story," he said. "Let me tell you what Maggie's employer, Levitt, did when she stood up for herself. Maggie complained to the Equal Employment Opportunity Commission, by filing a written Charge of Discrimination, on April 5th. She had worked for Levitt for almost five years. *One week* after complaining to the EEOC about the sexual harassment, Levitt fired her. One week."

He watched the woman take it in. Her jaw actually dropped. Jason had known that fact for so long that he'd forgotten how incredibly damning it was for Levitt. Good facts were like anything else. You got used to them and after a while they didn't make as big an impression. It was nice to see someone take it in for the first time. One week! That was such a good fucking fact!

Jason moved to the next person, a white male in his fifties who worked as a trucker and looked a bit rough. Jason didn't expect sympathy from him. He was going to have to make him angry at someone, preferably Levitt. Jason found it feasible that he could persuade a trucker to be wrathful toward a mega-rich law firm. The kind of firm that looked down on the little guy, that thought it could get away with anything.

"It gets worse," Jason told the trucker directly. "Levitt didn't want to look like it was firing Maggie outright. That might look bad." The trucker smirked. "So you know what it did? It fired *six people* without any cause and called it a layoff, making Maggie one of those six. It was not only willing to fire Maggie for complaining, it was willing to fire five other people for no reason other than to attempt to cover up what it was doing. Five other people who had nothing to do with this case. Five other people who were just minding their own business. And Maggie. They were all 'laid off'"—(air quotes)—"the same day. The man who made this decision is in the courtroom today. His name is James Peters. He's sitting with the defense. He is the Managing Partner of Levitt's Atlanta office. To this day."

Jason pointed directly at Peters, who looked up with a delightful combination of shock and terror before he was able to compose himself. The entire jury saw it. Most of them looked back at Jason again. Not the trucker, however. The trucker continued to stare at Peters. Jason thought, perhaps optimistically, that he saw anger in the man's eyes.

He moved to the next person, a homemaker seated to the right of the trucker. He was worried that she was going to dislike Maggie when it came out that she was (at least) an attempted adulterer. "This is where the story turns even more tragic," he told her directly. He had every last fraction of her attention. What would she think if she knew the other version of The Truth? Or if she knew there were competing versions of The Truth? Jason hoped very much that he would never find out.

"As part of James Peters's cover up of Maggie's firing," he told the woman, "he decided to fire a man named Donald Jeffries, who worked in Levitt's Atlanta office. I don't know whether Peters knew it or not at the time, but it turned out that Donald Jeffries was unbalanced mentally. There's a police report. You'll see it. When Donald Jeffries was fired, he pulled out most of his hair in the office. Levitt terminated him anyway. And did nothing. Offered no help with therapy or other support. Just fired him and turned him out on the street. Next thing they knew, Donald Jeffries showed up at the office with a gun. Levitt banned him from the building, but, again, didn't try to get him any help."

The Prick

Jason shook his head in disgust. "Donald Jeffries, ladies and gentlemen, suffered a mental breakdown. He blamed Robert Spelkin for getting him fired, when he really should have blamed James Peters. James Peters made the decision!" Jason pointed back at poor, hapless Peters. "But it was Mr. Spelkin that Donald Jeffries blamed. And so tragedy struck. One day last summer, Donald Jeffries tracked down Mr. Spelkin. He shot him in the street with his mother's handgun. Mr. Spelkin died right there, on Peachtree Street. His children lost a father. And his wife lost a husband. Because of what Levitt did. And then Donald Jeffries took his own life. Right there in the street. Because of what Levitt did."

"Now I told you before that I am not here to tell you Mr. Spelkin was an evil man. What he did was surely wrong, immoral, disgraceful. But he didn't deserve that. His family didn't deserve that. And I feel true sadness for his family."

The majority of the jurors were staring at him, nodding along. The trucker was still fixated on Peters. The housewife was looking at the judge, for whatever reason.

Jason spread his arms, open palms. "We're here today because Levitt must be held accountable. It must be held accountable for what happened to Maggie. We need to send a message that this conduct is entirely intolerable and we will not stand for it!" He clenched his right hand. "Thank you."

Jason walked back and sat next to Maggie. The inside of his suit was drenched in sweat and his hands were shaking with adrenaline. But he thought he had pulled it off. Maggie glanced at him, trying to gather some indicator of how it had gone. He gave her a slight nod and braced himself. It was Clifford's turn.

He watched as Clifford gathered his notes and sauntered up to the podium. Clifford glanced over at him on his way with a look that was ... curious? Appraising? Bemused? It was obvious that Jason had at least done something unexpected. Which was half the battle. He hoped.

*****

"Maggie, we've only got a few more minutes," her young attorney urgently and unhelpfully informed her. There was panic in his voice. "We need to get composed and go back in there. The judge only gave us fifteen minutes."

It was an interesting thing to hear someone panicking and telling her to compose herself simultaneously. But she understood. That was the position she'd put both of them in.

Maggie was back in a familiar place, a bathroom stall, doing a familiar thing, crying into a toilet, hearing a familiar sound, her lawyer asking her to brave the world outside of the stall. She'd promised herself she wouldn't do this, but, of course, she had, and in spectacularly appalling fashion.

Jason's presentation had gone well, at least as far as she was able to discern. He'd mentioned to her that he had shifted the strategy somewhat to deal with the change in what he called "the dynamics" of the case, which she understood to refer to the crazy guy killing Robert on Peachtree Street while she'd been crying in another bathroom stall across town. Maggie tried to listen for the change in Jason's argument, but she couldn't make it out. It all sounded the same as before.

At any rate, she found herself losing track of what he was actually saying because she was overcome with the intense desire to do whatever she could to just stop the whole thing, escape. She had started this, kind of. Couldn't she stop it? Everyone was staring at her. Even the judge. Even the deputies. Even the man in the suspenders who represented Her, Mrs. Spelkin.

The Prick

And then the man in the suspenders got up and started speaking. He had a slow Southern drawl, charming in a way that showed he knew it was charming.

"Well folks, a small part of what the young man told you was true. Mrs. Moxley here"—he pointed his chubby finger right at her—"accuses Mr. Spelkin of a horrible sexual act. She *claims* that he got drunk and forced himself upon her." His words were just dripping with skepticism. If he suggested in that tone that she didn't exist, she would question her very being.

The suspendered man moved close to the table she and Jason were sitting at. He blocked Jason from the jury's view, and Maggie was immediately to his left. The jury just saw Maggie and her suspendered torturer. Their eyes darted back and forth between the duo. "*She,*" he continued, pointing again with the chubby finger, "*claims* that she told him no, resisted these supposed sexual advances, but he *insisted* that *she* quote 'put it in her mouth.' There are no corroborating witnesses to this story, conveniently. *Nobody* else saw this happen."

"Now, you folks are going to hear a lot about this lady over the course of this trial, but let me tell you about Robert Spelkin, the man she accuses of such a horrible act. And let me tell you the part of Mr. Hunter's statement that was true. Mr. Spelkin is not here to defend himself against this woman's accusations. He was gunned down by a mentally ill man while he was walking down the street in midtown Atlanta." Clifford shook his head. "He's not here to tell you that what this woman says didn't happen. He's not here to defend his honor."

Clifford turned, pivoting toward her. He was maybe five feet from Maggie. He glared at her directly, pointedly. "Robert Spelkin *was* an *honorable* man," he declared, directly *at* her. Everyone in the jury was staring. Clifford

329

The Prick

glared at her, as if he was daring her to challenge that statement. The moment seemed to stretch and stretch in time. Maggie looked at Jason pleadingly. Make it stop, she wanted to ask him. Call the whole thing off, she wanted to beg him. But he just kept his poker face. The same poker face he had told her so many times to maintain during these statements. He nodded at her as if to say, it's okay, keep it together. But his eyes looked scared. Scared of how it was going or scared of what she was going to do, she didn't know.

"Robert Spelkin," Clifford repeated, still staring at her, "was an *honorable* man. He was a lawyer in good standing for over twenty-five years. He was a husband, married for over fifteen years. He was a father of two beautiful children. You saw them in the courtroom. They were ushered out at Mr. Hunter's request before he repeated *this woman's* scandalous allegations against that honorable man, who is no longer able to defend himself. I hate to think of the *pain* that her allegations must have caused him when he was still with us on this Earth."

Maggie heard someone sob. It was a big, oxygenated sob, and loud. She wanted to see who it was but kept looking straight ahead, the way Jason had told her. Then she heard it again. She couldn't help herself and looked around. Clifford had stopped talking. She scanned the other side and the rows behind and couldn't locate the crier.

Jason put his hand on her shoulder and whispered something unintelligible to her. She looked down at his hand and, in horror, realized where the sobbing was coming from. Her. And then she felt the hot tears streaming down her cheeks and felt the heat rush to her face. Jason's hand was on her back now, rubbing in a circular motion, and he was whispering in her ear, "It's okay, pull it together, it's okay ..." But she couldn't stop. It was getting worse. Huh

The Prick

huh huh. Jason's whispering was becoming more urgent, but she couldn't understand the words. Huh huh huh. She had to get out. Huh huh huh. She tried to push herself out of the chair, but there was something holding her down. Was it Jason? "Let me go!"

He said something else. Her ears were filled with the sound of blood rushing—it sounded like the ocean. She couldn't get out. Someone was grabbing her. "Let me go!"

She tried to wrestle free and felt the chair leg slam against the table, heard the loud crack it made. She was able to stand up a little but couldn't fully straighten her legs. She looked down. The chair was caught on her hips, its back legs touching the ground, and it wasn't letting her go. Jason, wild-eyed, was trying to yank the chair off of her by pulling down on the back of it. Everyone was gaping at the scene, some of their mouths wide open in shock.

Jason tugged and tugged at the chair. Huh huh huh. "Calm down," he was saying "calm down." She pushed down on the arms again and heard a rip. The right side of her blouse had torn, exposing some of her fleshy side. Jason yanked again, and finally the chair came free. Maggie grabbed the torn part of the blouse and pushed past Jason, knocking him into his chair and off balance.

She pushed through the little wooden doors that separated the courtroom from the audience. Huh huh huh. The ocean was roaring in her ears. She focused on the doors to the hallway and moved toward them as fast as she could. Escape. Huh huh huh. She knew what she must look like. Crying, red, ripped blouse, waddling away as fast as she could down the aisle. But she had to get outside.

And then it started. The laughter. She didn't know where it began (Mrs. Spelkin?) but it swept through the courtroom like a brush fire. She saw all the reporters laughing, fully and directly in her face. So cruel. So cold. She stared at one of them, trying to find some humanity as she waddled as quickly as possible toward the doors. There was no sympathy in his face. If anything her stare seemed to further inflame his laughter. A few more steps to the door as the chorus of laughter smashed down upon her. Ha ha ha ha ha ha.

She pushed through the door and out into the hall. But the laughter still pursued her. And somewhere in there, somewhere in that raucous madness, she thought that she heard, just for a second, Robert Spelkin, laughing at her again.

When she made it through the doors, she nearly ran over his children, who stared up at the large, bawling woman with wide eyes before someone whisked them out of her path.

And so here she was again, in a bathroom stall, the horrific scene playing on repeat in her head. That couldn't have actually happened, could it? She couldn't have gotten stuck in a chair while crying and trying to flee the courtroom. They couldn't have all laughed at her, could they?

"Two minutes, Maggie," a voice said over her head. Had her attorney gotten on a speaker system? No, he had gone into the next stall and climbed up on the toilet to peer in. How many times had he had to try to force her out of a bathroom in the last year? This must be a nightmare for him. She must be the worst client he'd ever had. He must hate her.

She looked up at him. "I'm so sorry."

*****

Climbing onto the toilet, Jason was enveloped in the same powerful emotion that had overcome him when Maggie's uncontrollable sobbing had started and intensified during her most inglorious escape from the courtroom, that

The Prick

is, a potent mixture of rage, humiliation, and panic. But when he ascended the toilet to look down into the next stall, which was struggling to contain his hysterical client, the absurdity of the situation expelled this emotional cocktail from his mind. Not bad, Universe, he thought. This is quite a magnificent disaster you've cooked up for me. He found himself actually suppressing a laugh and looked down on Maggie with pity for a few seconds. Laughter would probably be the worst medicine at this juncture.

"It's okay, Maggie. Look, the worst has happened now. There's nothing else to be afraid of, or nervous about. The case is almost certainly lost, if it wasn't before we got here today. Let's both just go out there, relax, and see it through. It'll be over in a few short days and then I'll get us both a good bankruptcy attorney."

"They laughed at me."

"Yes, they did," Jason said. "The Widow started it."

"She's a cruel woman," Maggie said, craning her neck to look at him. She was in a clump on the floor with her arms around the toilet, into which she had been literally crying when Jason first got his aerial view.

"I expect that's true."

"Robert was not an honorable man," she said, pushing herself to her feet.

"No," Jason said, "he wasn't."

Maggie unlocked the bathroom door. Jason waited until she exited the stall before he carefully stepped down off the toilet. He reached down and took Maggie's damp hand.

"Listen," he told her, "we are going to walk back into that courtroom together, and you are going to keep your head up. It takes strength to do what you're doing. Be proud of that. From here on out you are immune to what they say about you. You are above it. It doesn't touch you."

"Okay." She lifted her chin. Her head was literally up.

The Prick

He squeezed her hand, and she smiled at him. He realized that she might not have received any kindness at all from anyone for some time.

"Ready?"

"As I'm going to be."

Jason held the door open for her. He had been in women's restrooms more times during the Moxley case than in the rest of his life combined. She walked through it, head still upwardly inclined. There were some reporters and a few enemy attorneys milling around in the hall, and they all stopped what they were doing and stared at them. Jason stared back, hoping to shame them or at least guilt them into some slight contrition for laughing at this poor woman, but he saw neither shame nor guilt, just intense interest and glee that the show was about to go on.

Jason pushed through the courtroom doors and held them open for Maggie. The jurors had been sequestered in the jury room and the judge was back in chambers. The only people in the courtroom were the army of defense attorneys and attendants, The Widow and family, and the reporters. All noise and motion stopped dead and everyone turned to look. Even the kids.

Maggie walked, steadily and without making eye contact, up the hallway through the pews and through the doors separating the pews from the active courtroom. She sat right back down in the chair that had been her captor and tormentor. She smiled at Jason and took a deep breath.

He looked over at the defense side. Trent smiled her shark smile at him and Clifford winked. They thought that they'd already won. And they were probably right. An absurd thing to lose a case on—a fleeing fat woman with a ripped blouse and tears streaming down her face. But Jason's one and only witness had lost any credibility she'd had. Probably.

The Prick

"All rise!" the courtroom deputy bellowed. All complied. Judge Barnes and her clerk entourage came back in through the side door that connected with the judge's chambers, and the judge resumed her position at the bench. She scanned the courtroom though her glasses.

"Be seated," she said. "Counsel, approach."

Jason, Clifford, and Trent walked up to the side of the bench. Judge Barnes looked at Jason. "Counsel, is your client ready to proceed?" Her voice was low so that only the attorneys at sidebar and the court reporter and clerks could hear.

"Yes, Your Honor," said Jason. "I would request that, given what happened, we select a new jury. This one will certainly be biased because of this afternoon's incident. I don't believe that we'll be able to get a fair trial."

Judge Barnes put a hand up to silence Clifford and Trent, who both had started to speak at once. She leaned over. "I had considered that, Mr. Hunter, but it seems to me we spent an entire morning selecting this jury and I am not inclined to waste all of that time *and* spend additional hours selecting another just because your client decided to flee the courtroom and the—let's just say unfortunate—circumstances that occasioned her departure."

Jason saw in the judge's eyes what Jason already knew: his case was dead and the judge wasn't going to screw up her calendar to resuscitate it.

"Your Honor, I must then state my objection for the record. I don't believe that the jury will be able to fairly evaluate the facts of the case in light of what happened."

"We're not going to start over just because your client is unable to face the truth without suffering a meltdown," Trent interjected sharply. Clifford stayed quiet. But his face said it all: no reason to interrupt when you're winning.

The Prick

"That's enough, Ms. Trent," Judge Barnes said. "These are emotional issues, I'm sure, for Mrs. Moxley and I'm sympathetic to that." Judge Barnes looked at Jason. "Counsel, when I bring the jury back in, I will instruct them regarding the ... scene ... that they witnessed. I would instruct *you* to tell your client that further disturbances will not be tolerated. If she must cry, she will cry at the counsel table until she is excused. Is that understood?"

"Yes, Your Honor."

"Good," the judge said. "Now here's what's going to happen. Mr. Clifford is going to conclude his opening statement. And listen, Joe, stop shouting at the poor woman. You've made your point."

Clifford nodded with a hint of a smile. Jason appreciated the instruction but wasn't a big fan of the first-name basis.

Judge Barnes scowled at Trent. "When Joe is done, Ms. Trent will give her opening statement. I expect no theatrics. Understood?"

"Yes, Your Honor," Trent answered with obvious annoyance.

"Okay," Judge Barnes said. "After that, plaintiff will call her first witness. If that witness is the plaintiff, as I suspect, that should take us through the end of the day. I expect complete professionalism and decorum from all sides, and I expect the proceedings to occur in an orderly manner. Is that clear?"

"Yes, Your Honor," they said.

They returned to their seats, and the judge instructed the deputy to retrieve the jury. He returned shortly with them in tow, and all of the lawyers rose to greet them. Jason scanned them carefully. They all looked more subdued than he'd been expecting. He hoped that, in their minds and in the time during the break, Maggie had metamorphosed from a creature of ridicule to one of pity. Some of them had

336

The Prick

been laughing, he knew, during Maggie's horrible escape. But that didn't mean they didn't feel sorry for her. That was a third of the plan, after all. Pity her, hate Levitt, forget about Spelkin. The compromised trifecta litigation strategy, as he had taken to calling it inside his head and to no one else.

"Be seated," the judge said. Everyone sat.

"Now," Judge Barnes began, addressing the jury directly, "before we took our break, you all witnessed an unfortunate incident. These are emotional issues in a very emotional case and I instruct you jurors that you must evaluate the case based on the evidence that is put before you, not on what happened during Mr. Clifford's opening statement. Just as with the other attorneys, what Mr. Clifford said is not evidence and Mrs. Moxley's reaction is not evidence. You are instructed that what happened does not mean that Mrs. Moxley's allegations in this case are true, and it does not mean that they are false. You will make that determination at the close of the evidence based on the witnesses' testimony and the other evidence that is introduced. Certainly you must judge Mrs. Moxley's character, but *not* based on that incident."

After this confusing and somewhat contradictory statement, the jurors looked exceedingly nonplussed. Jason found the judge's instruction rather unhelpful in that, among other things, she seemed to be indicating that it *would* be prejudicial to Maggie if her character were judged on the incident. Her instruction to give no weight to it drew more attention to it and would cause the jurors to assign more weight to it. Human Nature 101. But the whole goddamn thing was Maggie's fault anyway, and the judge was in the very tricky position of having to de-prejudice an irretrievably prejudiced jury with the only tool at her disposal, specifically a judicial instruction to override their innate instincts and disregard the incredibly engrossing thing they had personally witnessed.

But Jason was young. He could always seek out another line of work when this whole thing inevitably ended in catastrophic fashion. He looked down at Maggie and wondered how much of this she was getting. She was staring straight ahead with her chin pointedly inclined.

"Now," the judge said, having completed construction of her verbal maze, "is there any member of the jury who feels that they cannot fairly evaluate the case in light of the incident during Mr. Clifford's opening statement?"

As if. As if anyone on the jury would admit to such a character failing, the absence of rationality. Especially when this case already promised so much in the way of entertainment. No, they were in it for the long haul. Nobody raised their hand.

"Very well," Judge Barnes said, seemingly pleased with the verbal anesthetic she had administered. "Mr. Clifford, you may proceed. You have twelve minutes remaining."

Clifford stood up and issued a knowing grin to the jury. It said, "I've already shown you who this woman is, haven't I?" He strolled over to the podium.

"I will only take one or two, Your Honor," he said. His voice, so booming before Maggie's meltdown, was mellow and soothing now. "Ladies and gentlemen of the jury, I will conclude my remarks by simply saying this: it did not happen. Nothing of what Mrs. Moxley claims happened actually did. She is entitled to nothing. You will surely draw this same, correct, conclusion for yourselves once all of the evidence is presented. I look forward to spending the next few days with you all and presenting the events as they *actually* transpired. Your job is the most important in the judicial system, to find the truth. *My* job is to make your job as easy as possible. And I will endeavor to do so."

The Prick

Clifford smiled at the jurors and they smiled back at him. Judge Barnes was smiling as well, and the clerks and the court reporter. All filled with such fine feelings toward this suspendered truth-elucidator. Jason morbidly wondered what would happen if he ran out of the courtroom crying. He would love to hear the judge's curative instruction on that one.

Trent stood up. Jason had been so preoccupied with this disintegrating case that he had not given Trent's outfit the attention that it was due. She sported a *lime green* pantsuit that was at least—at least—two sizes too big. Her shoulder pads looked like a football player's. Some of the jurors gave her the once-over as well. There had to be some ingenious strategy behind Trent's ill-fitting, bizarrely colored outfits, but Jason would be damned if he could figure out what it was.

She walked stiffly over to the podium with a stack of notes and placed them precisely and neatly in front of her. "Good afternoon."

This was the first time that Trent had interacted directly with the jury. Jason watched their reactions. She was the smartest lawyer in the courtroom, but there was legal intelligence and then there was social intelligence. Sometimes lawyers endowed with large portions of the former were strikingly deficient in the latter. Trent was not a warm person.

"I represent Levitt, Bennett and Taylor, the law firm that formerly employed both Mrs. Moxley and Robert Spelkin. Levitt employs over a hundred persons in Atlanta. It has never before been named as a defendant in a lawsuit alleging sexual harassment or retaliation in its Atlanta office. Robert Spelkin was a partner in the Atlanta office for years. His reputation was sterling. As my colleague Mr.

The Prick

Clifford explained, Mrs. Moxley accuses the late Robert Spelkin of immoral and reprehensible conduct. She's lying."

Anger radiated off Trent when she said this and her light blue eyes scanned the jury, like a teacher making sure the entire class was paying attention. "She's lying. She asks you to believe that Robert Spelkin, a married man with two children, risked everything, his career, his marriage, his reputation, to engage in extramarital relations with her. *And* she asks you not only to award damages against Mr. Spelkin's *estate* for these false allegations, she asks you to award damages against the firm that employed her for years." This was said in the tone of "Can you fucking believe this bullshit?"

"She also insults your intelligence by asking you to believe that Levitt, a law firm that employs over a thousand people across the country, including some of the finest lawyers in America, was so concerned about her baseless claims that they turned around and not only fired her but fired five of her colleagues! She actually expects you to believe that Levitt would wantonly end the careers of its other employees because of *her*."

Trent gripped the sides of the podium and her voice dropped an octave or two. "And now it gets even worse. Her lawyer, Mr. Hunter"—she said his name with abject contempt—"comes in here today and blames the death of Mr. Spelkin on Levitt. He actually had the gall to say in his opening statement to you all, his introduction, that it was Levitt's fault this great man is dead. That is the worst kind of lawyering and I say shame on him and shame on—"

Jason shot up. "Objection, Your Honor, that is completely—"

"Improper," Judge Barnes said. "That is enough, Ms. Trent. Conclude your remarks."

The Prick

Trent glared at the judge for a full five seconds. "Thank you, Your Honor."

"Carry on," Judge Barnes instructed.

"Yes, Your Honor." Trent turned back to the jury, now with sprained credibility. "What actually happened, ladies and gentlemen, is that Levitt underwent routine downsizing following the resolution of a big case. While Mrs. Moxley was laid off, it had nothing to do with her baseless allegations against Mr. Spelkin. The idea that it was connected was concocted by her attorney in a desperate attempt to add additional claims to this frivolous case. In fact—"

"Your Honor," Jason said, standing again, "Ms. Trent—"

"Is finished with her remarks," Judge Barnes said. "Thank you, Ms. Trent. We've concluded opening statements and the plaintiff will call her first witness."

Trent looked at the judge in shock. The judge looked back at her. Then Trent snapped out of it and turned to the jury. "Thank you." She picked up her papers and walked back to her table, stone-faced.

The judge looked at Jason. "Counsel, proceed."

Here we go, Jason thought.

The Prick

Chapter 15

Monday, December 10th
United States District Courthouse
Northern District of Georgia, Atlanta Division

"Plaintiff calls Margaret Moxley."

Jason said a silent thank you to God as Maggie extracted herself from her chair without incident and ambled up to the witness stand. They had practiced this tens of times, down to drawing a map of the courtroom and charting out where she would walk and sit down. Maggie managed to ascend the witness platform without any problems and was immediately sworn in.

Jason went up to the podium and turned it so he was facing Maggie, with the jury on his left.

"Maggie, please introduce yourself to the jury."

"Maggie Moxley," she said timidly.

"How long have you lived in Georgia, Maggie?"

"All of my life. Forty-two years."

"Are you married?"

"Yes. My husband's name is Pete."

"How long have you been married?"

"About nine years."

"Maggie, have you ever cheated on your husband?"

"Oh, no."

"Why not?"

The Prick

"I love him. And it's, you know, wrong to cheat. Morally wrong," she said softly. The jurors were craning forward in their seats to hear her.

"Yes," Jason agreed. He wished she'd been a bit stronger with that. In the rehearsals, it had been a strong condemnation of infidelity. But she was so meek up there, so scared. She wasn't about to give a strong condemnation of anything. He also noted unhappily that her "you know" tic had worked itself back into her diction.

"How long did you work for the Levitt law firm?"

"Almost five years."

"What was your position?"

"Legal assistant, which is essentially a secretary. Legal secretary, really."

"Who did you report to?"

"Well, technically all of the legal assistants reported to the Office Manager, Arthur Jensen. But our real bosses were the attorneys we were assigned to support."

"Last year, until the time that Levitt terminated your employment, how many attorneys were you assigned to support?"

"Four."

"Was Robert Spelkin one of those attorneys?"

Maggie swallowed. "Yes." Jason eyed the Kleenex box to the right of the witness stand so he could rush up and hand one to her when it became necessary, a near certainty.

"Was he the most important attorney you supported?"

Clifford stood. "Objection, Your Honor, vague and calls for speculation."

"Sustained," Judge Barnes said. "Rephrase, counsel."

"Yes, Your Honor. Maggie, did you consider Mr. Spelkin to be an important attorney at the firm?"

"Oh, certainly."

"Why?"

The Prick

"Well, he was a partner, and everyone knew that he was one of the biggest business generators at the firm."

"How long did you report to him?"

"Four years."

"Now, Maggie, we're going to talk about the night in question in a minute. But before we do, before that night happened, did Mr. Spelkin ever approach you sexually in any way?"

"No," Maggie said, shaking her head. "He never did. Some of the other girls around the office talked about how he looked at us, you know, the—"

"Objection, Your Honor, blatant hearsay!" Trent all but yelled from her table.

"Just the hearsay objection by itself is fine, Ms. Trent," she said. "Sustained. The jury will disregard the statement regarding what the other female employees discussed with respect to Mr. Spelkin."

Jason nodded, satisfied. The jury would just as easily cleanse the office gossip that Spelkin was a perv as they would the image of Maggie fleeing from the courtroom with her ripped blouse in the breeze.

"All right, Maggie, let's talk about the day in question." Jason wanted to get right to it and cover it fully before the jury was released for the day. Give the people what they want! And give them the whole night to think about it, ruminate on it, tell their families about it against the judge's instructions, before they came in the next day and Clifford and Trent carved Maggie up like a duplicitous Thanksgiving turkey.

"What day of the week was it?"

"Wednesday."

"Did you stay late that day?"

"Yes."

"Why?"

The Prick

"Mr. Spelkin told me that I had to stay late to finish entering edits to a brief he wanted to file that night."

"Did you feel that you could say no to that request?"

"Oh, no," Maggie said, "it wasn't a request. Mr. Spelkin didn't request. He told you."

A few of the jurors laughed a little at that. Good.

Jason smiled. "So Mr. Spelkin told you, directed you, that you had to stay late?"

"Yes."

"And you complied?"

"Yes."

"Did he tell you how late you would have to stay?"

"Until I finished."

"Right," Jason said. "Please tell the jury what happened at the end of that Wednesday."

This was it. He had no doubt as to what version of The Truth she was going to tell. He just wanted it to come out right, genuine, honest. What Levitt did was still wrong, he had told himself over and over. Maggie had made the decision to lie and he had made the decision to let her. Now she had to deliver.

"Well I was alone in the office, in my cubicle. Everyone else had left for the day or was upstairs at the bar."

"What do you mean, upstairs at the bar?"

"Mr. Spelkin, Mr. Nichols, and some of the others had gone up to the bar to celebrate. They'd just settled a big case, made a lot of money for the firm. I'm not supposed to say how much but it was a lot."

"There's a bar in the building?"

"Oh yes, the Peachtree Club. Mr. Spelkin and some of the others belonged there as members. Mr. Spelkin would give me receipts from there to expense. Sometimes he would take clients."

The Prick

"So Mr. Spelkin and the others were up at the bar and you were downstairs working?"

"Yes. He told me to email him when I was done and that he would come down, read it over, and then I would file it."

"After he'd been drinking?"

"Yes."

Jason glanced at the jury. Some of them were writing notes. The Asian man was shaking his head, maybe disapprovingly.

"Okay," Jason said. "You can tell the jury what happened next." He said it in the way that a therapist would assure a patient that it was safe to explain a traumatic event. This is a safe place, et cetera. The jurors would be entrusted with this information; Maggie would relive this painful memory for their benefit.

"Well, I was working on the brief, putting in his changes in my cubicle."

"Was anyone else there?"

"No, the office was deserted. All the lights were out except the one right over my desk."

"What happened next?"

"I heard him coming down the hall. There was banging against the wall. You could tell, you know, that he was stumbling. And then he came up to the desk. I could smell the booze on him."

"And then what happened when he got to your cubicle?"

"That's when he reached down and unzipped his pants. And he took it out."

"Took what out, Maggie?"

Maggie, who had been maintaining eye contact with Jason and Jason only (disregarding wholly Jason's repeated instructions in prep to look at the jury), now looked down at her lap.

"His penis."

The Prick

"Speak into the microphone please, Mrs. Moxley," Judge Barnes said.

Maggie moved her head closer to the microphone and said, loudly and clearly so that it reverberated through the courtroom, "He took his penis out of his pants. It was erect."

Jason nodded and looked at the jury. Maggie's hold on their attention was total.

"Then what happened?"

"He told me to put it in my mouth," she said into the microphone. "He said it was a project that he needed me to work on. He had a big smile on his face, you know, when he said it."

Maggie sniffed, and Jason could tell the waterworks were starting. He didn't mind them as long as she was able to get her story out. He walked up and handed her a tissue from the conveniently placed box of Kleenex.

Jason walked back to the podium and faced Maggie again. "When your boss cornered you in your cubicle after hours and told you to put his erect penis in your mouth, what did you do, Maggie?"

It was the greater-than-million-dollar question.

"I told him no," she said. "I told him no, I couldn't. And he said that I could and that I had to and that he knew I wanted to. He told me that nobody would find out."

"And then what happened?"

"Well, he wouldn't take no for an answer and I was trapped in the cubicle, so I just said no again and turned around in my chair towards my computer. I hoped that he would just ... go away."

"Did he?"

"No," Maggie said into the microphone. "He didn't."

"What happened next?"

She looked down again, at her lap. "I felt it."

"Into the microphone please, Maggie."

The Prick

She picked her head up and put her mouth an inch from the microphone. "I felt his erect penis pressed against my neck."

"What did you do?"

"Well, I moved, of course, I turned around and looked up at him. And he told me again that I had to put it in my mouth. He said that I had to do it or that I was fired."

"What happened next?"

"I said no again and I pushed past him. He tried to grab for me but he missed. He was very drunk," Maggie said into the microphone. "I ran away down the hall to the women's room."

"Anything else?" Jason asked. The laughing, damn it, bring up the laughing.

Maggie looked at him confused and then her eyes lit with understanding. She put her mouth back up to the microphone. "When I was running away down the hall, I heard him laughing. He was laughing at me."

"Laughing," Jason repeated. He looked at the jury and saw that they understood. They understood how terrible Spelkin was and how terrible it had been for the entire courtroom to laugh at poor Maggie that afternoon. But no need to guilt-trip them too long. Time to move on.

"Maggie, did you report this event to anyone?"

"I filed a Charge of Discrimination with the EEOC, and they said they would tell Levitt about it and that they would investigate."

In front of Maggie was a binder full of exhibits that the parties had submitted in advance of the trial so that the judge could rule on any evidentiary objections. "Maggie, please turn to tab one of the Exhibit binder," Jason said. "Is that the Charge of Discrimination that you signed and filed with the EEOC?"

"Yes."

The Prick

"Permission to publish the exhibit to the jury, Your Honor."

"Granted."

Jason put it up on the screen, and each juror looked at the image on the screen for their individual seat. The version of The Truth that Maggie had just described was consistent with the Charge version and Jason loved watching them read it. Even though the allegations were coming from the same source, it was still an official-looking document confirming everything Maggie had just said. Several of them nodded along as they recognized factual assertions they had just heard.

"Maggie, what was the date that you signed and filed this Charge?" Jason asked.

She looked down at the paper. "April 5th."

"And what was the date that Levitt terminated your employment?"

"April 12th"

"One week later." Jason shook his head in disgust. "Who told you that you were terminated?"

"Mr. Jensen, the Office Manager."

"I want to talk about that termination meeting, Maggie, but first I want to show you a few more documents, okay? Can you please take a look at tab two? What is that document?"

"My performance review from my first year," Maggie said, paging through it.

"Permission to publish, Your Honor."

"Granted."

Jason put it up on the screen. The jurors could navigate through the whole document.

"Do you see who signed this document?"

"Me, the Office Manager, and ... Robert Spelkin."

"And what was your overall performance rating?"

The Prick

"Meets Expectations," Maggie said.

Jason spent the next forty-five minutes painstakingly reviewing and publishing each of Maggie's performance reviews from her career at Levitt, all of them signed by the Office Manager and Spelkin, and each consistently reflecting that Maggie was an adequate performer who always met expectations.

"Seems like you always met the expectations of your job?" Jason said. It was a leading question, but he went for it anyway. No objection was forthcoming from the defense, and Maggie nodded. "Yes."

"Were you ever disciplined for any reason?"

"No."

"Had you ever received a performance review that was lower than 'Meets Expectations?'"

"No."

"But they terminated you a week after you filed your Charge anyway?" Jason was going to do everything possible to hammer home that time frame.

"Yes."

"Tell the jury about that termination meeting, Maggie."

"Well, Mr. Jensen called me on my office line and asked me to come see him. I thought he was going to ask me what happened with Mr. Spelkin because, you know, I'd just filed the EEOC Charge, so I was really nervous. I didn't want to, you know, talk about it. So I went into his office and he closed the door. He told me that Levitt was going to lay me off. I asked why, and he said it was budgetary and it wasn't anything about me personally."

She had started crying again. Jason happily watched the judge's law clerk hand her a Kleenex.

"Go on, Maggie."

"I said, 'Can you please tell me the reason this is happening?' And he said, 'All the information I have is that we're conducting a layoff. It's a not-for-cause termination.' He said I was, you know, an 'at will' employee, and my employment could be terminated at any time, and that the company was exercising its right. He was very cold." Maggie sniffled. "I asked if there was anything I could do, you know, to keep my job. I needed the income. And he just said no."

"Did he say anything else?"

"They—he—gave me an agreement to sign. A severance agreement. They offered to pay my salary for a few months."

Jason smiled. "In exchange for what?"

"If I would agree to release all of my claims against the company," Maggie said.

Jason looked at the jury. Most looked back at him and then over at the defense side. A few were scribbling notes. He hoped to God they understood.

"Did Mr. Jensen tell you to discuss the agreement with your lawyer?"

"No," Maggie said, "he just asked whether I was going to sign it."

"So Levitt terminates you out of the blue for no reason one week after you file your Charge and then asks you to sign an agreement to keep some income for a few months if you'll release all claims against the company?"

Clifford and Trent both stood and objected at once. It was a very objectionable question indeed but a nice little summary for the jury, if Jason did say so himself.

"Sustained." Judge Barnes said. She motioned for Clifford and Trent to sit down and glared at Jason.

Jason nodded. He walked up to Maggie, who was still sniffling, and handed her another Kleenex. She was going to go through the whole box by the time this trial was over. He looked at his watch. 4:43 p.m. Perfect.

The Prick

"Your Honor," he said, "I'm about to get into another line of inquiry. Perhaps this is a good place to stop for the day."

She nodded. "Very well. We will resume at 9:30 a.m. tomorrow. Jurors are reminded not to discuss the case with anyone and are further reminded not to do any independent research. Do not read, listen to, or watch any news coverage on this case, and do not do any Internet research. Court is adjourned." She pounded the gavel and it was.

*****

That goddamn little snot with his goddamn bullshit client with that motherfucking goddamn Judge Barnes and goddamn moronic Jimmy Peters gifting them an airtight retaliation claim that a law student couldn't screw up, which that goddamn piece-of-shit punk had decided to target, and that goddamn Spelkin wife giving the defensible part of the case to that fucking pompous windbag Clifford, and then getting shut down by that vindictive Judge Barnes in front of all of those goddamn reporters writing down everything that happened and asking her if she fucking thought the fucking day went poorly for her fucking noncompliant stupid-as-fuck client, who she would primarily have to defend by and through the dumb-as-a-goddamn-motherfucking-brick got-myself-shot-in-my-fat-ass Jimmy Peters.

Rebecca could feel anger pulsing through her body with every heartbeat. It was overpowering. She couldn't concentrate on anything the meek sycophants gathered around her were saying.

It was 9:35 p.m. and she was in her firm's main conference room, which had been transformed into a war room for the duration of this fiasco of a trial. With her was associate Maria Chan, an even lesser associate named John for Rebecca and Chan to assign grunt work to, and two paralegals.

Rebecca had debriefed with Clifford for an hour in the lawyer's lounge of the federal courthouse, and they had gone their separate ways to prepare for Trial Day 2. She and Clifford both knew that Rebecca had the much tougher road to hoe. Even if the jury didn't believe that Spelkin had sexually assaulted that blubbery mess, they could still enter judgment against Levitt on the retaliation claim if they found that Levitt terminated her because of the Charge. Which it clearly had. Which Peters clearly fucking had. Rebecca had even seen Judge Barnes raising her eyebrows at the timing of the termination, which that fucker Hunter pointed out every third sentence. Judge Barnes had looked directly at her when it sunk in that Levitt had retaliated, which was right around the time that Moxley was describing the termination meeting with the nitwit Office Manager. Rebecca knew what the judge was thinking: that she had recommended and been a party to retaliation. Nothing could be further from the truth, you fucking simpleton, Rebecca wanted to tell her.

But she had just glared back. Fuck her. She never should have been appointed to the federal bench in the first place, which is why Rebecca had lobbied against her nomination. But that fucking severance agreement! Jesus Christ! That had played so poorly, asking the woman to release all her claims without consulting a lawyer. The jury currently hated Levitt, she was sure of that. Fuck that fat fuck Jimmy Peters for putting her in this position. And fuck that fucking widow for giving the good part of the case to media hound Joe Clifford. And, really, fuck that cowardly Jason Hunter for focusing on the slam-dunk, low-value retaliation claim instead of the high-value, high-risk sexual assault claim. She

The Prick

was going to publicly lose this case to a twelve-year-old representing an obese attempted adulterer.

"Enough!" Rebecca shouted and slammed her hand on the table, ending all conversation and making everyone in the room jump. She had been brooding in silence for ten minutes.

She stood up, towering over them. "It's all bullshit! Levitt created this retaliation claim for Hunter and now Hunter has decided to make that the primary claim in the case. The only way we win this is if the jury dislikes and distrusts Moxley *and* the jury likes and trusts us. I know we can destroy Moxley. What I don't know is whether Peters can come across as the motherfucking competent good guy here." Rebecca pointed at the phone in the center of the table. "Call that motherfucker right now," she directed the young male associate who was so clearly terrified of her.

He jumped up and started dialing. It rang three times before Peters picked up.

"He—hello?"

"Jesus Christ! Have you been sleeping?"

"Oh, hi, yes ... Rebecca. I'm trying to be well rested for tomorrow. I expect Hunter is going to call me."

"Of course he's going to call you! We all know that! You should be up going over your testimony!"

"Maria and I have gone over it at least ten times, and I—"

"No! You are not going to lose this case for me. You are going to get up right now, put your clothes on, and come down to the office. We're going to drill you on this until you have it fucking down."

"I'm in bed, Rebecca. And I live two hours outside of town. I can't—I'm not going to—"

"Do it, now. Bring a bag and you can stay in my guest room. You put all of us in this position and I'm not going to listen to your excuses or any other bullshit. I will expect to see you here by 11:30."

"But I ... okay." The phone went dead.

Rebecca reached into her pocket and threw two hundred-dollar bills at the young male associate. "Go get us some food."

"Sure," he said. "What—"

"Just go!"

*****

"Apart from one horrendously terrible incident during Clifford's opening statement involving Maggie and her chair, which I can't even stand to think about, the day actually went well," Jason said.

"Good," Weston said gruffly. Jason had reached Weston on his cell phone while he was on vacation on Sea Island off the Savannah coast. "Her testimony come out credibly?"

"So far, so good, I think. Speaking of credibility, Judge Barnes completely shut down Trent in her opening statement. It was amazing. I've never seen anything like it."

"I'm not surprised. There are very few judges in this town that woman hasn't rubbed the wrong way at one point or another."

"She obviously doesn't care much for her."

"How are you going to deal with the weight issue?" Weston asked.

"I've got a plan."

The Prick

Chapter 16

Tuesday, December 11th
United States District Courthouse
Northern District of Georgia, Atlanta Division

"Maggie, when we broke yesterday, we were talking about how Levitt terminated your employment the week after you filed your EEOC Charge. Now I want to talk about the impact that had on you and your life. How did you feel when you heard the news that you would be terminated?"

"I was both shocked and devastated," Moxley said in a heavily rehearsed manner. Jason had gone over it with her too many times.

"Devastated how?"

"Well I felt like my whole world was falling apart. First my boss does, you know, that to me, and then I lose my job for no reason. Pete and I needed that income. I thought, what am I going to do? What are we going to do? Are we going to lose our house? We're already behind on the mortgage payments."

"I see," said Jason. "And what impact did that have on you, physically?"

"I just felt so worthless and I became, I don't know, depressed. And then I ... it's hard to say it, but I guess it's obvious to anyone who looks at me. And it was really obvious yesterday. I developed an eating disorder."

"An eating disorder?"

The Prick

"Yes," Maggie nodded sadly. Jason hoped to God this was coming off genuinely and not like something her lawyer had instructed her to say. "I've gained probably a hundred forty to a hundred forty-five pounds since Levitt fired me."

"How do you know?"

"Well, I've always struggled with my weight, and I weigh myself every day."

"Has that weight gain affected your marriage?"

Here it was. Jason's gambit to make the attempted adulterer appear sympathetic.

"Yes," Maggie said between breaths. She was crying again.

"I know this is hard for you to talk about, but how?"

"Well, you know, I can't blame him really, but I'm afraid that Pete doesn't find me sexually attractive anymore."

There was a derisive snort behind Jason to his right and he turned in surprise. It was The Widow! She sat there with a smug expression, shaking her head.

What a fantastic and unanticipated development. Jason raised his eyebrows to the jury. All of the women were glaring at The Widow. Glaring! Clifford whispered something in her ear. He could guess what it was. The Widow's face resumed its ice-queen visage.

Maggie, of course, was looking down at her lap like a beaten dog.

"Maggie," he said gently, "I know this is hard for you. But I think we need to talk about it because I suspect that defense counsel is going to bring it up on cross-examination. Has your weight gain, your eating disorder brought on by depression, caused you to do anything you regret?" Jason braced for it and watched the jury out of the side of his eye.

"Yes," Maggie said, reaching for another tissue, still looking at her lap.

The Prick

"What?" He was going to have to pry it out of her.

"I was feeling so low and Pete—Pete didn't want me anymore—and so I did a stupid thing. I put up a profile page on a dating website."

Jason saw some of the jurors look at each other.

"When, Maggie?"

"About six months ago," she sniffed. "I did it one night when I was feeling so ... neglected. I just wanted some attention. I just wanted someone to think that I was ... desirable again."

"I understand," Jason said. "Now this is important. Have you ever once cheated on your husband?"

Maggie raised her head and said clearly into the microphone, "No, I never went on any dates or even talked to any other man. I took the profile down after about a month or so. Nothing happened."

"Thank you, Maggie," Jason said, as if praising her for being so courageously honest. "Now, had you *ever* signed up for any kind of dating website before Levitt terminated your employment?"

"No, never."

"Have you been looking for employment since your termination?"

"Yes, every day. I can't even remember how many applications I've sent out."

"Any luck?"

"None. Not a single interview or even a call. I think that when the employers Google me they, you know, find out about this case."

Jason nodded. "Is this the first time you've been unemployed since graduating high school?"

"Oh yes," she said, "I've always had a job."

"And what was your ending salary with Levitt?"

"Fifty-eight thousand a year."

The Prick

"Thank you, Maggie."

Jason was done. He walked back to the plaintiff's side table and took his front-row seat for Joe Clifford and Rebecca Trent's inevitable devouring of poor Maggie Moxley.

Judge Barnes looked over at the defense side. "Mr. Clifford, I believe your cross is first, is that correct?"

Clifford stood up and buttoned his jacket. "Yes, thank you, Your Honor."

He picked up a yellow pad and pen and glided over to the podium. He stood there for a few seconds, looking at Maggie. She looked back at him, blinking and dabbing her eyes with her latest tissue.

"Now, Mrs. Moxley, I'm going to ask you some indelicate questions this morning. And I apologize for those indelicate questions, but this is an indelicate subject matter we're dealing with in the lawsuit that you chose to file."

"I understand," Maggie said.

"All right. "Now we just heard you say that you've put on some weight lately, is that correct?"

"Yes."

"And you attribute that weight gain to an eating disorder you developed following the termination of your employment with Levitt and the associated depression you've experienced?"

"That's correct."

"Now I was a bit surprised to hear that for the first time today, Mrs. Moxley. Are you under the treatment of a psychiatrist?"

"No, I'm not. I don't have the money to see anyone."

"I see. So this eating disorder is your own self-diagnosis, or perhaps the diagnosis of your lawyer?"

"Objection, Your Honor," Jason said. "Argumentative."

"Sustained."

The Prick

"Very well," said Clifford. "Mrs. Moxley, has any medical care provider diagnosed you with an eating disorder?"

"No."

"What about the depression diagnosis—any medical authority for that one?"

"No. But I know that I'm depressed."

"Have you ever previously received any psychiatric treatment, Mrs. Moxley?"

"No, never."

"Hmmm. I see," Clifford said. "You said something interesting this morning, ma'am. You said that you, a married woman, joined a dating website—Tinder, I believe it is—in order to get attention. Is that right?"

"Yes. I guess I was looking for some ... validation of my looks, now that I look like this."

"I'm curious. When you, as a married woman, signed up for Tinder to validate your current looks, as you say, did you use a current picture?"

Maggie paused and looked at Jason. Just answer the fucking question, Jason attempted to communicate with his eyes. "No."

"So you wanted some validation as to how you looked ... before?"

"Yes, I guess so," said Moxley.

"Really what you wanted was attention, right, Mrs. Moxley?"

"Yes," she said into her lap.

"Maybe make your husband jealous?"

"Yes," she said again, eyes downcast.

"Ummm hmmm," said Clifford. "And that—to make your husband jealous—is *exactly* why you made up the whole story about Robert Spelkin risking his career and marriage to come on to you in the office, isn't it Mrs. Moxley?"

The Prick

"No! That happened! Like I said it did!" Maggie said this loudly into the microphone and, in Jason's estimation, was sufficiently outraged at the suggestion that she made it all up.

"I hate to ask a lady this and my mama would probably slap me if she heard me, but since you brought it up, how much do you weigh Mrs. Moxley?"

Maggie stared at him for a few seconds. "About three forty-five now. This morning, the scale said three forty-five."

"Ummm hmmm. And I believe you said that you gained about a hundred forty-five pounds since your employment with Levitt ended?"

"One forty to one forty-five."

"So during your employment with Levitt, when you say that Robert Spelkin risked his life and career to sexually proposition you, you were about two hundred pounds?"

"Two hundred to two ten, probably."

"Two hundred to two ten," Clifford repeated. "Do you have a driver's license on you, ma'am?"

"Yes ..."

"Would you mind taking it out?"

"Oh ... okay."

"When was the driver's license issued?"

Maggie looked. "About a year ago."

"And what is the height listed?"

"Five five."

"Is that your correct height?"

"Yes."

"What is the weight listed?"

"One ... one eighty."

"Hmmm ... twenty to thirty pounds lighter than what you just testified."

"It fluctuates," Maggie said defensively. "And everyone, every woman, I think, lies a little bit on the driver's license."

The Prick

"Some people lie a lot bit about a great many things," Clifford observed.

"Objection, Your Honor."

Clifford looked up. "That wasn't a question, Your Honor, but if Mr. Hunter takes issue with the suggestion that some people are dishonest, I will withdraw it."

"Ask your next question, Mr. Clifford," Judge Barnes instructed.

"For example, Mrs. Moxley, when you filled out your Tinder app dating profile, you told the Internet community at large that you were single and a hundred eighty pounds, isn't that correct?

"I—I don't remember."

"Well, we can help you out with that, I believe. Please turn to tab eight of that binder in front of you. Permission to publish, Your Honor."

"Granted."

And there it was. Pulled up in front of every juror was Maggie's Tinder profile, with her status listed as single, her weight listed as 180, and the picture she'd uploaded of herself in a low-cut shirt in her bathroom. The jurors stared at it and looked up at Maggie. Jason could feel their feelings about her changing.

"Does this refresh your recollection about the information you provided?"

"Yes," Maggie said quietly.

"So some innocent man who's reading this might reach out to you for a date, not knowing in so doing he might be helping you commit adultery?"

"I never went on any dates."

"You're sure about that?"

"Yes."

"You did fill out this dating profile voluntarily, correct?"

"Yes."

The Prick

"And you did fill it out while at home in the house that you shared with your husband?"

"Yes."

"And you expect us to believe that you signed up for a dating website, but not for the purpose of dating?"

"I said before why, yes. I just—"

"Yes, you said before that you've always been faithful to your husband, correct?"

"Yes."

"And is your husband with us today in the courtroom?"

"No."

"Why not?"

"He had to work?"

"Hmmm … Are you still living with your husband, Mrs. Moxley?"

"Umm, not right now."

What! What the fuck was this?!?! Jason fought back the urge to glare at his client, who was looking over at him with a look that was apologetic and pleading.

"Are you and your husband separated, Mrs. Moxley?"

"Not … I'm staying with my sister right now."

"Is that because Mr. Moxley was upset about the Tinder dating profile?"

"No."

"I find that hard to believe, begging your pardon. Your husband was not upset when he found out that you had signed up for a dating website? Did you tell him?"

Maggie looked down. "No."

Jason tried to maintain the poker face but it was impossible. Maggie had said she'd told Pete about the Tinder profile, they'd had a big fight about it, and he eventually forgave her. Jason wasn't going to call Pete to the stand for other obvious reasons, but the jury didn't know that. Jason felt the hatred for Maggie seeping back into him. Did anything ever happen the way she said it did?

Clifford looked at the jury. "You didn't tell your husband. And when this horrible thing allegedly happened to you at work, when Robert Spelkin, a distinguished attorney, loving husband, and father allegedly *sexually assaulted* you, you didn't tell the police, did you?"

"No."

"And you didn't tell anyone at work."

"No."

"And you didn't go to Human Resources with it."

"No."

"And you didn't tell your direct supervisor, Mr. Jensen."

"No."

"Instead, what you did was, you took your story down to Ponce De Leon and you sold it to a lawyer."

"Objection, Your Honor.

"Sustained."

"Mrs. Moxley, or maybe Ms. Moxley now, why is it that the jury should believe you about the late Mr. Spelkin's alleged infidelity when you lie to the government, you lie to people who read your dating profile, and you lie to your husband?"

"Objection."

"Overruled," said the judge. "Answer the question, Mrs. Moxley."

"I—it—it happened. It happened to me."

"So you say. Is there anyone else in the world who can verify your story? Any other evidence that you aren't simply lying about an honorable man who has left this world?"

"I ... no."

Clifford looked at the jury. "No indeed," he said. "Your Honor, that's all the questions I have for the plaintiff at this time."

The Prick

Judge Barnes nodded and finished some notes that she was making. She looked at Jason. "Redirect, counsel?"

"None, Your Honor." That had obviously been incredibly damaging but there was nothing Jason could think of to do about it, and he wasn't about to give Clifford another shot at Maggie on re-cross. Besides, none of that, absolutely none of that, should impact the retaliation case—if the jury followed the law.

"Very well," said the judge. "Ms. Trent?"

Trent rose. "Thank you, Your Honor," she said brusquely.

Clifford had hit the high points in terms of making Maggie look like an unfaithful, lying, immoral, willing-to-say-anything, starved-for-attention strumpet. Everything Clifford had used, Jason had expected and done his best to prepare Maggie for, except for the petty license bullshit. He hadn't seen the marital separation coming but that was on Maggie, not him. Clifford hadn't looked surprised. They almost certainly had a private investigator following her around.

And now Trent. He had no idea what was coming. Every damn interaction he had with her, she rained down pain on him with ammunition he never anticipated. Those manila folders and the destruction they unleashed. She had some with her at the podium. Jason stared at them, not even distracted by today's abominable pantsuit, a burnt orange.

"Good morning, Mrs. Moxley," Trent began.

"Good morning, Ms. Trent," Maggie responded.

"One of the claims you brought in the lawsuit that you filed against Levitt is that your layoff was retaliation for your filing a Charge of Discrimination with the EEOC. Do you understand that?"

"Yes."

The Prick

"And you are aware that at the same time that Levitt laid you off, it laid off five other employees?"

"Yes. They terminated six of us."

"So did Levitt lay off those other employees in retaliation for you filing a Charge of Discrimination?"

"They—that was part of the cover-up."

"So your theory is that as part of a conspiracy to retaliate against you individually, Levitt ended the careers of five other employees who had nothing to do with the EEOC Charge?"

"Yes," Maggie said. "It would be too obvious if they just fired me."

Good. Maggie was doing very well so far. They had practiced for these questions tens of times. Jason waited for the trap.

"I see. So you're so important that Levitt was willing to put five other people out of work?"

"I'm not important," Maggie said. "Robert Spelkin was important. More important than everyone Levitt fired."

Touchdown. Jason couldn't have written that response any better himself. In fact, he had written that response himself in anticipation of that very question, nearly verbatim, in preparation.

"I see." Trent looked just for a second like she knew she'd been stung. "And tell us, do you have any evidence besides your own speculation that Levitt terminated your employment in retaliation for your EEOC Charge?"

"Well, there's the fact that it happened just one week after I filed it, with no warning whatsoever, and the fact that I had always met expectations and had never been disciplined."

Another score for Maggie. That was another question that Jason had practiced with her countless times. What the hell was going on here?

"So, no, you don't have any other evidence besides your own speculation?"

Jason stood up. "Objection, Your Honor, she just answered that question. Ms. Trent didn't like the answer and is now harassing the witness."

"Sustained," Judge Barnes said. "Move on to the next question, Ms. Trent."

"*Thank you*, Your Honor," Trent said. Was that a hint of sarcasm? Jason looked at the judge, who raised her eyebrows—in surprise?—but didn't say anything further. Clifford shook his head—in disapproval?

Trent took one of her manila folders out and walked around the podium, closer to the witness stand but not so close that she had to ask permission to approach. His eyes were on the folder. He glanced up and saw Maggie staring at it as well. After the depositions, she was as scared of them as Jason was.

Trent held the folder in her right hand and tapped it with her left. "Mrs. Moxley, you understand that the testimony that you are giving here today is under oath?"

"Yes."

"And you understand that it is subject to penalties of perjury?"

"Objection, Your Honor," Jason said, standing. "Is this really necessary?"

"Probably not," Judge Barnes said, sounding a bit annoyed. "But go ahead and answer the question, Mrs. Moxley."

"Yes, I do, I do understand that." Maggie said.

"And you understand that there are criminal penalties to perjury, that lying under oath can get you jail time."

Jason did not object but looked at the judge. She nodded to him as if to say, I will let her ask this last one but will stop anything further. Trent was glowering at Maggie, still tapping the folder.

"Yes," Maggie said, swallowing.

"Good," Trent said. "With all that in mind, I'm going to ask you a very simple question. Have you committed adultery in the past year?"

Maggie looked at Trent for a second and blinked, but didn't hesitate too long before saying loudly into the microphone, "No."

Trent nodded at her and smiled her shark smile, and Jason's stomach did Olympic-level gymnastics. Trent opened the folder, the contents facing her but shielded it so that only she could see what was inside.

"So your testimony under oath is that you have been with no man besides your husband for the past year?"

Maggie looked confused. "I have been with no one but Pete."

Trent's voice rose. "That's what you're going to sit here and tell the jury under oath?"

Jason got back up. "Objection, Your Honor, this is harassment."

Trent wheeled around to glare at him and then swung back to the judge. "I am entitled to cross-examine her thoroughly regarding her alleged incorruptibility, Your Honor. I'm sorry these questions are making her counsel uncomfortable but they go to the heart of the case."

Judge Barnes shook her head. "You've already asked her that question several times now, Ms. Trent. If you have something there that you believe impeaches her testimony, feel free to share it with us. But she has answered the question."

"She has *not* answered the question, Your Honor," Trent yelled, actually yelled, back at the judge.

The Prick

"Ms. Trent, mind your tone. The objection is sustained. Move on to the next question."

Trent glared at Judge Barnes and then trained her laser sights back on Moxley. "So you're going to sit here and tell these good people that you haven't cheated on your husband, under oath?"

"Your Honor!" Jason interjected.

"That is enough, Ms. Trent," the judge said loudly and forcefully. "Either introduce an exhibit or ask another question."

Trent stood completely still, glaring at Maggie for what must have been thirty seconds. Maggie looked around uncomfortably but didn't make a sound.

Then, incredibly, Trent said, "No more questions, Your Honor."

Maggie and Jason exhaled simultaneously and hopefully not too noticeably. It had been a bluff. The whole thing had been a bluff! And that was it. That was Trent's cross. It was over. She was done. It was like a hurricane that had been threatening to hit shore and destroy everything in its path suddenly veered off to spin itself out harmlessly over the Atlantic. Had she scored some points and Jason had just missed it? Judging from the look on Trent's face, no, he hadn't missed anything. She had tanked.

Even Judge Barnes seemed somewhat surprised. "Okay," she said. "Any redirect?"

Not a chance. "No, Your Honor."

"We will break for lunch. I expect that the plaintiff may be able to conclude the presentation of her witnesses in the afternoon."

She banged the gavel and they all stood up. Maggie had survived, somewhat intact.

*****

The Prick

Arthur Jensen quaked in his witness chair and punted, as Jason had expected he would. He testified that he was only following orders, that Peters had told him exactly who would be fired or "laid off" without providing any rationale as to why those particular individuals were to be terminated.

"It's the part of the job I hate the most," he said.

"I understand. The decision wasn't yours to make."

"No," the Office Manager said, "it wasn't."

Jason dismissed him. There was no redirect from Trent. Clifford, who had no stake in this part of the case, stayed in his seat and made notes.

Then Jason called Peters, the man he'd identified as the trial villain. The retaliator. Peters lumbered up to the stand and settled in uncomfortably.

"Good afternoon, Mr. Peters."

"Good afternoon."

"What is your current position?"

"Managing Partner of the Atlanta office of Levitt, Bennett and Taylor."

"To whom do you report?"

"The Levitt board of directors."

"But in terms of Atlanta, you're the boss."

"I guess ... I guess you could say so."

"Well, would you say so?"

"Yes."

"In Atlanta, the buck stops with you, so to speak?"

"I—yes."

"How long have you been the Managing Partner of the Levitt Atlanta office?"

"Nearly twelve years."

"Was Robert Spelkin a partner there the entire time?"

"Yes."

The Prick

"Was he one of the most profitable partners in that office?"

"Profitable ... in terms of—"

"You know what profitable means, Mr. Peters. Did Robert Spelkin bring in more money than most other partners in the office?"

"I would need to look at the books ..."

Jason stared at him and Peters shifted in his seat.

"But yes, he did."

"Can you identify any other partners in Atlanta who generated more money for the firm than Mr. Spelkin?"

"I would need to look at the books, but ... I don't think so, no."

"Let's get four things out of the way right off the bat, okay? First, you directed Arthur Jensen to fire my client, Maggie Moxley."

"It was a layoff, ten percent staff layoff."

"I understand that's the official public release of Levitt, Mr. Peters, but I would like an answer to my direct question. You expressly directed Arthur Jensen to terminate the employment of Maggie Moxley, correct?"

"Yes."

"Thank you. That's the first thing. Second, at the time that you directed Mr. Jensen to fire Maggie Moxley, you knew that she had filed a Charge of Discrimination with the EEOC alleging that she had been sexually assaulted by one of your most profitable partners, correct?

Peters, very much a bewildered buffalo, turned to look over at the defense table, blinking.

"You don't need help with this answer, Mr. Peters. You know it."

"Objection, Your Honor, argumentative," Trent said.

"Sustained," Judge Barnes said. "But answer the question, Mr. Peters."

"It—it was a ten percent layoff, that's it."

Jason smiled. "I don't think you heard the judge's instruction. She told you to answer the question. The question was this, if you need it again: at the time that you directed Mr. Jensen to fire Maggie Moxley, you knew that she had filed a Charge of Discrimination with the EEOC alleging that she had been sexually assaulted by one of your most profitable partners, correct?"

Peters looked at him. He did not like the question.

"I can show you the EEOC's email expressly informing you about the Charge if you would like, Mr. Peters. It's in the exhibit book."

"No," Peters said. "I just didn't think it was a fair question. I knew about the Charge."

"And to be very clear, you knew that Maggie Moxley had filed an EEOC Charge alleging that Robert Spelkin sexually assaulted her before you directed that her employment be terminated."

"Yes, that's what was in the Charge. But we didn't believe the Charge."

"You didn't believe the Charge. At the time that you directed that my client be terminated, what investigation had you done into whether the allegations in it were true?"

"I ... we talked to Robert about it."

"I see. So the married man accused of sexually assaulting his married assistant denied doing so?"

Some of the jurors laughed at that. Peters looked over at them and then glared at Jason.

"Yes," he said, "he did."

"Have you ever done a sexual harassment investigation in which the accused admitted to the Charge?"

"I don't do sexual harassment investigations."

The Prick

"Clearly," Jason said. "Anything else you did to satisfy yourself that the allegations in Mrs. Moxley's Charge were false before you directed that she be terminated?"

"No, and she wasn't terminated for cause. It was a layoff."

"A layoff that just so happened to result in the termination of Maggie Moxley and just so happened to occur immediately after Mrs. Moxley filed a Charge of Discrimination with the EEOC."

"I—it was a layoff. Ten percent layoff," Peters stammered.

"I feel as if I've heard that line somewhere before," Jason said, to the jury's amusement. "So, regardless of what we call it, you made the decision to terminate my client's employment after you found out she had filed an EEOC Charge alleging that Robert Spelkin, one of the most profitable partners in your office, had sexually assaulted her?"

"Objection, Your Honor," Trent said. "How many times is he going to ask the same question? The witness has answered it already."

"I would like one direct answer to that question, Your Honor. The witness is refusing to answer it directly."

The judge nodded. "Overruled, but last time. Mr. Peters you are directed to answer the question."

Peters looked up at the judge and then at Jason. "Yes."

"Thank you," Jason said, with an it's-about-time tone. "On to the third thing. You made the decision to terminate Maggie Moxley's employment less than a week after you found out that she'd filed the EEOC Charge, correct?"

There was no fighting that one; the dates were the dates. "Yes."

"Thank you," Jason said. "Now the fourth. At the time that you chose to terminate Maggie Moxley's employment, there were no issues with her job performance, correct?"

"Mrs. Moxley performed her job adequately."

"And because she performed her job adequately, as you say, the decision to terminate her employment had nothing to do with her job performance, correct?"

"Correct."

"Thank you. Now let's talk about the selection of employees for this so-called ten percent layoff that we've heard so much about."

"Your testimony as I understand it, is that ten percent of the administrative workforce in the Atlanta office was laid off and that Mrs. Moxley was part of that ten percent, is that correct?"

"Yes."

"And how many people in total were laid off?"

"Six"

"So that would mean that prior to the layoff there were sixty administrative employees in the Atlanta office?"

"Approximately."

"Approximately. And whose decision was it to do this ten percent downsizing?"

"Ah ... mine. I mean, mine and Washington's."

"What do you mean, Washington's? You mean the Levitt's board of directors in Washington, DC?"

"Yes."

"And who communicated to you that the Levitt board of directors was of the opinion that you should lay off ten percent of the Atlanta office's administrative staff?"

"Will Simmons."

"The firm's general counsel. Interesting. Any idea why the firm's general counsel was involved in an operational administrative decision?"

The Prick

"No. He didn't tell me."

"Did you ask?'

"No."

"Had Mr. Simmons ever previously directed you to terminate any employees?

"No."

"Whose job was it to select the ten percent? Whose job was it to decide who'd be terminated?"

"Mine."

"So Washington named the number and you decided upon whom the axe would fall?"

"I wouldn't put it like that."

"How would you put it?"

"It was my job to determine which ... which ... who we had to let go."

"It was your job to determine which employees would have their employment terminated?"

"Yes."

"And how did you make that determination? Based on performance?"

"No."

"Not based on performance? How about tenure with the company?"

"No."

"No? How about disciplinary history? Assess which employees had the most write-ups?"

"No."

"Hmmm, what else, what about salary? Try to let go those employees who were earning the most in their positions?"

"I ... no ..."

"So, not performance, not tenure, not disciplinary history, not earnings. What methodology, pray tell, did you use to select the individuals who would be terminated?"

"I did it randomly. Through random selection."

"Through random selection," Jason repeated. "Please tell the jury exactly how you picked these people."

Peters sighed. "I had the Office Manager bring me all the personnel files for the administrative staff. I knew that we would be laying off Moxley, so I took her folder out and then I selected the five others without looking at the names. I thought that was the fairest way, just by chance."

Time stopped.

Jason looked at Peters. Peters blinked back at him, clearly not realizing what he had just said.

"Your Honor, can we have a short recess?" Trent asked somewhere in the periphery off to Jason's right.

"No," Judge Barnes said.

Peters looked over at Trent. Concern spread across his face as he read the expressions of the defense counsel. Jason didn't look back at them. He looked instead at the jury. Some of them, maybe even most of them, looked like they had gotten it.

All of them had to get it.

"You took Mrs. Moxley's file out first, before you did the random selection, because you knew that you were going to fire her?"

"Objection, Your Honor, mischaracterizes the witness's testimony."

"Overruled."

"That's not what I said," Peters protested, shaking his head. You could hear the panic in his voice.

"That's exactly what you just said." Jason dropped his notes on the podium and walked toward him. "Madam Court Reporter, please read back the witness's last answer."

She did. Peters went pale.

"I misspoke," he said.

The Prick

"No, I don't think you did. I think you finally told the truth."

"Objection, Your Honor!" Trent yelled out.

"Overruled," Judge Barnes said. "Sit down, Ms. Trent."

Jason ignored the interchange completely. He was trained on Peters.

"You are under oath," he said. "You are an officer of this court and you are under oath. You have given your word to tell the truth. The penalties of perjury are criminal. You know that. Now answer this question truthfully. You selected Maggie Moxley for termination before any random selection, isn't that so?"

Peters looked over at the defense table for help. There was none. He looked back at Jason.

"Answer it," Jason commanded.

Peters dropped his head and heaved a huge sigh.

"Yes."

Trent stood again. "Your Honor, I request a sidebar or a recess. The witness is exhausted."

"No," Judge Barnes said. "Sit down now."

Jason raised his voice. "You selected Mrs. Moxley for termination first because she filed the EEOC Charge against Levitt, didn't you, Mr. Peters?"

Peters lifted his head and looked not at Jason but at the defense table. His face took Jason aback. He was no longer afraid; his expression was charged with another primal emotion: anger.

"Yes," he said, nodding and glaring over Jason's shoulder. "They made me do it. They wanted someone to blame."

"Levitt made you fire her in retaliation for her EEOC Charge, correct?"

"Yes."

The Prick

"And then Levitt told you to come to court and lie about it to the jury."

"Yes," Peters said. "They did."

"Your Honor, that's all the questions I have for this witness."

*****

Waffle House
Piedmont Road, Buckhead

The hours after his testimony had been interesting. The entire Levitt defense team had marched back to the lawyers' lounge. They all sat in silence for at least ten minutes.

Peters watched their faces. Nobody would make eye contact with him. Except Trent. He believed she would actually kill him if she could get away with it. If society had not illegalized murder, Rebecca Trent would try to murder him in that very room. He outweighed her by at least two hundred pounds but he was confident she would beat him in any fight.

The silence was broken when Clifford entered the room. He looked at Peters and shook his head. He asked to speak with Trent outside. They were gone for maybe five minutes. Then Trent came back in alone.

The night before, she had kept him up all night in her office, screaming at him regarding (1) the fact that Levitt had decided to terminate Moxley in the first place; (2) the fact that he had "lost" Spelkin originally when he fled to New Orleans; (3) the way in which he had conducted the terminations; (4) the fact that he had terminated Rossi (which sent her into another screaming fit about the Rossi settlement); (5) the fact that he had terminated the lunatic Don Jeffries; (6) the fact that he hadn't had Don Jeffries committed; (7) the fact that he hadn't tried to stop Jeffries when he was firing at the great Robert Spelkin (she called

The Prick

him a "fat fucking chickenshit" during that particular diatribe); (8) the fact that Spelkin's widow had decided to move the "defensible part of the case" to that "blowhard Clifford" and left her the "dogshit retaliation case" which Levitt had allegedly funded through the Rossi settlement; and, finally, and most vociferously and most animatedly and most crudely (9) the fact that he never, ever gave answers to her preparatory questions that she deemed satisfactory.

She'd grilled him for hours and hours while the associates and paralegals in the room looked on in terror and exhaustion, and then, following each answer, she verbally eviscerated and emasculated him in front of the audience. And he had just taken it. Toward the end of the night, around roughly five a.m. or so, he'd been permitted to sleep on a couch in one of the partner's offices. He couldn't sleep, though, not after that. He just lay there and trembled, listening to her rant and rave in her corner office down the hall about his incompetency and idiocy. He'd been so afraid about what was going to happen.

But when Trent came back into the lawyers' lounge after the trial day was over and started in on him again, he realized something wonderful. Life-changing.

He didn't give a goddamn shit.

His breakdown on the stand had been because of her, not Hunter. When he started telling the truth up there, a weight lifted off of him and he was hit with sudden clarity as to what he had been doing: lying on the stand, committing perjury, to protect a firm that didn't respect him and to advance the interests of a woman who had just spent an entire night and really an entire year verbally abusing him.

So when she came back in the room and starting screaming again, he stood up, smiled at her, and walked out. His time with Levitt was done. His time with Trent was done.

The Prick

And so he sat in the corner booth of the Waffle House on Piedmont and realized that he was free.

The waitress came over. "Can I get you anything else, hon?"

"Yes," he said. "You can."

The Prick

Chapter 17

Wednesday, December 12th
United States District Courthouse
Northern District of Georgia, Atlanta Division

> *Rule 404. Character Evidence; Crimes or
> Other Acts*
>
> **(a) Character Evidence.**
> **(1) Prohibited Uses.** *Evidence of a
> person's character or character
> trait is not admissible to prove
> that on a particular occasion the
> person acted in accordance with
> the character or trait.*

The retaliation case against Levitt almost assuredly in the bag due to Peters's incredible misstep and subsequent stroke of righteous honesty, Jason spent the morning, along with the rest of the courtroom occupants, listening to what a great man Robert Spelkin had been. The estate and The Widow were putting on their defense to the tort claims filed against Spelkin individually. They of course had no actual witnesses to the alleged events, or nonevents, so the defense consisted of essentially a stream of character witnesses—including David Nichols—giving almost exclusively impermissible character evidence. Nobody had any clue

The Prick

what had actually happened that night. But they thought, given what they knew about Robert Spelkin—with the undertone of what they could see of Maggie Moxley—that the story wasn't credible. That was essentially the testimony, hour after hour, witness after witness. Jason objected to this nearly unapologetic character evidence each time for each witness, but not vociferously, and Judge Barnes grudgingly allowed it over Jason's objection but kept Clifford on a tight enough leash so as not to appear biased, and Clifford made quick work of each witness without belaboring the points.

Still, it was a parade of bullshit witnesses who testified what a stand-up guy Robert Spelkin was before The Widow was called to the stand, a foundation upon which to build her testimony. Jason was annoyed but he also understood. What was Judge Barnes supposed to do, deny them any defense witnesses? The accused couldn't defend himself because a maniac murdered him in the middle of a workday on Peachtree Street. Jason had made his record, and Judge Barnes and the defense—or Clifford at least—knew it. Might even be enough of a threat on appeal for a small settlement if and when the claims against the estate were lost.

And then came The Widow. Stunning. Pale white skin, black cloth, red-rimmed, crying eyes. Clifford was ever so gentle with her, cradling her with soft words. They talked for about three hours. About the Spelkins' wedding day, about their kids, about who Spelkin was as a man. By the end, they had all of the women jurors crying. Two of the men, too.

And then Clifford was done. Jason got up to cross-examine this person in black. This grieving snow angel. To walk the tightrope of giving Maggie's individual claims a chance in hell while not alienating the jury clearly so enamored with this person. He had his retaliation claims

The Prick

against Levitt to protect. Couldn't risk the jury hating his guts for beating up on the bereaved.

"I'm sorry that we're here under these circumstances, Mrs. Spelkin."

"You're the reason we're here," she said.

Ouch. Score one for The Widow. But would that hostility play with the weeping jury? Hard to tell. Jury tea leaves were notoriously fickle flora.

"I suppose in a way that's true," Jason said. "You talked a lot about your husband just now, Mrs. Spelkin. And I gather you had a happy marriage."

"We did."

"Did you sleep in the same bed?"

"Of course."

"Did you sleep in the same bed on the night of March 21st?"

"I don't remember."

"You don't remember whether your husband slept in your bed that night?"

"No. There were nights that he had to work late and he slept on his couch at work instead of driving home."

"I see. You heard the previous testimony from not only Mrs. Moxley but one of your own witnesses, David Nichols, that Mr. Spelkin had been drinking that night. Were there nights that he also drank late and didn't come home?"

"I don't know."

"Right. You *don't* know."

A few seeds of doubt were Jason's only goal. The Widow was grieving and oddly perfect and she had two little perfect children to support ... but she really had no earthly clue what her husband had been up to.

"How many nights a month would your husband not sleep at home?"

"I don't know. It was rare."

The Prick

"I understand from your direct testimony that you trusted your husband and considered him incapable of infidelity."

"That's right," The Widow said. "Robert would never cheat on me. Not in a million years."

"But isn't it true that you considered divorcing him in the past year?"

"Absolutely not," The Widow said, voice rock hard. "When I read about the allegations, I was mad, but not at him. I knew they were lies. I was mad at you. And her." She glared at Maggie.

"All right," Jason said. He was pretty sure that was a lie, at least according to what Trent had told him. But there was no way to prove it. Jimmy Peters would likely end up being the only truly honest witness at the trial.

"One last question, Mrs. Spelkin. Do you have any personal knowledge regarding what happened at Levitt's office on the night of March 21st?"

"I was at home with my children."

"So no?"

"Robert wouldn't do what she said he did."

"So no?"

"No. I wasn't there. But I knew my husband."

"So no," Jason said, looking at the jury to underscore that point, which was really all he had. "That's all the questions I have for Mrs. Spelkin, Your Honor."

Clifford stood. "No redirect, Your Honor."

"Very well," Judge Barnes said. "Mrs. Spelkin, you are excused. Does the estate have any additional witnesses to call?"

"No, Your Honor," Clifford said.

"We will take a short recess," said Judge Barnes. "The jury is excused. I will talk to the lawyers at the bench."

The Prick

Jason stole another glance at Jimmy Peters as he walked up. He had found himself looking at Peters throughout the day. The heavy man seemed much lighter somehow, and there was a strangely serene smile on his face. He should be devastated—his career at Levitt was almost certainly over. But maybe his was the joy of a clean conscience.

Jason, Clifford, and Trent lined up to the right of the bench and Judge Barnes looked down at the trio from on high. "How many witnesses does Levitt expect to call?" she asked Trent.

Trent looked terrible. "None," she said quietly.

"None?" Judge Barnes said.

Trent shook her head.

They all looked at her for a few seconds.

"Well, all right," said Judge Barnes. "That *is* your prerogative. I expect both sides will be moving, as is customary, for judgment as a matter of law. I am going to deny any such motions. All claims are going to the jury. If you believe the jury gets it wrong, you can renew your motions. We'll break for ten minutes and then I will hear any motions, maximum of ten minutes of argument each, and then we will bring the jury back in, have closing arguments, take care of the jury instructions, and then give the case to the jury." She banged her gavel. "Court is in recess. Ten minutes."

Greatly comforted that the judge wouldn't grant any defense motions from the estate and slightly annoyed that he wouldn't get judgment as a matter of law on the retaliation claim, Jason walked back to the lawyers' table and saw the reporters scramble out into the hallway. At the beginning of the trial, he couldn't stop thinking about the feral pack of journalists who kept rushing in and out of the courtroom, but now he kept forgetting that they were even there. He wondered if Peters's confession had made the evening news—he hadn't checked. From the beginning of the trial he had turned his personal phone off and had no idea whether people had been trying to contact him. He had a burner phone for trial purposes, and the only people he'd given the number to were Moxley, Weston, the court, Clifford, and Trent. Not even Rossi had it. No distractions. No more phonehead fiascos.

Trent gathered her team and Clifford gathered his. Why hadn't Trent made a settlement offer? Potentially she couldn't bring herself to do it.

"What did the judge say?" Maggie asked.

"The parties are done presenting evidence," Jason said, sitting down and looking over his closing notes. "We'll break and then we'll give closing statements. Then the jury gets the case."

Maggie nodded and looked down at her purse. "Do you think we'll win?"

"We should win the retaliation claim. The assault and battery claims probably aren't going to make it."

"The retaliation claim is the one against Levitt, right? The one you said Mr. Peters lost for them?"

Jason shook his head. If he had a dollar for every time he had explained that to Maggie, he wouldn't have to worry about winning the case. Come hell or high water, at the end of this trial, he and Maggie were going on a break.

"Yes."

"Good," Maggie said. "They were the ones who really were in the wrong."

Jesus. What the fuck did that mean? Better not to ask or to think about it.

"Be quiet, Maggie."

He closed his eyes and visualized his closing. He saw himself in front of the jury, confident, strong, persuasive, provoking sympathy, empathy, and anger at will. Saw them writing down his words on their pads and thinking up big dollar signs. The ten minutes flew.

Judge Barnes came back in, the parties moved for judgment as a matter of law, and Judge Barnes, true to her word, denied all motions.

"This is it," Jason said under his breath as the jurors filed back in.

Judge Barnes explained to the jurors that they would hear closing arguments, that nothing the lawyers said was evidence, that she would then give them instructions, and then they would meet to decide the case. Satisfied that she had delivered all necessary instructions and directives, she nodded at Jason.

"Mr. Hunter," she said, "please proceed."

"Thank you, Your Honor." Jason walked around the bench to the podium. "And thank you, ladies and gentlemen of the jury. I know this is a great time commitment and I have greatly appreciated the attention that I have observed you all paying throughout the case." Half of them had been visibly doodling and/or dozing off at one time or another during the trial. But flattery is seldom rejected on the grounds that it is untrue.

"It is very important that you recognize that there are two parts to this case. First, there is Mrs. Moxley's claim against Levitt. This is the retaliatory termination claim. To prove the retaliation claim, Mrs. Moxley must prove, by a preponderance of the evidence, that Levitt terminated her employment because she filed a Charge of Discrimination with the EEOC. Whether or not you believe Mr. Spelkin did what Mrs. Moxley told you he did is irrelevant to this claim. It doesn't matter. All that matters is whether Levitt terminated Mrs. Moxley because she filed that Charge."

Jason paused and looked at all the jurors to make sure they were paying attention to this part. "You don't have to speculate or draw any inferences as to whether retaliation occurred here. Mr. Peters, the man who made the decision to terminate Mrs. Moxley, sat right over there and told you directly that Levitt terminated Mrs. Moxley because of the Charge. He confessed, ladies and gentlemen. He confessed. That confession is the only thing that makes sense, given that Mrs. Moxley had always performed satisfactorily, had never been disciplined, and was fired *one week* after she filed that Charge, accusing one of the most profitable partners in Levitt's Atlanta office of sexual assault."

"I cannot stress this enough, folks: *he told you that he did it*. He admitted it! I urge you, therefore, to find for Mrs. Moxley and against Levitt on the retaliation claims. And we request that you award her lost wages, interest, and compensatory damages for her emotional distress and all of the turmoil it has caused in her life. We also request that you assess punitive damages against Levitt to punish it for this grossly unlawful behavior and to deter it from committing such egregious acts in the future."

Jason nodded in agreement with himself. He put up his right index finger. "That's the first claim," he said. "It is independent of the second claim." He put up his left index finger. He would beat into the jury the separateness of the two claims and the two defendants if it killed him. The claims were so distinct that they could not even be different fingers on the same hand. "The second claim is the claim against Robert Spelkin, and because Mr. Spelkin is no longer with us—he was killed by a deranged man who Levitt fired in the cover-up—this claim is against Mr. Spelkin's estate. Specifically, Mrs. Moxley alleges, as she told you on the stand, that Mr. Spelkin came into her cubicle when he was drunk, propositioned her, and sexually assaulted her."

"Now, you heard Mrs. Moxley testify about what happened. She told you directly. I expect that you will hear some talk in the defense's closing about her getting on Tinder, et cetera. That is entirely beside the point, ladies and gentlemen. Nobody is perfect, and certainly Mrs. Moxley is not. But that doesn't excuse her boss drunkenly demanding fellatio from her, and it doesn't excuse him putting his erect penis on her neck and telling her to put it in her mouth or she's fired. Whether she put a picture on a website months after this happened, after she developed an eating disorder, doesn't matter. This woman was sexually assaulted by her drunken boss."

"Now I'm sure you remember the defense witnesses, who all said such laudatory things about Mr. Spelkin. But think about this. None of them were there. None of them saw what happened. Mrs. Moxley, my client, is the only one who was. And think about what the defense witnesses said. They admitted Mr. Spelkin was drinking that night. They admitted that they didn't know whether he went home that night. They admitted that they didn't know whether he spent the night in his marital bed. Mrs. Moxley is the only one in this courtroom who knows what happened. And she told you directly. We therefore also ask you to also find for Mrs. Moxley on the sexual assault and battery claims against Robert Spelkin, now his estate."

One more time and he was done. "And, again, regardless of what you determine about that second claim, you still must conclude that Levitt retaliated against Mrs. Moxley. They told you straight out that they did. Thank you. I'm confident that you will do the right thing."

Jason nodded to the jury and went to his seat. An immense feeling of relief washed over him. His role was finished. He had done the best he could with the obese and pathological hand he'd been dealt. He looked at Maggie and wondered what she was thinking. She was staring at Clifford, her frequent tormentor, who had seized center

The Prick

stage and was again spouting off something about Spelkin being an honorable man. Jason couldn't give a shit. He pretended to listen, wrote down "honorable man" on his notepad, and glanced over at Trent. Clifford's closing statement wrote itself—play up Spelkin's character and tear down Moxley's. But he had no idea what Trent was going to do. What the hell could she do? Her defense had always been a leaky vessel; now it was the Lusitania.

Clifford's tone switched to what was assuredly the end of his remarks and Jason tuned back in.

"The young man, Mr. Hunter, was correct in that there was only one eyewitness to the alleged event who was able to testify. But I submit to you, honorable citizens, that you cannot trust a word this plaintiff says about the late Robert Spelkin. Remember, she lied to the state, she lied to the public on the Internet, and she lied to her husband. She also, I'm afraid, lied to you. You saw that firsthand. So I ask you to protect Robert Spelkin's reputation. I ask you to protect the memory of that honorable man. And I ask you to protect his family. We ask for a complete defense verdict. Thank you."

Clifford walked confidently back to his table and nodded to Jason on the way. Jason optimistically interpreted the nod as a sign of some modest respect, and perhaps it was.

"Thank you, Mr. Clifford," said Judge Barnes. "Ms. Trent?"

Trent stood. For the occasion, she had selected a sky-blue pantsuit that was about three sizes too big. Even in the high tension of the moment, Jason could not help but appreciate how stupendously bad Trent's fashion sense was, and with such remarkable consistency. He supposed everyone in her life was simply too terrified of her to offer any criticism, constructive or otherwise.

The Prick

She walked to the podium. She had nothing in her hands, which were behind her back.

"I've been a lawyer for almost thirty years," she began. "I've had over twenty-five jury trials, most of them in this courthouse. Never before have I been so convinced that the plaintiff is lying about the salient facts of the case. I find myself, however, and my client finds itself, in an unenviable position: that is, our primary witness, James Peters, got up on the stand, took an oath to tell the truth, and then he lied as well."

She shook her head. "In a cowardly attempt to explain his own managerial ineptitude, Mr. Peters attempted to blame innocent individuals whom he claims told him to terminate Mrs. Moxley because of retaliatory animus when in fact it was his decision alone. I would ask that you not give Mrs. Moxley a windfall simply because one bad actor, Mr. Peters, made the decision—"

"Ha!" Jimmy Peters said, at the end of the defense table. "That's rich! *My* decision!" Peters let out a great booming belly laugh.

Trent looked back at him, shocked. Peters continued to shake with laughter. "My decision!"

The jury was watching the interaction with pure delight. They weren't buying this new spin at all, Jason saw, and they liked newly-designated-scapegoat Jimmy Peters standing up for himself. They were laughing, actually laughing at Trent. One woman hid her face behind her notebook; others covered their mouths with their hands. But they were laughing.

Trent looked at Judge Barnes pleadingly. In a priceless moment that Jason would remember forever, Judge Barnes just looked back at her and shrugged.

The Prick

Trent turned back to the jury, wide-eyed. "I assure you, ladies and gentlemen, that this is no laughing matter. This is an incredibly serious situation and—"

The jury erupted in laughter. Trent just stood there, staring at them.

The Prick

Chapter 18

Thursday, December 13th
United States District Courthouse
Northern District of Georgia, Atlanta Division

Three and a half hours. After all of that madness, the jury was out for three and a half hours. Judge Barnes, after somewhat regaining control of the courtroom following Trent's performance the previous afternoon, had called it a day and directed that jury deliberations would resume at 9:30 a.m. the next day, following instructions.

The jury had reached a resolution suspiciously close to the end of the free lunch. The verdict was in.

Jason and Maggie had huddled in a little, overheated conference room, waiting. With them was a resurfaced and hungry-looking Pete Moxley.

"How much do you think we'll get?" he asked Jason roughly 6,000 times.

"I really can't estimate that at this point, Pete, if we win," Jason said, again and again.

"I bet we get millions," Pete always responded. "Goddamn rich pervert motherfuckers."

Maggie looked at her purse.

When the deputy mercifully knocked on the door to let them know that a result had been reached, Jason took a deep breath. "Let's go."

The Prick

Maggie took a deep breath as well. Pete rubbed his hands together like he was getting ready for a big Christmas dinner.

They followed the deputy down the hall, into the elevator, and into the courtroom. Nobody said a word. The deputy held the door open for them and Jason walked through first, nodding to the gaggle of five reporters, to whom he had refused to speak during the proceedings. He led Maggie back up to their table and instructed Pete, quietly but firmly, to sit in the pews.

Maggie sat down and continued to breathe heavily, like she was in labor. Jason could feel her pain. He glanced over at the defense table and saw similar anxiety-ridden looks on everyone except Clifford, who looked like he was fly fishing.

Clifford caught his eye. "Good luck, son."

"Yeah," Jason said. Trent didn't make eye contact. She didn't look like she intended to make eye contact with anyone.

"All rise!" the deputy shouted, and everyone did. Judge Barnes entered from the side door. "I am informed," she said, "that the jury has reached a verdict on all claims and that it is unanimous. I will now bring the jury in, confirm that this is accurate, and then read the verdict. I expect full decorum from everyone in this courtroom, including all of you fine members of the press in the back. I will hold anyone who does not adhere to this directive in contempt. Are there any questions?"

There weren't any questions.

Judge Barnes nodded. "Deputy, please bring in the jury."

They were led in. Some of them smiled at Jason, and at Maggie. He was greatly comforted.

"Foreperson, have you reached a verdict?" Judge Barnes asked.

The Prick

The trucker, of all people, stood up. "Yes, Your Honor," he said gruffly.

"Is it unanimous?"

"Yes."

Judge Barnes nodded her approval. "Very well," she said. "Deputy, please bring me the completed verdict form."

Jason watched the large man in the tan uniform take the piece of paper from the trucker—potentially the most valuable piece of paper Jason had ever seen—and deliver it to the judge.

The judge received the paper, unfolded it, and read it to herself. She cleared her throat and leaned closer to the microphone.

"With respect to Count I, Mrs. Moxley's retaliation claim against Levitt, Bennett and Taylor, in response to the question of whether Mrs. Moxley proved by a preponderance of the evidence that Levitt terminated her employment because she filed an EEOC Charge, the jury answered: Yes."

Jason felt Maggie's damp hand grab his and squeeze.

"In lost wages," the judge continued, "the jury awards the plaintiff 174,000 dollars, representing one year of back wages and two years of front wages.

"In compensatory damages on the retaliation claim, the jury awards the plaintiff one million dollars."

Maggie's grip on Jason's hand got much, much tighter.

The judge cleared her throat again. "In punitive damages on the retaliation claim, the jury awards the plaintiff fifteen million dollars."

Maggie gasped, and there was a large commotion in the back of the room. The judge pounded her gavel and glared. Everyone fell silent. Few of them understood what this actually meant. Jason had a vain hope that Maggie and Pete understood, given that he had explained it to them at least ten times, but he would bet sixteen million dollars that they didn't.

Judge Barnes turned the page. "With respect to Count II, to the question regarding whether Mrs. Moxley established by a preponderance of the evidence that Robert Spelkin committed the civil tort of sexual assault, the jury answered: Yes."

"Holy shit," Jason whispered.

"In compensatory damages on the sexual assault claim, the jury awards the plaintiff one thousand dollars."

"Oh," Jason said.

"In punitive damages on the sexual assault claim, the jury awards the plaintiff one dollar."

The judge looked up, as if daring someone to cause a disturbance. There were no takers.

"Finally, with respect to Count III, the question regarding whether Mrs. Moxley established by a preponderance of the evidence that Robert Spelkin committed the civil tort of sexual battery, the jury answered: Yes."

"In compensatory damages on the sexual battery claim, the jury awards the plaintiff one thousand dollars."

"In punitive damages on the sexual battery claim, the jury awards the plaintiff one dollar."

Judge Barnes looked at the jury. "Is that your verdict?"

"Yes," the trucker said.

"Very well," Judge Barnes said. "The jury is thanked for its service and excused. Post-trial motions, if any, will be heard tomorrow morning. Court is adjourned." She pounded her gavel.

Pandemonium. Everyone started talking at once and someone hit Jason with a crushing bear hug. It was one Pete Moxley.

The Prick

"We did it!" Pete Moxley yelled in his ear. "We fucking did it!"

*****

They were back in the little, overheated room. It was Jason's hope to break the news gently to Maggie and Pete before they had any interaction with the outside world, and in particular the media.

"But the judge said that we get sixteen million dollars!" Pete yelled.

"Yes, I understand that, but that was on the Title VII retaliation claim."

"So the fuck what?"

"Well, as we've, ah ... discussed before, Title VII has a cap on compensatory and punitive damages."

"What in the goddamn fuck does that mean?"

"It means that the jury couldn't award more than a total of 300,000 of non-economic damages for that claim."

"But they gave us sixteen million," Maggie said. She was sitting in the corner.

"Yes, but they weren't authorized to."

"Who didn't authorize them to?" Pete asked.

"Congress."

"But they did it anyway."

"It doesn't matter."

"So what does that mean?" Maggie asked. "How much do we actually get?"

"The judge will reduce the compensatory and punitive damages award down to 300,000," Jason said.

"You got to be fuckin' kidding me," Pete said. "Did you know? Did you know that would happen?"

"Well I knew what the cap was," Jason said. "That's the law."

"So how much do we get?" Maggie asked.

"The total will be about 474,000."

The Prick

"After the jury awarded sixteen million fucking dollars?" Pete said.

"Well ... after the attorneys' fees, the net amount to you will be around 284,000."

"You've got to be fuckin' kidding me," Pete said.

Perhaps that hadn't been the opportune time to bring up fees.

"No," Jason said, "that's the deal, I'm afraid. But look, we won. The jury found for us on everything."

"Doesn't feel like it," Maggie said.

"Sure the fuck doesn't," Pete said. "Can we, you know, appeal this shit?"

The Prick

Chapter 19

Friday, December 21st
The Law Offices of Jason Hunter, Esq.

Jason spent a week holed up in his apartment drinking beer, ordering pizza, and playing Call of Duty. Maggie never called him. Weston did quite a few times. As did the reporters. They wanted to know how he felt about only getting $475K on a multimillion dollar verdict, according to their voicemails. He didn't return any calls.

He tried Jessica a few times, but she didn't pick up the phone or respond to calls or texts. He assumed that she was pissed that he had ignored her during the trial, or disappointed that he hadn't lived up to her millionaire expectations, or both.

Finally, he forced himself to shower, get in his car, and drive to his office. All his plants had died and someone, likely him, had neglected to empty or clean the coffeepot, which was now sustaining a great deal of bacterial life.

He walked back out and headed down the street to the Krispy Kreme. After ordering a large coffee and a box of donuts, he redirected back to the office. Someone was knocking on his door. As he drew closer, he recognized the figure and groaned. It was David Nichols.

Nichols grinned at him as he approached. He was holding a manila envelope. "You look great," he said to Jason. "Breakfast of champions."

The Prick

"The fuck do you want?"

"Invite me in and I'll tell you."

Jason handed him the box of donuts. "Hold this."

"Can I have one?"

"You can have two," Jason said, turning the key and pushing the door in. "Come on in, make yourself at home."

"Jesus, Jason, this place is really a shithole," Nichols observed, taking a Krispy Kreme.

"Correct," Jason said, taking a seat behind the desk. "I'm planning to move once I get that Levitt check."

Nichols sat down and took a bite. "Not that great a check, really, all told. But I'm sure you'll find some way to make do."

Jason grunted and turned on his computer.

"Not that you'll be seeing it for a while. We'll surely appeal."

"Correct," Jason said.

"Tell me, Jason, how did that blob take it when you told her that her sixteen million dollar verdict was worth less than a half million?"

"Better than her husband."

Nichols laughed. "I suspect that's true." He put the half-eaten donut down on Jason's desk.

"Tell me, Jason, off the record, did he do it? Did Robert actually do it?"

Jason stared at him and Nichols stared back.

"The jury said yes." Jason sipped his sugary coffee.

"That's what I thought," Nichols said. "You have no fucking idea."

"Do you?"

"Off the record?"

"Sure."

"No," Nichols said. "I don't"

"Well, I guess we'll just have to trust the enlightened conscience of the jury," Jason said. "Listen, Nichols, no offense, I enjoy your company, but what the fuck are you doing here?"

Nichols laughed. "I have something for you. Are you familiar with the phrase 'what goes around comes around'?"

"Somewhat."

Nichols got up and handed Jason the envelope. "Open it."

Jason complied. It was a Complaint in state court. But he didn't read past the caption.

SUPERIOR COURT OF THE STATE OF GEORGIA
COUNTY OF FULTON

JESSICA ROSSI,	CASE NO. 24-CV-18260812
Plaintiff,	**VERIFIED COMPLAINT**
vs.	
JASON HUNTER, THE LAW OFFICES OF JASON HUNTER, P.C.,	
Defendants.	

Jason put it down on his desk and closed his eyes.

"Breach of fiduciary duty," Nichols said. "You took advantage of your position of power to coerce her into sexual intercourse with you. I decided to take the case. Pro bono, as they say."

The Prick

"You know this is bullshit."

"Says the man who told a room full of people I forced that nympho to have anal sex for the first time."

Jason nodded. "Get out."

"All right," Nichols said. "Let me know if you want to talk settlement. I can see if Bass is available to mediate. I hear he's effective in these types of cases."

"Out," Jason said, opening his eyes and feeling murderous rage.

"Okay, I'm leaving," Nichols said, backing up, hand in the air. He opened the door and turned, giving Jason a big smile.

"You'll probably want to get a lawyer."

The End

About The Author

D C Wales

D.C. Wales has litigated hundreds of cases, including bench and jury trials. He has published articles in legal journals, edited a leading treatise, and filed countless briefs with federal and state judges across the United States. *The Prick* is his first novel, written over the course of years in time not devoured by the ever-demanding practice of law.

The Prick tours the series of events set in motion by one (alleged) egregious and cataclysmic action, set in the battleground of Atlanta employment litigation, a venue Wales knows and loves. The self-inflicted catastrophe, denial, wrath, retaliation and redemption–attempted at least–that play out in the novel have all been present in these cases for decades, and with stunning regularity.

Wales lives outside of Atlanta with his wife and son.

If You Enjoyed This Book
Visit

PENMORE PRESS
www.penmorepress.com

All Penmore Press books are available directly through our website, amazon.com, Barnes and Noble and Nook, Sony Reader, Apple iTunes, Kobo books and via leading bookshops across the United States, Canada, the UK, Australia and Europe.

JAKE FOR MAYOR

BY

LOU AGUILAR

Ken Miller is having a bad run of luck. After torpedoing his career as a campaign manager, he drives through tiny Erie, Colorado, when a homeless beagle named Jake causes a series of mishaps that lands him in jail. Ken is granted bail on two conditions: that he not leave town before his trial in three weeks and—much to his chagrin—that he not let Jake out of his sight until then. Stuck in Erie as it prepares for a mayoral election, he's drawn into the local politics by a waitress who vehemently opposes incumbent Charles Dunbar, the only candidate on the ticket.

Unable to resist political adventure, Ken gets a brainstorm. If he can exploit the dog's popularity among the townspeople and get them to elect Jake as a protest candidate, the publicity will put him back on top. But things don't go exactly as planned. Ken warms to the dog, falls for the waitress, and employs her teenage son and his gang as campaign aides in a madcap battle with Mayor Dunbar ... who has no intention of losing to a dog.

PENMORE PRESS
www.penmorepress.com

SAVED BY THE BANG

BY

MARINA J. NEARY

Welcome to 1980s Belarus, where Polish denim is the currency, "kike" is a pedestrian endearment, and a second-trimester abortion can be procured for a box of chocolates. Antonia Olenski, a catty half-Jewish professor at the Gomel Music Academy, wavers between her flamboyant composer husband, Joseph, and a chivalrous tenor, Nicholas. The Chernobyl disaster breaks up the love triangle, forcing Antonia into evacuation with her annoying eight-year-old daughter, Maryana.

After a summer of cruising through Crimean sanatoriums and provoking wounded Afghan veterans, Antonia starts pining for the intrigues and scandals of the Academy. When the queen of cats finally returns home, she finds that new artistic, ethnic, and sexual rivalries have emerged in the afterglow of nuclear fallout. How far will Antonia go to reclaim her throne?

PENMORE PRESS
www.penmorepress.com

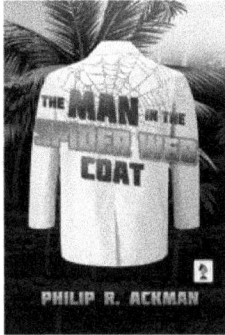

THE MAN IN THE SPIDER WEB COAT
BY
PHILIP ACKMAN

Titus Buchanan, a professor who runs a think tank at Williams College, believes he's figured out how to stage a successful revolution. When the United Nations adopts a historic vote spelling the end of colonialism, Buchanan seizes the opportunity to test his theory. His laboratory will be the Splendid Islands, a collection of palm-fringed cays scattered across three quarters of a million square miles of the South Pacific. Its inhabitants will be his lab rats.

But complications arise. The Splendids belong to New Zealand, and New Zealand has no intention of giving them up. The United States has its own secret "space age" agenda for the islands. The Queen of England is bound to support New Zealand, but she doesn't want Britain to fall out with the Americans, who favor independence. Meanwhile, the islanders, gripped with revolutionary fever, have ideas about self-rule. Reverend Geoffrey Brown, originally recruited by Buchanan to run the revolution, joins forces with an unlikely crew of locals and sets out to match wits with powerful opponents.

PENMORE PRESS
www.penmorepress.com

DC Wales

Penmore Press

Challenging, Intriguing, Adventurous, Historical and Imaginative

www.penmorepress.com